INDIAN BLANKETS AND THEIR MAKERS

A Navaho Weaver.
(Photo by A. C. Vroman.)

Indian Blankets
and Their Makers

BY
GEORGE WHARTON JAMES

*With Numerous Illustrations and
Colored Plates*

Dover Publications, Inc.
New York

Published in Canada by General Publishing Company, Ltd., 30 Lesmill Road, Don Mills, Toronto, Ontario.

Published in the United Kingdom by Constable and Company, Ltd., 10 Orange Street, London WC 2.

This Dover edition, first published in 1974, is an unabridged republication of the 1920 edition of the work originally published by A. C. McClurg & Co., Chicago, in 1914.

International Standard Book Number (clothbound):
0-486-23068-6
International Standard Book Number (paperbound):
0-486-22996-3
Library of Congress Catalog Card Number: 73-90526

Manufactured in the United States of America
Dover Publications, Inc.
180 Varick Street
New York, N. Y. 10014

INTRODUCTION

THE art development of the human race is a fascinating study, and one that has long engaged the attention of some of our most profound philosophers. Whence springs the love of beauty, and the desire for its reproduction or imitation in the work of human hands? The answer seems obvious, whether it is regarded from a standpoint interior or exterior to man. If interior, man is a spiritual being with power to discern all beauty, and Nature, with her multiform manifestations of beauty, is but the complement of that spiritual nature, given to him to afford exercise for the faculties of his soul. On the other hand if the subject is regarded as exterior to man then the beauty of Nature must be regarded as the exterior objects that develop within him a love for the beautiful. Once a sunrise, a sunset, a flower, strikes man's inner vision and awakens a love for its rare appearance, he experiences the dawn of the art instinct, and its development is merely a question of time.

The instinct once aroused and development begun it becomes as natural to seek to imitate as it is to observe. The power of the artist transfixes the beauty of the moment and makes it a permanent joy. He "carries over" the glory of today into all the tomorrows. But it is essential that the artist be a good and faithful worshiper at the shrine of Nature. Morning, noon, evening, and through the silent watches of the night he must reverently remain at his post.

The aboriginal man was perforce a keen observer of Nature. He could be no other. Upon his observing powers his very existence depended. As I once elsewhere wrote:

In the days of his dawning intelligence, living in free and unrestrained contact with Nature, his perceptive faculties were aroused and highly developed by the very struggle for existence. He was compelled to watch the animals, in order that he might avoid those that were dangerous and catch those that were good for food; to follow the flying birds that he might know when and where to trap them; the fishes as they spawned and hatched; the insects as they bored and burrowed; the plants and trees as they grew and budded, blossomed and seeded. He became familiar, not only with such simple things as the movements of the polar constellations and the retrograde and forward motions of the planets, but also with the less known spiral movements of the whirlwind as they took up the sand of the desert; and the zigzags of the lightning were burned into his consciousness and memory in the fierce storms that, again and again, in darkest night, swept over the exposed area in which he roamed. With the flying of the birds, the graceful movements of the snakes, the peculiar wrigglings of the insects, the tracks of insects, reptiles, birds, and animals, whether upon the sand, the snow, the mud, or more solid earth he soon became familiar. The rise and fall of the mountains and valleys, the soaring spires and wide spreading branches of the trees, the shadows they cast, and the changes they underwent as the seasons progressed; the scudding or anchored clouds in their infinitude of form and color, the graceful arch of the rainbow, the peculiar formation and dissipation of the fogs, the triumphant lancings of the night by the gorgeous fire weapons of the morning sun, the stately retreat of the Day King as each day came to its close, all these and a thousand and one other things in Nature he soon learned to know in his simple and primitive manner, and, when the imitative faculty was once aroused, and the art faculty demanded expression, what more natural than that he should attempt, crudely at first, more perfectly later on, the reproduction of that which he was constantly observing, and which was forcefully impressed upon his plastic mind.*

Here then, we have the origin of the art *motifs* of the aborigines. The North American Indians — the Amerinds, as Major J. W. Powell called them — became experts in several arts and crafts, chief of which were those of pottery, basketry, and blanket weaving. This book deals entirely with the latter.

While several tribes have engaged in rude and primitive weaving, the Pueblo Indians of Arizona and New Mexico weaving their cotton garments exquisitely and artistically long prior to the coming of the Spaniards in 1540, it was left for the Navaho of our historic time to develop the art to a high degree, so that we find writers of note, and authorities, declaring that his is the best blanket in the world — neither Ottoman fingers nor British machines have ever produced its peer.

The Franciscan Fathers of St. Michaels, Arizona, than whom no one has studied the Navaho more, assert that the modern Navaho blanket is not one whit behind its predecessors of sixty or seventy years ago. They say, in addition: "The Navaho blanket is today the only thing of its kind in the world. No other people, white, red, black, brown, or yellow, turn out a textile fabric that can be placed beside it. It is true, Oriental rugs are woven in much richer patterns than the Navaho blanket, but, while the former bewilder the eye by their over-rich and over-crowded designs, the latter, by their very barbaric simplicity of design and well chosen colors, please and rest the eye at the same time."

Hence it will be seen that Navaho blanket-weaving is not "a lost art," nor are the weavers a vanishing race. In these pages I shall show, and with a thousand blankets selected from those made this year it can be demonstrated, that *as good blankets are being woven today* by the Navahos as were ever fashioned in their history, and the fact that there are over thirty thousand of these Indians on their reservation in this year of grace 1914, where twenty years ago there were less than twenty thousand, is proof that they are not decreasing.

Yet the Indian — the Navaho, as well as all others — *as an Indian,* is rapidly disappearing from the land. He is slowly changing; not into a civilized being comparable with ourselves, but into a peculiar nondescript,

* *Indian Basketry,* Chap. XII, p. 198.

in whose life aboriginal superstitions linger side by side with white men's follies, vices, habits, customs, and conventional ideas. Hence it is well to gather together all that we possibly can of his aboriginal modes of thought and life, his social and tribal customs, religious ceremonies, dances, and legends ere it is too late. In the doing of this the thoughtful mind soon discovers how large a debt we owe to the aborigine, and how far along the path of civilization his inventive genius and indefatigable industry thrust us. For we learn, not that "we" taught the Indian how to weave, but that "he" taught "us."

In the far-away dim ages of the past when the aboriginal man was seeking for some means of carrying in one receptacle the several articles of his hunting-craft — such as flint arrow-points, lance-heads, skinning knives, gut for his bow, sinew for his arrows, his fetich to make his hunting sure — and his wife desired a similar "hold-all" for her treasures, the basket was a necessity. The bird's nest, possibly, was the first suggestion of the basket, and bark, twigs, flexible roots, and fibre of shrubs and plants were woven together in rude imitation of the nest, and *the art of basketry was born*. Once created, imitation, experience, and rivalry soon developed the art until the Amerind became the greatest exponent of basket-making the world has ever known. Indeed, experts assert that there is not a known stitch now produced by the deft fingers of Parisian, London, Berlin, or Italian fingers, or warp and weft, no matter how cunning, sent forth to delight the eye from the most complicated weaving-machine of modern time that cannot be duplicated in the fragments of baskets, matting, and cloth exhumed from graves that were centuries old in this American land long before Columbus sailed from the harbor of Palos.

Is it not somewhat humbling to our haughty pride to know that these "savage, dirty, loathsome, filthy, disgusting" people — with a score other rude epithets which I have heard applied to them — gave us the weaving art in such high perfection, and that we are indebted to them for all the useful, beautiful, and luxurious products of our modern looms?

Prior to 1892 the *modern* Navaho blanket was almost unknown. As I shall show in the chapter on the early history of the blanket, there were rare, fine, and wonderful blankets made early in the last century that today are the envy and desire of the collector, but it was not until after 1892 that the blanket began to be made on a large scale as a commercial article. Then came a rapid deterioration of the art that was as unnecessary as it was lamentable and regrettable, for it gave crude, thick, coarse, degraded specimens of blanketry to the world and thus worked the art long-time detriment and injury. But, like many another evil, it grew to such proportions that it became its own slayer. Out of the mere instinct of self-preservation the Indian trader sprang into the breach he himself had made and refused to buy the inferior specimens of the loom, for, as no one would buy them, they remained as dead and unprofitable stock on his shelves. The result is that, today, as fine blankets are being woven as were ever produced in the palmiest days of the art, and among the nearly *million dollars' worth* of blankets the United States Government officials report as the product of the Navaho looms in 1913, there are scores, nay hundreds, and perhaps thousands, that would be the pride of any trained and expert collector, or grace the hall, den, library, or bedroom of the most fastidious, exacting, and artistic housewife in the land.

During the past twenty years interest in the life of the North American aborigine has so increased that everything connected with him has taken on an added value. The collecting of Indian "curios" has passed through all the successive stages of the popular "fad," and blankets, baskets, bead-work, pipes, drums, head-dresses, and many etceteras have each taken a more or less exalted place for a longer or shorter time in the public estimation. But to a comparatively limited few, who, however, are slowly but surely growing in number, there has come a true appreciation of the marvelous work of certain Indians along the lines of textile and basket weaving. Upon the latter subject I prepared a popular work some years ago,* (now in its sixth edition), which is largely used by those seeking further information in this fascinating branch of aboriginal industry. In the pages that follow I have endeavored to do for the art of blanket-weaving what that book sought to do for the art of basket-making. If thereby I shall bring to a larger circle of American and other students a more intimate knowledge of the Indian who weaves the blanket and a deeper sympathy with him in his life problems, I shall feel that my endeavors have been eminently successful.

It will be observed that I follow the Americanized and rational form of spelling the name *Navaho.* Why people should consent to use the misleading and unnecessary Spanish form of the name, *Navajo,* is beyond me. Every stranger to the Spanish tongue—and there are millions who are thus strange—naturally pronounces this *Na-va-joe,* and cannot be blamed. Yet it does give the One-who-knows the opportunity to laugh at him, and perhaps this is the reason the Spanish form is retained. Were the name one of Spanish origin we might be reconciled to that form of spelling, but as it is a name belonging to a tribe of Amerinds who were found here, and had been here for centuries when the Spaniards came, there is no reason whatever why they should have fixed upon them forever a European method of spelling their name.

For upwards of thirty years I have known the Navaho Indian. I wrote and published for the first Indian trader who made a specialty of the Navaho blanket the first blanket catalogue ever issued. I have carefully watched the various developments of the art, have bought many hundreds of blankets, know personally scores of the best weavers of the tribe, and as late as the winter of 1912-13 spent over three months visiting

* *Indian Basketry.*

them, watching them work, engaging in their ceremonies, sleeping in their *hogans,* eating their food, riding their ponies, and listening to their legends, and the following pages are the result of this long-continued study and personal association. To understand the blanket *aright* and *fully,* the student must understand the Indian; hence my introduction in the Appendix of much that to the superficial may seem unnecessary and extraneous matter. To the "knowing," however, I am assured that every line will justify its presence, and it is for these that I find the joy of writing.

In this, as in all my other books, I have cared less about being thought an *original* writer than of giving all possible information about the subject presented. Hence I have gleaned from every known and available source. As a rule these sources are stated, but if in any place I have failed to give the fullest possible credit it has been through inadvertence, and I hereby extend my apologies and acknowledgements and freely and fully express my obligations.

Pasadena, 1914.   George Wharton James.

CONTENTS

ILLUSTRATIONS

*Asterisks indicate that the illustration is in the color
plate section, which follows page 10.*

xiii

ILLUSTRATIONS

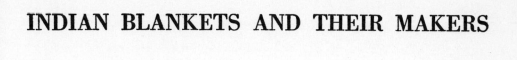

INDIAN BLANKETS AND THEIR MAKERS

INDIAN BLANKETS AND THEIR MAKERS

CHAPTER I

Where Navaho Blankets Are Made
Navaho Houses and Their Songs of Blessing

ONE of the great surprises to him who travels over the Navaho reservation for the first time is that he never sees villages, towns, settlements, or groups of houses of the Navahos. Indeed, he may wander for months and seldom see a *hogan* unless he watches trails carefully and follows those that seem to be traveled. The Navaho is not a gregarious animal in his home life. He wants his own about him and no more. Association with his fellows he obtains at the trading-store, or at the many ceremonial chantings, dancings, or prayers that his "singing, prayer, and medicine men" provide for him.

Following one of these trails the visitor may be led into a small arroyo — or dry stream, and there close to the wall, perhaps, is the summer *hogan*. It may be in the woods, or in the shelter of some rocks, but seldom in the open.

The older Navahos tell us that in the "far-away days of the old" they used to live in mere dugouts, with a rude covering of a grass and yucca mat secured with yucca cords. This was entered by means of a ladder which was drawn in after use. When a change of domicile was desired both yucca mat-roof and ladder were made into a roll and carried to the new location.

But as conditions improved, the type of dwelling correspondingly improved until the present forms of *hogans* (pronounced ho-gán) were modeled. The builders claim, however, that these types are sacred and are constructed after legendary designs. There are, broadly speaking, two types, the summer and the winter *hogan*. Both are miserably crude structures and wholly at variance with the exquisite blankets designed and manufactured therein. One would naturally think that, with the art instinct highly developed in one line, it would assert itself in others, and espe-

I

cially in the structures erected for their homes. Yet as one studies the inner life of the Navaho he may find full explanation of this apparent contradiction. In the first place the Navaho is a partial nomad. Never until now has he really felt himself able to settle down anywhere. He had few or no possessions and his home, therefore, needed to be only a temporary shelter which he might have to leave at a moment's or an hour's notice. Hence, why should he make it beautiful, and have his heart grieved at being compelled to forsake it. Superstition also requires the Navahos to burn the *hogan* after a death has taken place in it. Then, too, the Navaho does not regard the *hogan* as a white man does his home. The latter lives in his house and goes out of doors as his business or his pleasure demands. The Navaho, on the other hand, lives out of doors. That is his *home*. He uses his *hogan* as a convenient place of storage and a stopping place, with the addition, of course, in winter, that it is a comfortable sleeping place which he can make warm. But *our* idea of a house being a home never enters his mind. He loves the beauty of the out-of-doors. He regards that as his own, and the poetry of his conceptions in a variety of ways is remarkably influenced by the glories of Nature. These, then, are reasons against the making of a more beautiful and permanent dwelling.

Who but a Nature poet, even in his legends, could have conceived of a house *(hogan)* made as follows, resplendent and magnificent, as did the Navaho creator of the original *hogan:*

The poles were made of precious stones such as white-shell, turquoise, abalone, obsidian, and red stone, and were five in number. The interstices were lined with four shelves of white-shell, and four of turquoise, and four of abalone and obsidian, each corresponding with the pole of the respective stone, thus combining the cardinal colors of white, blue, yellow and black in one gorgeous edifice. The floor, too, of this structure was laid with a fourfold rug of obsidian, abalone, turquoise, and white shell, each spread over the other in the order mentioned, while the door consisted of a quadruple curtain or screen of dawn, sky-blue, evening twilight, and darkness. As a matter of course the divine builders might increase its size at will, and reduce it to a minimum, whenever it seemed desirable to do so.*

Nor is this the only gorgeous *hogan* of the poet's imagination. There are others which were the prototypes of other styles in use today, and also for *hogans* for especial ceremonial use.

While Father Berard states that the present custom does not require special dedicatory ceremonies at the completion of a *hogan,* Cosmos Mindeleff, in the *Seventeenth Report of the Bureau of American Ethnology,* gives a full account of them, and they are so wonderful, for a wild and barbaric people, that I cannot refrain from extracting largely.

* Father Berard in *An Ethnologic Dictionary.* The Franciscan Fathers, St. Michels, Ariz.

Personally I have witnessed some of these ceremonials, have recorded some of the songs in my graphophone, and have felt that I would like to give to the American civilized, Christian world, a ceremony for the dedication of its houses based on what I have seen and learned of the home-dedication rituals of these heathen, uncivilized, unchristian (!) people.

Brotherly helpfulness is the rule in the erection of a Navaho *hogan,* and the assistance of friends generally makes it possible to complete the structure in one, or at most two or three days. The wife then sweeps out the interior with a grass broom, and she or her husband lights a fire under the smoke-hole. Then, taking a saucer or bowl-shaped basket she fills it with white corn meal which she hands over to the head of the household. He proceeds to rub a handful of meal on each of the five principal timbers of which the *hogan* frame is formed, beginning always with the south doorway timber. He rubs the meal on one place, as high up as he can easily reach, and always in the following order: south doorway, south, west, north timbers, and the north doorway timber. All keep reverent silence while this is being done. Next, with a sweeping motion of his hand, sunwise, he sprinkles the meal to the outer circumference of the room, at the same time in a low, measured, chanting tone saying:

> May it be delightful, my house;
> From my head may it be delightful;
> To my feet may it be delightful;
> Where I lie may it be delightful;
> All above me may it be delightful;
> All around me may it be delightful.

Then, flinging a little meal into the fire he continues:

> May it be delightful and well, my fire.

Tossing a handful or two of meal up and through the smoke-hole:

> May it be delightful, Sun, my mother's ancestor, for this gift;
> May it be delightful as I walk around my house.

Now, sprinkling two or three handfuls out of the doorway he says:

> May it be delightful, this road of light [the path of the Sun], my mother's ancestor.

The woman of the house now advances, makes a meal-offering to the fire, and says, in a quiet and subdued voice:

> May it be delightful, my fire;
> May it be delightful for my children; may all be well;
> May it be delightful with my food and theirs; may all be well;
> All my possessions well may they be made.
> All my flocks well may they be made [that is, may they be healthful and increase].

Let me quote Cosmos Mindeleff for the remainder of the description:

Night will have fallen . . . all now gather inside, the blanket is suspended over the door-frame, all the possessions of the family are brought in, sheepskins are spread on the floor, the fire is brightened, and the men all squat around it. The women bring in food in earthen cooking pots and basins, and, having set them down among the men, they huddle together by themselves to enjoy the occasion as spectators. Everyone helps himself from the pots by dipping in with his fingers, the meat is broken into pieces, and the bones are gnawed upon and sociably passed from hand to hand. When the feast is finished tobacco and corn husks are produced, cigarettes are made, everyone smokes, and convivial gossipy talk prevails. This continues for two or three hours, when the people who live near by get up their horses and ride home. Those from a long distance either find places to sleep in the *hogan* or wrap themselves in their blankets and sleep at the foot of a tree. This ceremony is known as the *qogán aiila,* a kind of salutation to the house.

But the house devotions have not yet been observed. Occasionally these take place as soon as the house is finished, but usually there is an interval of several days to permit the house builders to invite all their friends and to provide the necessary food for their entertainment. Although analogous to the Anglo-Saxon "house-warming," the house devotions, besides being a merrymaking for the young people, have a much more solemn significance for the elders. If they be not observed soon after the house is built bad dreams will plague the dwellers therein, toothache (dreaded for mystic reasons) will torture them, and the evil influence from the north will cause them all kinds of bodily ill; the flocks will dwindle, ill luck will come, ghosts will haunt the place, and the house will become *batsic,* tabooed.

A few days after the house is finished an arrangement is made with some shaman (devotional singer) to come and sing the ceremonial house songs. For this service he always receives a fee from those who engage him, perhaps a few sheep or their value, sometimes three or four horses or their equivalent, according to the circumstances of the house-builders. The social gathering at the house-devotion is much the same as that of the salutation to the house, when the house is built, except that more people are usually invited to the former. They feast and smoke, interchange scandal, and talk of other topics of interest, for some hours. Presently the shaman seats himself under the main west timber so as to face the east, and the singing begins.

In this ceremony no rattle is used. The songs are begun by the shaman in a drawling tone and all the men join in. The shaman acts only as leader and director. Each one, and there are many of them in the tribe, has his own particular songs, fetiches, and accompanying ceremonies, and after he has pitched a song he listens closely to hear whether the correct words are sung. This is a matter of great importance, as the omission of a part of the song or the incorrect rendering of any word would entail evil consequences to the house and its inmates. All the house songs of the numerous shamans are of similar import, but differ in minor details.

The first song is addressed to the east, and is as follows:

> Far in the east far below there a house was made;
> Delightful house.
> God of Dawn there his house was made;
> Delightful house.
> The Dawn there his house was made;
> Delightful house.
> White corn there its house was made;
> Delightful house.
> Soft possessions for them a house was made;
> Delightful house.
> Water in plenty surrounding for it a house was made;
> Delightful house.
> Corn pollen for it a house was made;
> Delightful house.
> The ancients make their presence delightful;
> Delightful house.

Immediately following this song, but in a much livelier measure, the following benedictory chant is sung:

> Before me may it be delightful;
> Behind me may it be delightful;
> Around me may it be delightful;
> Below me may it be delightful;
> Above me may it be delightful;
> All (universally) may it be delightful.

After a short interval the following is sung to the west:

> Far in the west far below there a house was made;
> Delightful house.
> God of Twilight there his house was made;
> Delightful house.
> Yellow light of evening there his house was made;
> Delightful house.
> Yellow corn there its house was made;
> Delightful house.
> Hard possessions there their house was made;
> Delightful house.
> Young rain there its house was made;
> Delightful house.
> Corn pollen there its house was made;
> Delightful house.
> The ancients make their presence delightful;
> Delightful house.

The song to the west is also followed by the benedictory chant, as above, and after this the song which was sung to the east is repeated; but this time it is addressed to the south. The song to the west is then repeated, but addressed to the north, and the two songs are repeated alternately until each one has been sung three times to each cardinal point. The benedictory chant is sung between each repetition.

All the men present join in the singing under the leadership of the shaman, who does not himself sing, but only starts each song. The women never sing at these gatherings, although on other occasions, when they get together by themselves, they sing very sweetly. It is quite common to hear a primitive kind of part singing, some piping in a curious falsetto, others droning a deep bass.

The songs are addressed to each of the cardinal points, because in the Navaho system different groups of deities are assigned to each of these points. The Navaho also makes a distinction between heavy rain and light rain. The heavy rain, such as accompanies thunder storms, is regarded as the " male rain," while the gentle showers, or " young rains," coming directly from the house of Estsanatlehi, are regarded as especially beneficent; but both are deemed necessary to fertilize. A distinction is also made between " hard possessions," such as turquois and coral beads, shell ornaments, and all articles made from hard substances, and " soft possessions," which comprise blankets and all textile substances, skins, etc. The Navaho prays that his house may cover many of both hard and soft possessions.

The songs given above are known as the twelve house songs, although there are only two songs, each repeated twelve times. These are sung with many variations by the different shamans, and while the builders are preparing for this ceremony they discuss which shaman has the best and most beautiful words before they decide which one to engage. But the songs are invariably addressed to the deities named, Quastceyalci, the God of Dawn, and Qastceqogan, the God of Twilight; and they always have the same general significance.

After the " twelve songs " are finished many others are sung: to Estsanatlehi, a benignant Goddess of the West, and to Yol'kai Estsan, the complementary Goddess of the East; to the sun, the dawn, and twilight; to the light and to the darkness; to the six sacred mountains, and to many other members of a very numerous theogony. Other song-prayers are chanted directly to malign influences, beseeching them to remain far off; to evil in general; to coughs and lung evils, and to sorcerers, praying them not to come near the dwelling. The singing of the songs is so timed that the last one is delivered just as the gray streaks of dawn appear, when the visitors round up their horses and ride home.*

Father Berard, whose knowledge is profound, and whose care in making assertions is equal to his knowledge, contends that these songs are only incidentally connected with a ceremony of house dedication, but are essential to the Vigil or Rite of Blessing which is performed frequently in the same *hogan*, in order that the blessing may be renewed upon the members of the family and all their possessions. He goes further and states:

Moreover, it is in accordance with good custom to have other ceremonies performed in a new *hogan* previous to the invocation of the house songs. In fact, this

* Cosmos Mindeleff, *Navaho Houses*, pp. 504-509, in *Seventeenth Annual Report Bureau of Ethnology.*

Fig. 1.
A Summer Hogan.
(Photo by A. C. Vroman.)

Fig. 2.
A Winter Hogan.

custom suggests that at times the new *hogan* is built for the purpose of having a desirable ceremony performed, For, while greater convenience makes a summer and winter home desirable at different points, and such natural causes as scarcity of range and water frequently decide a change in location, this change is at times due to an evil spell which may haunt a vicinity. Should this continue, despite all efforts to dispel such influence, a new dwelling is erected in some other locality, and its occupation inaugurated with some effective and purifying ceremony.*

In Fig. 1 we have a good representation of a summer *hogan*. This is invariably near the cornfields or other farming place, and as convenient as possible to the sheep range. Suitable corrals are constructed for the care of the sheep during the night time, and where possible the close proximity of a spring, running stream, or pool of water is desired.

It is in the selection of the site and the erection of the winter *hogan* (Fig. 2) that the Navaho shows the greatest care. He must see that there are no red ant hills near by, as, aside from the perpetual discomfort of too close proximity to these pests, his legendary lore has taught him that it was these small but annoying creatures that separated First Man from the Gods. There must be an unobstructed view to the east from the doorway, as the beneficial influences of the God of Sunrise are much appreciated by the devout Navaho.

Now the five chief timbers must be found, three of these to terminate in a spreading fork, the other two, for the doorway, being selected for their straightness. As there is no standard of size, the poles need not be any set size, but they are generally from ten to twelve feet long.

Few white men would call the Navaho *hogan* beautiful, for there is seldom, if ever, the slightest attempt made to adorn it, yet to the Indian it is beautiful in accordance with his myths and the closeness to which he adheres to the ancient model in its construction. Strength of timber, dryness, warmth, and smoothness of floor, good bark and other material to allow the piling over it of the earth covering, these make the *hogan nijoni* — the house beautiful — of the Navaho. And surely when he recalls the stories of the first *hogans* made by the gods, if he sees in his own rude and primitive dwelling any of the charm and glory associated with those early houses he must see great and wonderful beauty in them.

* From *An Ethnologic Dictionary*.

CHAPTER II

The Birth and Growth of the Art of Navaho Blanket-Weaving

WHAT would civilized mankind do without its textile fabrics — goods woven from wool, cotton, flax, and other fibers? Imagine the world of today without its cottons and calicoes for dresses, shirts, waists, sheets, and the thousand and one things for which they are used; its linens; its woollens; its silks; its carpets; its manillas, and its scores of other materials woven into specific shapes, or in the piece for cutting out and making into the objects required. Destroy the art of weaving and in one month civilized mankind would send up such a wail of deprivation and distress as would resound from pole to pole and completely encircle the earth.

Whence, then, came this useful, this necessary art? To whom do we owe its introduction? Necessarily, it is one of those arts which only the highest civilization could have evolved; it must have come from the French, the Germans, the English, or, if slightly less modern, from the Greeks and Romans!

Nay, nay!

Then it is an oriental art, brought to us from the Arabs, or the Hindoos, the Japanese, or Chinese?

Nay, it is not from these.

It goes back to the primitive little brown woman, the aboriginal mother, who sought for something more than mere skins to clothe her helpless babe and herself when the rigorous storms of winter quickened her intellect through her maternal affection — or instinct, if her affectionate nature had not yet evolved.

There is much evidence to prove that long, long before the art of making pottery was discovered, weaving had attained a fair degree of perfection. Ropes twisted, braided, and knotted were used; nets had long been in use for carrying small objects; mats, sandals, doorway coverings, etc., were made of yucca fiber, cedar bark, and other fibers, and prior to the coming of the Spaniards the Amerind had found out all about cotton, had learned how to grow it, to card, spin, and weave it, and many of our museums have specimens of cotton cloth in many weaves secured from graves that were ancient and the objects of tradition before the Spaniards arrived.

8

Too often have we imagined that human progress began with us. Human conceit does not lessen as we grow in years. This is a pity, for it shuts us out from closer knowledge and sympathy with the peoples of the past, fosters our own ignorance, which needs no fostering to reveal it as colossal, and, worst of all, it brings upon us the inevitable and evil results that always follow in the train of pride, conceit, and ignorance, whether these traits be manifested in a race, a nation, a state, or an individual. There are but few of the beneficial inventions that pertain to the home and personal life of mankind, the first steps of which — by far the most important — were not discovered by these patient, pathetic pioneers among the facts of human existence — the aborigines. In one phase of its author's thought this book is a humble and tardy, though none the less sincere, tribute to the worth and work of the aboriginal woman. Too long has the debt been unrecognized. The sooner we send out our song of thanks to her — no matter how many centuries may have elapsed since she passed on — the better for us. Unpaid obligations always weigh down those who have not paid, whether through ignorance, carelessness, indifference, or pride. In the case of ignorance its punishment is itself — more ignorance. In that of carelessness, indifference, and pride, the law of life is that "with what measure ye mete it shall be measured to you again." And ingratitude ever brings its own special train of evils upon the ungrateful.

It will be evident, therefore, that I propose that the weaving art of the Amerind shall speak for itself to the culture of the civilized races of today. It needs no apology; it stands upon its own worth. It came, a full-fledged art from their hands to us, and as recipients we shall do well to understand, as far as we may, the various steps through which it arduously climbed to its present stage of perfection.

It seems reasonable to assume that blanketry was an outcome of basketry. The latter approximates more nearly to natural processes, as in the weaving of twigs together to form the birds' nests, or the simple interlacing and intertwining of vines, etc., in their wild state. This art once commenced, and pliable and flexible twigs once used for the weaving of baskets, it could scarcely be called another art that the making of textile fabrics followed. It was simply the merging of the use of the less flexible and coarse into the more flexible and fine.

When all these processes actually began we do not know. The most ancient literature of all peoples took it for granted that readers were familiar with weaving and the varied products of the loom, as the art long antedated written language. When Moses was instructed to call upon the children of Israel for materials for the tabernacle he asked for fine linen and other spun objects, and we are told (Exodus 35:25),

"And all the women that were wise-hearted did spin with their hands, and brought that which they had spun, both of blue, and of purple, and of scarlet, and of fine linen."

The Navahos have a legend which claims divine origin for the art of weaving. It is related as follows in their "Moving Upward" chant:

The Spider Man drew some cotton from his side and instructed the Navaho to make a loom. The cotton-warp was made of spider-web. The upper cross-pole was called the sky-cord, the lower cross-pole the earth-cord. The warp-sticks were made of sun rays; the upper strings, fastening the warp to the pole, of lightning; the lower strings of sun-halo; the heald was a rock-crystal; the cord-heald stick was made of sheet-lightning, and was secured to the warp strands by means of rain-ray-cords.

The batten-stick was also made of sun-halo, while the comb was of white shell. Four spindles or distaffs were added to this, the disks of which were of cannel-coal, turquoise, abalone, and white bead, respectively, and the spindle-sticks of zigzag lightning, flash lightning, sheet lightning, and rain-ray, respectively.

The dark blue, yellow, and white winds quickened the spindles according to their color, and enabled them to travel around the world.*

Sheep perhaps were the first animals to be domesticated, and in the most ancient literature we find constant references to them, both as flocks and as individual animals. The patriarchs of the Old Testament owned sheep by the thousands, and lived very much like the Navahos of today, moving their homes from place to place as their sheep required fresh pasture and water. They used the flesh of the sheep for food, and their skins for clothing and to sleep upon. Later, when the art of weaving was invented the fleeces were spun and woven, even as the Navahos spin and weave them today. A fascinating chapter could be made up in this book of references to sheep, shepherds, sheep-folds, the habits of sheep, the shearing of sheep, weaving, dyeing, etc., from the Hebrew scriptures, nearly all of which could be applied with truth and force to the Navaho shepherd as he is today. And such a chapter would help to give to the reader a clearer comprehension of the life of the Navaho shepherd than any brief and cursory account could do.

Few biblical students think of the Navaho when reading the exquisite twenty-third psalm, yet few shepherds surpass these New Mexican aborigines in their care to see that their flocks are made "to lie down in green pastures," or led "beside the still waters."

In their sacred songs there are many references to sheep and their care, and a Navaho shaman might have been the original author of such passages as: "Be thou diligent to know the state of thy flocks, and look well to thy herds." (Proverbs, 27:23.)

From the day they are able to toddle young Navaho boys and girls

* From *An Ethnologic Dictionary.*

Fig. 4.
Rare Old Bayeta Blanket.
(Author's Collection.)   [PAGE 20]

Fig. 5.
Hopi Ceremonial Blanket.
(Collection of J. L. Hubbell.)
Showing lightning, rain cloud, and descending rain in the two outside diamonds.
[PAGE 21]

FIG. 7.

Bayeta " Chief's " Blanket.

(Fred Harvey Collection.)

A very old Navaho. The color of the bayeta, from years of usage and from the
action of water and the sun, has toned down to a most beautiful rose color.

[PAGE 32]

FIG. 8.

Fine " Chief's " Blanket of Bayeta.

(Vroman Collection.)   [PAGE 33]

FIG. 10.

Typical Navaho Squaw Dress of the Oldest Style.
(Collection of J. L. Hubbell.)   [PAGE 33]

FIG. 9.

Rare Type Old Bayeta Double Saddle Blanket.
(Fred Harvey Collection.)

Saddle blankets are the commonest type of Navaho weaving, though specimens like the above are rarer than larger blankets of the same type, and were usually made for some chief or person of distinction.   [PAGE 33]

[PAGE 35]

FIG. 16.
An Exquisite Bayeta.
(Vroman Collection.)

[PAGE 34]

FIG. 11.
Old Bayeta Saddle Blanket.
(Author's Collection.)

[Page 37]

Fig. 24.

Double Saddle Blanket of Soft Weave, Native Colors
and Native Wool.

(Author's Collection.)

[Page 35]

Fig. 17.

A Blanket About Which Experts Differ.

(Vroman Collection.)

FIG. 26.

A Beautiful Soft Piece of Weaving.

(Author's Collection.)

[PAGE 38]

FIG. 25.

A Good Specimen of an Old Style Native Blanket.

(Author's Collection.)

[PAGE 37]

FIG. 29.

Modern Navaho Squaw Dress.

(Collection of C. N. Cotton.)

[PAGE 41]

FIG. 30.

Unique Zuni Squaw Dress.

(Fred Harvey Collection.)

The design and color scheme in this blanket are entirely unique; so is its history. Two styles of weaving, different from the general type of Navaho work, and the introduction of two different shades of indigo blue, combine to make this a very rare specimen. [PAGE 41]

[PAGE 54]

Fig. 38.

Rare Old Moki Pattern.
(Fred Harvey Collection.)
The common type of so-called Moki blankets consists usually of the black or
brown and blue stripe, sometimes alternated with white stripes.

Fig. 32.

Pueblo-made Squaw Dress.
(Author's Collection.)   [PAGE 42]

FIG. 195.
Outline Blanket.
(Collection of C. C. Manning Co.)
Designed by Keh-yez-zhie Be-ma.

FIG. 195.
Outline Blanket.
(Collection of C. C. Manning Co.)
Designed by Keh-yez-zhie Be-ma.

FIG. 146.
Navaho Blanket of Symbolic Design.
(Author's Collection.)

[PAGE 124]

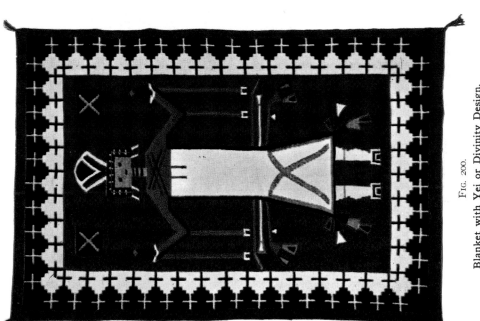

Fig. 202.

Yei Blanket from a Painting.

(By permission of the owner, W. MacGinnies.)

[PAGE 141]

Fig. 200.

Blanket with Yei or Divinity Design.

(Courtesy of R. T. F. Simpson.)

[PAGE 140]

FIG. 217.

Standard Blanket.

(Courtesy of J. A. Molohon & Co.)

Woven by Be-leen Al-pi Be-gay Eh-son.   [PAGE 150]

FIG. 203.

Blanket with Sacred Symbols.

(Courtesy of J. A. Molohon & Co.)

Designed and woven by Dug-gau-eth-lun Bi-dazhie.   [PAGE 142]

FIG. 219.

Standard Blanket.

(Courtesy of the C. C. Manning Co.)

Gray base, with design in red, white, and black.   [PAGE 151]

FIG. 218.

"Extra" Blanket of Good Design.

(Courtesy of the C. C. Manning Co.)

Occasionally found in "Standard" quality.

Woven by Meh-li-to Be-day-zhie.   [PAGE 151]

Fig. 230.

"Extra" Native Wool Undyed Blanket of Striking Design.
(Courtesy of J. A. Molohon & Co.)
This weaver never duplicates her blankets.

[PAGE 153]

Fig. 228.

Native Wool Blanket   [PAGE 152]

FIG. 232.

Individualistic Design. Same Weave as Fig. 230.
(Courtesy of J. A. Molohon & Co.)
Showing the fertility of invention in the maker.   [PAGE 154]

FIG. 231.

Individualistic Design in "Extra" Blanket.   [PAGE 154]
(Courtesy of J. A. Molohon & Co.)

[Page 154]

Fig. 234.
Unique Design in "Extra" Quality.
(Courtesy of J. A. Molohon & Co.)
Designed by Yeh-del-spah Bi-mah.

[Page 154]

Fig. 233.
Simple and Pleasing Design.
Generally woven in "Extra" quality.

Fig. 236.

The Flood of Red in the Outer Body of This Blanket Gives It a
Rich and Warm Effect.

[Page 155]

Fig. 235.

Daring Design of Naturalistic and Geometric Figures.

[Page 155]

are taught the duties, privileges, joys, and responsibilities of the shepherd. On all my trips over the Navaho reservation this has been one of my great pleasures, to find, in a score of instances, young lads of ten, twelve, fourteen years, and sometimes girls of the same age, alone, in charge of a flock of a hundred, or several hundred sheep. Nor is attending to a flock of sheep a mere perfunctory task. There is much to do and much to know properly to care for them. Pasture must be found, therefore all the good and available ranges within the area of their roaming must be known to the young shepherd. Water also is as essential as grass, hence the apparently marvelous knowledge the Navaho youths possess of water-pockets, casual ponds, tanks-in-the-rocks, springs, etc. A score of times when traveling, my Navaho drivers have stopped the team, unhitched the horses, left me to my own devices in the heart of the desert, and ridden off with a wild whoop, carrying all the available canteens. In half an hour, an hour, and occasionally, even longer, they would return, the horses and themselves fully refreshed with the water they had found, and their canteens or *tusjehs* full of the precious fluid.

Dogs help them protect their charge from the attacks of coyotes, mountain lions, and other beasts of prey, and there are few of the shepherds who are not expert in the use of the shotgun. They also become astute interpreters of weather signs; they learn to read the changing face of the heavens, as one fierce and unprepared-for storm might rob them of their whole herd. Hence these youngsters, perforce, are weather-wise to a remarkable degree, and they know when the time has come for them to move from the open plains to the foothills, and thence to the higher ranges, where grass lingers, and when browse can be found in the chaparral long after the grass has been buried by winter's snows. For Navaho sheep soon learn that they must not be too choice and particular as to their diet. They must eat what they can get, rather than what they prefer.

Lambing time, too, requires no small knowledge and skill, and while the fathers and mothers aid at this and at all other needed times, it behooves the young shepherds to be ready for everything that may happen.

Their knowledge of the individual members of their flocks seems like magic, for, to a casual observer, it is impossible to tell one sheep from another in a flock of say five hundred, seven hundred and fifty, or a thousand animals. Yet many a time when I have wanted to buy a sheep, the juvenile shepherd has first gained his mother's consent to the sale, and then partaken in a discussion as to which animal should be delivered over to the slaughter. Then, with sure and certain movements, he proceeded to search out, find, and steal upon the selected creature, with ·a knowledge as certain as that of a mother in designating her children.

But however interesting sheep and shepherds may be to us, we must now return to a consideration of the art of weaving. That it was known to the Amerind long prior to the time of Columbus is as clearly established as any fact in history.

The fabrics woven and used in the making and decoration of pottery, according to Holmes, consisted generally of

the fibre of bark, flax, hemp, nettles, and grasses, which were spun into thread of various sizes; or of splints of wood, twigs, roots, vines, porcupine quills, feathers, and a variety of animal tissues, either plaited or used in an untwisted state. The articles produced were mats, baskets, nets, bags, plain cloths, and entire garments, such as capes, hats, belts, and sandals.*

When cotton made its appearance in America is not known, yet it must have been quite early, for in the ruined and prehistoric Cliff Dwellings many cotton fabrics have been found. Holmes, Bandelier, Nordenskiold, Fewkes, and others have described the cottons thus found. At Awatobi, one of the ruined pueblos of the Hopi, fragments of cloth of cotton and agave fibre, and of cotton alone were gathered.

When the European first discovered the American Indians of the Southwest he found them wearing blankets and other garments of their own weaving, mostly made of cotton, which they grew, cleaned, carded, spun, and dyed themselves. Cabez de Vaca, in his *Relacion,* states that he found the natives wearing linen and woolen cloths, and at one place fine cotton shawls, all of their own weaving.

Fray Marcos de Nizza, when he made his memorable reconnoissance into New Mexico in 1538, says that the natives were dressed in cottoncloth, and that the men of Cibola wore long cotton gowns which reached to their feet.

When Coronado reached the seven cities of Cibola (Zuni) in 1540, he found the people wearing cotton blankets. Castañeda says: "The women wear blankets, which they tie or knot over the left shoulder, leaving the right arm out. These serve to cover the body." This is an exact description of the Pueblo Indian woman's dress of today.

Later, when Don Pedro de Tobar went to explore the Province of Tusayan—the home of the Hopi—and the Indians barred his pathway, he fell upon them and vanquished them. Then they brought gifts, among which were cotton cloth of their own manufacture.

About forty-five miles west of Oraibi, in the Province of Tusayan, the Hopis had a fairly large area of cultivable land which to this day is known to the Navahos as "the cotton-planting ground."

The Pueblo Indians, in the ancient days, used blankets in their larger

* W. H. Holmes, in *Third Annual Report, Bureau of Ethnology.*

doorways as covering for cold weather. There was no other provided way of closing them. Until a few years ago doorways existed where a slight pole, of the same kind as those used in the lintel, was built into the masonry of the jambs a few inches below the lintel proper. Upon this the blanket was hung.*

These blankets, however, were made up of agave fibre and cotton, or of one or the other alone — not of wool. For, prior to the coming of the Spaniards, wool was unknown in North America.

Sheep were first brought into New Mexico by Coronado in 1540, but his flocks were killed after his return to Mexico. Then when Juan de Oñate came he brought a fresh supply in which were some fine Spanish merinos, and since then sheep have never failed in New Mexico, in spite of the rebellion which drove out the Spaniards, nomad and thieving Indians, drought, and famine. Indeed, for many years New Mexico's chief dependence was upon its sheep. We are told that "in 1822 Francisco Xavier Chavez, then governor, better known as El Guero (The Blond), owned over a million sheep. These were let out on shares to men all over the territory. A later governor, Bartolomé Baca, had nearly as many. An old Mexican was living in 1899, who used to be one of Baca's majordomos, and had had charge of 500,000 sheep, with seven hundred shepherds under him. All the shepherds were armed with flintlock muskets, and frequently had to use them against the savages, as well as in keeping down the bears, cougars, wolves, coyotes, and other animals.

It is interesting in this connection to enquire whence gained the Navaho his flocks and herds of sheep and goats. This question opens up a very interesting phase of early Spanish and Pueblo history. When the Spaniards came and the Franciscans began their work of Christianizing and civilizing the Indian, the roving Navaho never came much under their influence. But the sedentary Pueblo was material ready to hand, as it were, and the priests made the most of him. The result was churches were built in many of the Pueblos of New Mexico (including what is now Arizona), such as San Ildefonso, Zuni, Acoma, Awatobi, Oraibi, and other of the Hopi pueblos. This was not done without arousing the fiercest hostility, and in time, deadly hatred of the native shamans, medicine-men, or priests. Again and again the Hopis rose in rebellion against the "long gowns"— as they called the Franciscan friars — and the bearded warriors of Spain. On Inscription Rock, in New Mexico, we read the rude record, made on the yielding but retaining rock, of the expedition of Don Feliz Martinez, Governor and Captain General of New Mexico, for "the reduction of the Zunis." Padre Letrado was slain in Zuni at

---

* Cosmos Mindeleff, *Pueblo Architecture*, p. 182, in *Eighth Annual Report, Bureau of Ethnology*.

the incitement of the aboriginal priests. The whole pueblo of Awatobi was wiped out of existence because its leading men even tolerated and welcomed the presence of the padres. From six hundred to a thousand people thus perished, showing the extreme lengths to which the native priests would go to defend their own religion from extinction.*

Added to the fury of religious superstition was the anger of free peoples made subservient to the domination of outsiders. The Spaniards were not always kind and politic in their dealings with the peoples they subjugated, and in their treatment of the Pueblo Indians they were especially unwise.

They took the calm and unresisting demeanor of these Quaker-like people for poor-spiritedness and cowardice. Never were they more mistaken, as they found in the great Pueblo rebellion in 1680. At this time, largely instigated by a Santa Clara patriot named Popé — a true aboriginal Patrick Henry and George Washington rolled into one — the whole of the Pueblo population of New Mexico and Arizona arose against the hated invader, with his long-gowned priests, and drove all whom they did not slay out of the country. Then, fearful of the vengeance they soon began to expect at the hands of the Spaniards, the "rebellious people"— nay, nay, let us call them by their proper name — these true-hearted patriots who had arisen in defense of their hearths, their homes, the graveyards of their ancestors, their cornfields, their hunting-grounds, their religion, their ceremonies, their honor, their families, and the preservation of their national existence — hid themselves on fortified mesas in the old inaccessible cliff-dwellings and elsewhere until the storm should have passed. But the Spaniards were long in coming; therefore the fear of vengeance was long continued. One evil result of these constant conflicts and of this waiting for the avenging blow of the Spaniards to fall was that the Pueblo Indians were unable to care for the sheep and goats which the Spaniards had brought to them very early in their relationship. The Navahos had already secured some of these new animals. *Now* were chances many for materially adding to their four-footed possessions.

For centuries they had been at war with the Pueblo, and naturally everything owned by him was regarded as legitimate prey. Doubtless soon after sheep were brought to the country they learned the flavor of mutton, and thenceforth found it easier to steal sheep than to go out on long, wearisome deer, antelope, and coyote hunts for their food. Then, too, sheep were surer of capture than wild animals.

Nor was it alone from the Pueblos that the Navahos learned to steal. They had no love for the Spaniard and Mexican. How could

* This interesting story is fully told in my *Old Franciscan Missions of New Mexico, Arizona, and Texas.*

they have? The possessor of a land seldom loves those who come to dispossess him, and the Navahos' predatory instincts were not long in asserting themselves in their dealings with the newcomers. Indeed, every page of the history of Spain's and Mexico's dealings with New Mexico is interlined with records of Navaho raids and thefts, and corresponding losses of sheep, horses, and cattle.

It is an interesting fact to note in passing that the Hopi and other Pueblo Indians from whom the Navahos stole their first bands of sheep now freely acknowledge that, had it not been for these thefts, they themselves would have had no sheep later on. Here is their explanation. Soon after their subjugation by the Spaniards, who brought the sheep to them, the fierce Utes of the North and East used to swoop down upon them in relentless raids and steal everything upon which they could lay their hands. The semi-nomad Navahos, who did not accumulate household and other goods as did the Hopis, though they lived in the raided region, were less troubled by the rapacious marauders. Hence they never entered into any compact with the harassed Pueblo Indians for purposes of joint defense, although now and again they suffered severely. They held their land and defied their foes, and along the valleys of the South of the San Juan the edges of the numerous mesas are lined with stone-wall breastworks, and the remains are still to be seen of many rude but well-chosen defenses, erected by them to repel Ute attacks. Being better fighters than the Pueblos, they succeeded in guarding their flocks and herds from the enemy, whereas the Pueblos lost every sheep and horse they possessed. Hence, while the Navaho sheep were originally stolen from the Pueblos, or captured in their fighting affrays with them, it was the fact that they had guarded the stolen herds so successfully that enabled the Pueblos later on to obtain sheep again.

In seeking to find out from whence the Navaho learned the art of weaving the questioning mind naturally halts at this point and asks whether there is any relation between the stealing of Spanish and Pueblo sheep by the Navahos and their induction into the art of weaving.

American archæologists and ethnologists have all assumed that the art of weaving on the loom was learned by the Navahos from their Pueblo neighbors. All the facts in the case seem to bear out this supposition. Yet, as is well known, the Navahos are a part of the great Athabascan family, which has scattered, by separate migrations, from Alaska into California, Arizona, and New Mexico. Many of the Alaskans are good weavers, and, according to Navaho traditions, their ancestors, when they came into the country, wore blankets that were made of cedar bark and yucca fibre. Even in the Alaska (Thlinket) blankets, made today of the wool of the white mountain goat, cedar bark is twisted in with the wool of the warp. Why, then, should not the Navaho woman have brought the art of weaving, possibly in a very primitive stage, from her original Alaskan home? That her art, however, has been improved by her contact with the Pueblo and other Indians there can be no question, and, if she had a crude loom, it was speedily replaced by the one so long used by the Pueblo. Where the Pueblo weaver gained his loom we do not know, whether from the tribes of the South or by his own invention. But in all practical ways the primitive loom was as complete and perfect at the time of the Spanish conquest as it is today.

According to the Rev. Father A. G. Morice, O. M. I., for many years a missionary among the Dénés of British Columbia, doubtless a branch of the Navaho family, the loom used by these western Indians is much more crude than that of our Navahos. It consists simply of a foursquare heavy frame, the warp strings being attached to the top and bottom beams, with no method for tightening the warp. He states that the only weaving they did was of rabbit-skin blankets. The skins were twisted — corresponding to the spinning of yarn — by first soaking them in water and then twisting the strips by rolling them upon the naked thigh. Each skin was made to yield a single band, and each band was knotted end to end so as to form a continuous cord. This cord was then used both as warp and woof, and was of the simplest and crudest kind of weaving, no batten of any kind being used.

This is an important contribution to the literature of the Navaho blanket, for these western Dénés are the original stock of the so-called Athabascan tribes of our American Southwest. Hence it is reasonable to assume that if they now have a loom superior to those of their own people, it was gained elsewhere. As yet the Dénés of the West have not evolved it. The Navahos were familiar with the crude rabbit-skin blanket loom, for it is still to be found today in active operation among the Mohaves, Pimas, and Apaches. Fig. 3 is of a Mohave Indian wearing one of these rabbit-skin blankets, and they are by no means uncommon. This blanket and this loom, crude though they were, prepared them, however, for the ready and immediate adoption of a superior loom. Hence, just as they stole the sheep of the Spaniards, Mexicans, and Pueblo Indians, it is not unreasonable to suppose they stole the loom of the latter, and possibly compelled 'a captive of the tribe to instruct them in its more complex manipulation.

This loom and the varied processes of weaving are fully described in the chapter devoted to that purpose.

Whether the Navahos learned the art from the Pueblo or not, it is freely conceded that they are by far the better weavers of the two today. In quality of work and excellence of design all other aboriginal weavers

Fig. 3.
Mohave Indian Wearing Rabbit-Skin Blanket.
(Photo by George Wharton James.)

north of the Mexican line must yield to them. And not only is the Navaho weaver the best, but she has preserved her art freest from European influence. The Navaho is the great American conservative. He loves neither the white man nor his ways. He seeks to live his own life on his own reservation, unhampered and uncontrolled by the white race. He scorns nearly everything about the latter — his dress, his food, his houses, his habits, his opinions, his religion, his language — and merely tolerates him because he has to, and for the money he can get out of him for his blankets and the wool of his sheep, and for the guns he does not know how to make, yet loves to use.

While to those who know the Navaho and Pueblo Indian weavers it is a commonplace too well known even to repeat, it should not be overlooked by the general reader that in speaking of the Navaho as a weaver it is his womankind who do the actual work. The Navaho man is seldom a weaver. Now and again one is found who is accomplished in the art, but this is a rare occurrence. It is the Navaho woman who chooses the poles and sticks for the loom, who superintends the daily life of the sheep that provide the wool, who shears the sheep, washes, cards, and spins the wool, who prepares the dyes — whether the almost forgotten native dyes or the easily made anilines — who conceives the design, prepares the warp, actually weaves the blanket and generally disposes of it to the trader, or once in a while to the casual tourist who "happens along" at the time it is ready for sale.

With the Pueblo Indian it is generally the man who weaves, as the photographs of Pueblo weaving show. And it is a remarkable evidence of tribal habit that in one group of Amerinds the woman is the weaver, while in that of another, who live in practically the same region, the man does the work.

In the olden time there were several traditions in regard to weaving. One was that it must not be indulged in extravagantly, overdone, but only engaged in in moderation. A ceremony for the amelioration of the ill effects of overwork at the loom was provided for in a sacrificial offering to the spindle. The prayer of the gods was recited, and a prayer-stick was used made of yucca, precious stones (turquoise, etc.), bird and turkey feathers, tassels of grass, and pollen.

Maidens, before marriage, were also kept from weaving lest they should overdo, but of late years this idea of overdoing on the part of either married woman or maiden has practically disappeared.

The deterioration of the art of weaving among the Pueblos and its improvement with the Navahos, is a proof of the unconscious exercise of the law of following the line of least resistance and of the power of native tastes and talents. It is quite reasonable to assume that at the time of the Spanish Conquest the Pueblo weavers were by far the more accomplished — that is, assuming that the Navahos had already learned the art. The Navahos, in common with the Pueblos, were basket and pottery makers. The former, however, were nomads, wandering to and fro over an area now largely included in their reservation in Arizona and New Mexico. As I have elsewhere shown, this land is arid though not an absolute desert. The precipitation at an altitude varying from 5,000 to 7,000 feet amounts to only 14.10 inches (or less) during the year, and this is generally confined to two short seasons of moisture separated from one another by months of absolute drought, which, except in specially favored localities, would destroy any of the ordinary field-crops.

Naturally in such a country as this, material for basketry was scant, and what was found was of a poor quality. This in itself was a deterrent to the art of basketry, and rendered the Navahos indifferent towards it. On the other hand, the Paiutis of southern Nevada and Utah, living near flowing streams, where willows and other basketry material abounded, all of the finest quality, and the Havasupais of Cataract or Havasu (Blue Water) Canyon — living in a region so favorable to the growth of willows that Lieut. Frank H. Cushing, who visited them from Zuni in the early eighties, described them as the "Nation of the Willows"— became experts in the art the materials of which were so close to their hands. Being neighbors to the Navahos, the latter were able to trade with them for basket-work and thus secure by barter all they needed.

Pottery is never much in favor with a nomad people, especially the crude, fragile pottery of the aborigine. It is hard to transport, and is in constant danger of being broken; hence the Navaho never cultivated to any great extent the art of pottery, while the sedentary and home-loving Pueblos found it a far easier task to make pottery for the purpose of storing water, corn, flour, seeds, and other foods than basketry, and the same instinct for decoration that had led to the beautifying of the basket asserted itself in the heart of the Pueblo potter, and she began to make geometrical designs, scrolls, figures, symbols of such great diversity as to be "the wonder of the world of design," whenever and wherever studied. Let those who deem this statement exaggerated secure Part II of the *Seventeenth Report of the United States Bureau of American Ethnology,* and see therein Dr. J. Walter Fewkes's reproductions of the signs, symbols, designs, and patterns from the pottery of the ancient Hopi ruins of Sikyatki in northern Arizona, some of which are given in a later chapter of this book. In these designs, and those found on the basketry of the more progressive of the basket-making tribes, it is probable that the Navahos gained the suggestion, at least, of the designs which they have since incorporated into their blankets, and which, later, we shall more fully consider.

It will be apparent therefore from the foregoing considerations that as the Navaho could barter or trade for the baskets and pottery he needed, and his country and habits afforded him better advantages for the breeding of sheep and horses than his neighbors, he gradually abandoned the basketry and pottery-making arts and devoted his attentions to sheep and horse-raising, and also to the making of blankets.

His nomad life was eminently suited to lead him, naturally, to the work of the weaver. With a portable loom to weave the wool from the backs of the sheep into blankets, which were eagerly sought for in trade by other tribes, it was the most natural thing in the world for the Navaho woman to develop into the great weaver she has become.

In studying the development and growth of the art, however, other factors than mere usefulness — highly important and fundamental as it is — have to be considered. Usefulness was perfectly attained as soon as the weave of the blanket was made perfect, without any regard to variety in stitch, color of the material, variety in color, the introduction of a design, or the attaching of a symbolic meaning to the design. Whence came these important factors in the Navaho's art development?

Even the most barbaric people cannot fail to be sensible, more or less, to the beauties Nature presents to them on every hand. The love of beauty primarily comes from contact with beautiful things, and as soon as this love is once aroused the desire to produce its object seems to be almost an instinct. Hence the dawn and the development of aboriginal art. In basketry this showed itself in the coloring of certain splints and later in the use of designs, worked into the general texture by·means of these different colored splints. The Hopi, near neighbors to the Navaho, in all their villages made baskets, on the two nearest mesas using yucca splints and on the third mesa contenting themselves with willows. They became experts in the use of certain dyes, and produced geometrical figures and designs of symbolic significance in great variety in their yucca-fiber placques. At Oraibi the willow splints were colored and made into designs copying the masks of the Kachinas, or lesser divinities, and the Navahos, with their wide inclusiveness as to the gods of other peoples, trading for the baskets of the Hopi, introduced what they knew or imagined of the ceremonialism connected with the Hopi divinities into their own ritual, and thus accorded to these baskets an honored place in their ceremonial life. It can well be seen, therefore, that in time the Navaho cared little for his own home-made baskets but attached especial significance to the basketry of other peoples, especially that which appealed to him in the manner I have suggested.

CHAPTER III

The Early History of the Navaho Blanket

I HAVE already traced the broad and general development of the art of weaving among the Navahos both before and after the coming of the Spaniards. In this chapter let me show the condition of the art when the Americans first came in contact with the Navahos up to the time when blanket-weaving began to deteriorate.

Long before the country of the Navahos — New Mexico — came under the control of the United States, stories were told, now and again, by that intrepid race of men, the trappers, who have generally been the forerunners of civilization, of Indians who wove marvelous blankets, and — rarer even than the stories — a trapper would buy and bring home to his friends one of these remarkable specimens of aboriginal weave. As they somewhat resembled the fine serapes of the Mexican they were generally termed Serape-Navahos, or Navaho-Serapes, and were regarded as great curiosities, and by the informed as remarkable specimens of the weaver's art. But, as practically nothing was known of the Indians who wove them, nor of the primitive loom upon which they were constructed, their wonderful qualities were insufficiently appreciated even by those who realized somewhat of their superlative workmanship.

Josiah Gregg, in *Commerce of the Prairies* (New York, 1844), gives one of the earliest comments upon the Navahos and their blankets, viz.:

They reside in the main range of the Cordilleras, one hundred and fifty to two hundred miles west of Santa Fe, on the waters of the Rio Colorado of California, not far from the region, according to historians, from whence the Aztecs emigrated to Mexico; and there are many reasons to suppose them direct descendants from the remnant, which remained in the north, of this celebrated nation of antiquity. Although they live in rude *jacales,* somewhat resembling the wigwams of the Pawnees, yet, from time immemorial, they have excelled all others in their original manufactures; and as well as the Moquies [the Hopis], they are still distinguished for some exquisite styles of cotton textures, and display considerable ingenuity in embroidering with feathers the skins of animals, according to their primitive practice. They now, also, manufacture a singular species of blanket, known as the *Sarape-Navaho,* which is of so close and dense a texture that it will frequently hold water almost equal to hum-elastic cloth. It is therefore highly prized for protection against the rains. Some of the finer qualities are often sold among the Mexicans as high as $50 or $60 each.

Fig. 4*is a blanket of this type. For full description, see page 34.

* In color section.   20

When the conquest of New Mexico was undertaken the outside world began to hear further, and see more, of these specimens of aboriginal handicraft. In September, 1846, Major Emory, U. S. A., sent out on a military reconnoissance, visited the pueblo of Santo Domingo, New Mexico. He says:

We were shown into his reverence's parlor, tapestried with curtains stamped with the likenesses of the Presidents of the United States up to this time. The cushions were of spotless damask and the couch covered with a white Navaho blanket worked in richly colored flowers.

I have seen this very room and the blanket to which he refers. It was not a Navaho blanket, but a ceremonial blanket of Pueblo Indian weave, made of native cotton, and the "flowers" were the embroidered work in colors done by hand, exactly as the Hopis embroider their ceremonial blankets and kilts today. (Fig. 5.) *

A little later in his report Emory tells of meeting some Indians that he took for "Pimos-Apaches." He thus describes their spinning and the loom:

A woman was seated on the ground under the shade of a cottonwood. Her left leg was tucked under her and her foot turned sole upward; between her big toe and the next was a spindle about eighteen inches long, with a single fly of four or six inches. Ever and anon she gave it a twist in a dexterous manner, and at its end was drawn a coarse cotton thread. This was their spinning jenny. Led on by this primitive display, I asked for their loom by pointing to the thread and then to the blanket girded about the woman's loins. A fellow stretched in the dust, sunning himself, rose leisurely and untied a bundle which I had supposed to be a bow and arrow. This little package, with four stakes in the ground was the loom. He stretched his cloth and commenced the process of weaving.

J. T. Hughes, in his story, *Doniphan's Expedition,* 1847, thus tells of his colonel's reception and appreciation of several blankets:

The chief presented Colonel Doniphan with several fine Navaho blankets, the manufacture of which discovers great ingenuity, having been spun and woven without the advantage of wheels or looms, by a people living in the open air, without houses or tents. Of these the colors are exceedingly brilliant, and the designs and figures in good taste. The fabric is not only so thick and compact as to turn rain, but to hold water as a vessel. They are used by the Navahos as a cloak in the day time, and converted into a pallet at night. Colonel Doniphan designs sending those which he brought home with him to the war department at Washington, as specimens of Navaho manufacture.

Lieut. J. H. Simpson, in his *Report on the Navaho Country,* 1852, already takes it for granted that his readers are familiar with the Navaho blanket, for he says in one place:

* In color section.

It seems anomalous to me that a nation living in such miserably-constructed mud lodges should, at the same time, be capable of making, probably, the best blankets in the world!

In 1854 Dr. Letherman wrote to the Smithsonian Institution about the Navaho blanket as follows:

The spinning and weaving is done by the women, and by hand. The thread is made entirely by hand, and is coarse and uneven. The blanket is woven by a tedious and rude process, after the manner of the Pueblo Indians, and is very coarse, thick, and heavy, with little nap, and cannot bear comparison with an American blanket for warmth and comfort. Many of them are woven so closely as to hold water; but this is of little advantage, for when worn during a rain they become saturated with water, and are then uncomfortably heavy. The colors are red, blue, black, and yellow; black and red being the most common. The red strands are obtained by unravelling red cloth, black by using the wool of black sheep, blue by dissolving indigo in fermented urine, and yellow is said to be produced by coloring with a particular flower. The colors are woven in bands and diamonds. We have never observed blankets with figures of a complicated pattern. Occasionally a blanket is seen which is quite handsome, and costs at the same time the extravagant price of forty or fifty dollars; these, however, are very scarce, and are generally made for a special purpose. The Indians prefer an American blanket, as it is lighter and much warmer. The article manufactured by them is superior, because of its thickness, to that made in the United States, for placing between the bed and the ground when bivouacking, and this is the only use it can be put to in which its superiority is shown. The manner of weaving is peculiar, and is, no doubt, original with these people and the neighboring tribes; and, taken in connection with the fact of some dilapidated buildings (not of Spanish structure) being found in different portions of the country, it has suggested the idea that they may once have been what are usually called " Pueblo Indians." *

John Russell Bartlett, who was connected with the United States and Mexican Boundary Commission, in his *Personal Narrative of Explorations and Incidents in Texas and New Mexico,* 1854, thus speaks of the Navaho and his blanket:

On one occasion our camp was visited by a band of Navaho Indians, four hundred of whom were encamped on the banks of the Gila. This is a formidable, warlike, and treacherous tribe which descends from their strongholds in the canyons west of Santa Fe and robs the inhabitants of New Mexico of their cattle and sheep. They had heard of our party, and had taken advantage of the friendly manner in which the Apaches came to us to accompany them. With the exception of a different style in their boots, and in the manner of arranging their hair, their dress appeared the same. Their bows, arrows, and lances were the same, and the helmet shaped head-dress did not materially differ. The Navahos had a very fine description of woolen blankets of their own manufacture, which they used to cover their bodies when it was cold, as well as for saddle cloths. These blankets are superior to any native fabric I have ever seen; in fact, they are quite equal to the best English blankets, except

* *Smithsonian Report, 1855, p. 291.*

that they are without any nap. I have been told that they spin and dye the wool, which they raise themselves; though others assert that the richer colors are obtained by unravelling fine scarlet blankets of English manufacture, the threads of which are then used in the weaving of their own. Whether this is true or not I am unable to say. At any rate, even if true, this forms but a very small portion of the fabric, the remainder of which is undoubtedly spun and woven by themselves.

We had some little bartering with these people, giving them shirts and other wearing apparel for their bows and arrows and caps, and some of our party were so fortunate as to obtain some fine specimens of their blankets. I got a small one of inferior quality, but sufficient to show the style of their manufacture.

The "Boy Scout," William F. Drannan, who published in 1908 his *Thirty-one Years on the Plains and in the Mountains,* states therein that in 1865 he was scouting with Lieutenant Jacobson, of Fort Yuma, in southern Arizona and there saw an unusual Navaho blanket. Here is what he says, page 420:

One day, while I was out on a scouting tour, I ran on to a little band of Navaho Indians on their way to the St. Louis Mountains for a hunt. They had some blankets with them of their own manufacture, and being confident that the lieutenant had never seen a blanket of that kind, I induced them to go with me to our quarters to show their blankets to the lieutenant and others as well. I told the lieutenant that he could carry water in one of those all day and it would not leak through. He took one of them, he taking two corners and I two, and the third man poured a bucket of water in the center of it, and we carried it twenty rods and the water did not leak through it. The lieutenant asked how long it took to make one of them, and the Indian said it took about six months. He bought a blanket for five dollars, being about all the silver dollars in the command. The blanket had a horse worked in each corner, of various colors, also a man in the center with a spear in his hand. How this could be done was a mystery to all of us, as it contained many colors and showed identically the same on both sides.

In 1854 the Indian Commissioner's *Report* contained the following in speaking of the Navahos: "They are the manufacturers of a superb quality of blankets that are waterproof, as well as of coarser woolens."

It is evident, therefore, that over sixty years ago the Navahos were experts in the art of blanket-weaving, making an object "whose quality and artistic execution excited the attention and appealed to the esthetic tastes of cultured and educated men."

These are the rare blankets of the olden days that are so much prized today by museums and collectors. They are practically worth their weight in gold. Charles F. Lummis, in his *Some Strange Corners of Our Country,* thus speaks of their rarity and value:

The very highest grade of Navaho blankets is now very rare. It is a dozen years since any of them have been made; the yarn blankets which are far less expensive and sell just as well to the ignorant traveler, have entirely supplanted them. Only a few of the precious old ones remain — a few in the hands of the wealthy Pueblo Indians and Mexicans — and they are almost priceless. I know every such blanket in the Southwest, and, outside of one or two private collections, the specimens can be counted on one's fingers. The colors of these choicest blankets are red, white, and blue, or, rarely, just red and white. In a very few specimens there is also a little black. Red is very much the prevailing color, and takes up some four-fifths of the blanket, the other colors merely drawing a pattern on a red ground.

CHAPTER IV

The Bayeta Blanket of the Navaho

IN the preceding chapter practically all the blankets referred to or described were of a superior, indeed superlatively superior, weave, and of great commercial value. I have already quoted from Dr. Lummis where he speaks of the rarity of these older specimens. Here are two other quotations, the first from his book already referred to, and the latter from *The Land of Sunshine,* for December, 1896.

Speaking of the red groundwork of which so many of these fine blankets are mainly composed, he writes:

This red material is from a fine Turkish woolen cloth called *balleta.* It used to be imported to Mexico, whence the Navahos procured it at first. Later, it was sold at some of the trading-posts in this territory. The fixed price of it was $6 a pound. The Navahos used to ravel this cloth and use the thread for their finest blankets; and it made such blankets as never have been produced elsewhere. Their durability is wonderful. They never fade, no matter how frequently washed — an operation in which *amole,* the saponaceous root of the *Palmilla,* should be substituted for soap. As for wear, I have seen the latter blankets which have been used for rugs on the floors of populous Mexican houses for fifty years, which still retain their brilliant color, and show serious wear only at their broken edges. And they will hold water as well as canvas will.

A balleta blanket like that pictured elsewhere * is worth $200 and not a dozen of them could be bought at any price today. It is seventy-three inches long by fifty-six inches wide and weighs six pounds. You can easily reckon that the thread in it cost something, at $6 a pound, and the weaving occupied a Navaho woman for many months. It is hardly thicker than an ordinary book cover, and is almost as firm. It is too thin and stiff to be an ideal bed-blanket, and it was never meant to be one. All blankets of that quality were made to be worn on the shoulders of chiefs; and most of them were *ponchos* — that is, they had a small slit left in the center for the wearer to put his head through, so that the blanket would hang upon him like a cape. Thus it was combined overcoat, water-proof, and adornment. I bought this specimen after weeks of diplomacy, from Martin del Valle, the noble-faced old Indian who had been many times governor of the cliff-built "City" of Acoma. He bought it twenty years ago from a Navaho war-chief for a lot of ponies and turquoise. He had used it ever since, but it was as brilliant and apparently as strong as the day it was finished.

These finest blankets are seldom used or shown except on festal occasions, such as councils, dances, and races.

* Dr. Lummis here referred to a picture of a fine bayeta blanket which accompanied his article.

The second quotation is as follows:

The Navaho Indian of New Mexico and Arizona cannot vie with the modern Turk in rugs nor with the extinct Yunca in fringes; but when it comes to blankets he can beat the world. Or rather, he could — for it is nearly a generation since a Navaho blanket of strictly first class has been created. Here is a lost art — not because the Navahos no longer know how, but because they will no longer take the trouble. They make thousands of blankets still — thick, coarse, fuzzy things, which are the best camping-blankets to be had anywhere, and most comfortable robes.. But of the superb old *ponchos* and *zarapes* for chiefs — those iron fabrics woven from vayeta (a Turkish cloth imported specially for them and sold at $6 a pound, unraveled by them, and its thread reincarnated in an infinitely better new body), not one has been woven in twenty years. It is a loss to the world; but the collector who began in time can hardly be philanthropic enough to lament the deterioration which has made it impossible that even the richest rival shall ever be able to match his treasures.

There are still Navahos (20,000 of them), and there is still vayeta; and as there are people who would give $500 for an absolutely first-class vayeta blanket, you might fancy that the three things would pool. But that is to forget the Navaho. He is a barbarian, to whom enough is an elegant sufficiency. By weaving the cheap and wretched blankets of today — wretched, that is, as works of art — he can get all the money he desires. Why then toil a twelvemonth over a blanket for $500 (which is more coin than he can imagine anyhow) when a week's work will bring $5? You will think the Navaho is a fool, who will not put out his hand for money; but it is to be remembered that he *knows* you are one who burn your life for it. And a thousand efforts, by the smartest business men on the frontier, have absolutely failed to revive this wonderful old industry. They have at most succeeded only in getting some back-slidden *marueca** to weave an Americanized blanket which no connoisseur would have in his house.†

When Dr. Letherman described the Navahos as he found them in 1854 he thus speaks of bayeta or baize forming a part of their costume:

Some wear short breeches of brownish-colored buckskin, or red baize, buttoned at the knee, and leggins of the same material. A small blanket, or a piece of red baize, with a hole in it, through which the head is thrust, extends a short distance below the small of the back, and covers the abdomen in front, the sides being partially sewed together; and a strip of red cloth attached to the blanket or baize, where it covers the shoulder, forms the sleeve, the whole serving the purpose of a coat. Over all this is thrown a blanket, under and sometimes over which is worn a belt, to which are attached oval pieces of silver, plain or variously wrought.

I have given Dr. Lummis's statements in full, together with both his methods of spelling *bayeta,* not only because of his great knowledge upon the subject, but more because of his profound and deep interest in

* Navaho woman.
† I must apologize to Dr. Lummis for quoting him as spelling the word Navaho. He is as emphatic in demanding that it be spelt *Navajo* as I am that it be *Navaho*.

the Indians and all concerning them. Yet I am inclined to question both his spelling and his information in regard to bayeta.

Bayeta is simply the Spanish for *baize,* a kind of flannel with a nap on one side. Another authority than Dr. Lummis asserts that it was originally made in Spain, and was sold in Mexico as Spanish flannel, and by the Mexicans traded to the Indians.

Some twenty-five years ago I found it a common article of manufacture in certain woolen mills in Yorkshire, England, regularly sold by Manchester wholesalers to the Spanish, Turkish, Mexican, and United States trade, and by these latter dealers distributed to the Indian traders of the United States.

While in the early days there was little of any color but red used by the Navahos, bayeta was made in as many colors as there are dyes — red, green, yellow, pink, blue, orange, purple, etc., and there is no doubt whatever but that *bayeta* blankets *with English yarn of different colors* have been made for years by the Navahos. For I have spoken with both Mexican and Indian traders who have dealt in bayeta of different colors for many years, though all agree that the chief demand has always been for red.

The leading manufacturers of baizes in England today contend that they were never made in Spain, and "certainly never in Turkey." It is generally believed that the baize trade was originally introduced into England in the sixteenth century by refugees from France and the Netherlands. It is well known that religious persecutions almost destroyed the weaving industries of these two countries, and that the shrewd and awakening business sense of England took advantage of the situation by gladly offering hospitality to those whose very religious dogmatism and firmness made of them the most desirable kind of artisan citizenship. For over two hundred years one firm to which I have referred has dealt largely in baizes, and "Rossendale Valley baizes" are favorably known to the trade throughout the world.

There is a peculiar kind of baize, bearing an extra long nap, or face, with a lustrous and curly finish, which is known to the trade as *Pellons.* In Halifax, Yorkshire, England, is a lane known for over three hundred years as Pellon Lane, thus clearly indicating to the local antiquarians that a pellon mill was originally situated in this neighborhood, which today is largely occupied by the weaving industry.

Traditions still exist in the minds of the old members of the firms whose chief weaves are baizes, with whom I have conversed and corresponded, to the effect that the woven pieces were shipped to Spain — never direct to Mexico or South America — and by the Spanish dealers distributed to their compatriot customers throughout the world. Even now this custom is largely followed, it being well known that the English manufacturers and shippers are conservative and averse to changing long-established methods of doing business. It would not be "good form" to endeavor to secure the direct trade of the Mexican and South American dealers who, for centuries, have been supplied with their goods through wholesale houses in Spain.

From this fact that the bayetas and pellons were always and only secured through dealers in Spain undoubtedly sprang the impression that they were made in that country.

Another thing also aided in deepening that impression, namely: the names given to the various colors and shades in which these baize-pellons were made. Even in the English trade they were and are known by the Spanish labels, as, for instance: *Morado Subido,* strong violet or purple; *Rosa Bajo,* dull rose; *Oro,* gold; *Amarillo Tostado,* yellow with a light brown tinge; *Grana,* deep scarlet; *Dragon, Sajon Hermosa,* and a score of others.

Pellon-baizes were largely used in England in my boy days for making bags for carrying lawyers' briefs. England is a rainy country, and papers and documents that were needed in court must be carried back and forth, despite the weather. It was found that the long curly nap of the pellon threw off the rain very effectively, even when the clerk had to walk farther than usual. Hence when the trade extended to Spain and its North and South American dependencies or colonies, these baizes were much sought after for the making of *ponchos* which would shed severe rains and thus protect the wearer from becoming drenched by the fierce showers that so often descend unexpectedly in tropical climes. The open weave, under the long nap, also afforded abundant ventilation — a great desideratum in a hot country.

The colors in which baizes and pellons were dyed prior to the discovery of aniline dyes were bright scarlet and varying shades to deep maroon, blues, yellows, greens, etc. The reds were extracted from cochineal, Spanish *Cochinilla,* which, as is well known, is the female insect *Coccus cacti,* found in large numbers on various species of cactus in Mexico, Central America, and other tropical countries. These insects are gathered from the plant, killed by heat, and then exposed to the sun to dry. They then appear much like small seeds or berries of a brown or purple color, so for years were scientifically defined as the grain of the *Quercus coccifera.* The essential coloring matter is carminic acid, a purple red amorphous substance which yields carmine red. The varying colors produced from cochineal depended entirely upon the mordants used.

A mordant is any substance, such as alum, copperas, urine, which has a twofold attraction. It acts equally upon the organic fibres of wool, cotton, etc., and at the same time upon the minute particles of coloring matter, and thus serves as a bond to *fix* the dye in whatever substance the dyer is seeking to color.

Modern science — even that of a hundred or more years ago — in England, combined with many years of experimentation with dyestuffs, had led English dyers to the discovery of several excellent mordants, and to these discoveries and the care shown in the exercise of the dyer's art is owing the superlative colors and their unfading qualities in the priceless Navaho bayeta blankets of the early days.

When the Navahos began to dye wool for themselves they were dependent upon the less experienced Mexicans and Pueblo Indians for their knowledge of dyes and mordants; hence their gamut of colors and shades was much limited. Yet is it not remarkable that in a few years they succeeded in making dyes equal to those of the English?

Blue was made from indigo, which is procured from woad and other plants native to Asia, Africa, and America. This is one of the oldest dyestuffs known, and was used to color the faces of the ancient Britons, Queen Boadicea being said to have stained her face with woad after her defeat and capture by the Romans. The indigo, however, does not exist in the plants as such. It is obtained by the decomposition or fermentation of the *Glucoside indican.* It is a dark blue earthy substance, tasteless and odorless, with a coffee-violet luster when rubbed. It appears in commerce in dark-blue cubical cakes, varying very much in the quality of their composition, some containing indigo-red and indigo-brown, besides moisture, mineral matters, and glutinous substances. Consequently the color varies, especially when used as dye by one who is not an expert. This accounts for the varying shades of blue too often found in the wools dyed by the Navaho, while the older blankets, probably made from bayeta dyed blue by the English experts, is as perfect and almost as full of color today as when first it came from the dye pot.

The most popular of the reds was originally called, even in England (and still is) *Brazil* baize. As late as twenty-five years ago, "Brazil sticks" could be obtained in New Mexico. This is a very heavy wood, the *Cesalpinia sapan,* brought originally from the Orient, and known long before the discovery of America. It has a reddish color and dyes red and yellow. After the discovery of America it is said that King Emanuel, of Portugal, gave the name Brazil to the country on the Southern Continent on account of its producing this wood. It is now called *Cesalpinia Braziliensis,* although the best color is produced from the *C. echinata,* a leguminous tree, the heart-wood of which is used for this purpose. The word brazil is supposed to come from the Spanish *brasa,* a live coal, which the color produced closely approximated in the mind of the poetic southern nations.

Another red is that produced from the heart of the logwood, *Hematoxylon campechianum,* another South American wood, which contains a crystalline substance called *hematoxylon* or *hematein.* When pure this forms nearly colorless crystals, but on oxidization, especially in the presence of an alkali, it is converted into the coloring matter which is the base for lakes, yielding violets, blues, and blacks, according to the mordant used. Logwood comes into the commerce of today in the form of logs, chips, and extracts. When the chips are used they are moistened with water and exposed in heaps so as to promote oxidization or fermentation, alkalies, etc., being generally added to hasten the process, or "curing," as it is often called. The resultant decoction is a deep reddish-brown color.

The older dyers of Chimayó still call for " Brazil sticks " when asked to dye wool for a "native color" blanket, though the article has generally dropped out of every-day commerce since the introduction of the aniline dyes.

Fustic was the heartwood of certain West Indian trees, *Maclura tinctoria,* giving a rich lemon yellow. Sometimes the Spanish termed it *fustoc.* *Young fustic* is the heartwood of a native sumac of the Mediterranean, *Rhus cotinus,* which yields an orange-colored lake.

These were the principal colors used by the English in their dyeing of bayetas and pellons in the early days, and even now used occasionally for rare and special orders. But since the great chemical discoveries of Perkin in 1856, Verguin in 1895, and others, the aniline dyes have largely taken possession of the field.

It may be interesting to the curious reader to note that the word "aniline" is made from *annil,* the Arabic, which was the original name for a West Indian plant from which indigo was first made. It goes back even to the Sanskrit, *nila,* a dark blue, and *nili,* the indigo plant itself.

In the bayetas of modern make, samples of which I have before me as I write, there are all the original colors such as the reds, crimsons, maroons, black, blues, and greens; and, in addition, magentas, pinks, oranges, lemon-yellows, etc. Yet all of these are made from aniline dyes.

Hence an important question arises in dealing with the subject of bayeta blankets. It must be self-evident to the most casual of readers that, given the bayeta, and the Indian willing to unravel the yarn as was done continuously in the old days, bayeta blankets of *modern* dye may be made today.

Are such blankets made?

I think I can affirm most positively that there has not been such a blanket made for several decades. There is not an Indian trader or a dealer in the whole Southwest who keeps bayeta of any color in stock. There is no call for it. But even if there were, and the Indian could be found to unravel and use it, it would be an easy matter for any chemist to determine immediately, and with positiveness, whether the dye used were aniline, or one of the old vegetable dyes.

It may then be relied upon that the few blankets offered for sale *as old bayeta blankets,* are exactly what they profess to be. Yet the following is a question often asked by collectors: Is there any way of definitely, positively, certainly, stating what is and what is not a *bayeta* blanket? One of the greatest experts in New Mexico asserts that the only test is this: If a thread of a blanket is pulled to pieces and it shows a single strand, then it is *bayeta.* If twisted and consisting of three strands, it is Germantown yarn.

He seemed to overlook the fact, however, that now and again — not often it must be confessed — a Navaho weaver would take a fine thread of bayeta, and, being desirous of making a thicker and heavier blanket than the fine thread would allow, twisted two or three of them together, thus giving us a two or three-ply yarn of bayeta.

Another expert takes a piece of the yarn to be tested, sets fire to it and watches the results. If something occurs it is bayeta, if it doesn't it is something else.

Still another expert insists that the only way to determine whether a blanket is of bayeta is by the feel of the strand. If it is silky and yet hard and with a fuzzy or rough feel it is bayeta, while Germantown has a woolly and soft rather than a silky, hard, and rough feel.

Yet another determines bayeta by microscopic examination. Bayeta being made by machinery, he contends that it must be smooth and even in spinning, whereas all hand-made yarn is uneven and irregular. This seems to be conclusive, yet when I called his attention to these two facts, viz., that much bayeta is retwisted by the Navahos by hand, and, second, that Germantown yarn is made by machinery, and must therefore present the same evenness and regularity of spinning displayed by bayeta, he confessed that the difficulty still remained. For, while it may successfully reveal the difference between a native-spun and a machine-spun yarn, that difference does not always exist between the two machine-spun yarns of Germantown and bayeta.

To my own mind these discussions are more academic than profitable. Chemical analysis can speedily determine whether the dye used in the yarn of a blanket be vegetal or aniline. But even this is not necessary. While it might be hard to convince another, who was not as familiar with the various makes of Navaho blankets, the expert can tell almost to a certainty with his eyes shut which is an old bayeta and which is not. There is a feel that reveals the old weave, and when to this is added the ocular demonstration of age and color, the old vegetal colors of the ancient bayetas toning down to the richest shades of color harmonies, one can rest confidently in the judgment of an expert that he is viewing an old bayeta.

Of this character are the following blankets from three well-known collections — those of the American Museum of Natural History, of Fred Harvey, of Albuquerque, and A. C. Vroman, Pasadena, with added specimens that have been in my own possession for many years.

Fig. 6 is one of the earliest types of Honal-Kladi, referred to later in connection with Fig. 7. Long before any geometrical or other design was introduced into the blanket, the attempt to beautify these chiefs' robes was made by varying the width of the panels, changing their colors, and introducing bands of color across a portion of each panel. The effect, though simple, was pleasing, and made, as many of these blankets are, of the finest material, and woven with consummate skill, they are even more highly prized by collectors than later specimens of more elaborate design.

Fig. 7*is an exquisitely beautiful blanket of soft delicate tones, although the elaborate bands of black and white give it a striking character. The red of the bayeta, which forms the body color of the center design and the outer border, is toned down to a delicate rose tint which harmonizes in exquisite effect with the blue and black stripes introduced therein. It will be observed that this blanket is woven crosswise instead of lengthwise. Blankets of this character are spoken of as "Chief's Blankets," or by the Navahos are called *Honal-Kladi,* or *Honal-Chodi.* The peculiar design for this weave is undoubtedly found in the fact that the Navaho chief or leading men of the tribe desired to have their blankets of a different type from those worn by the ordinary men of the tribe. Blankets of this character are wrapped around the body broadside, which shows off the stripes to better advantage than if they had been woven in the other direction, as then the stripes would run up and down and be displeasing to the eye. This type of blanket is undoubtedly from one hundred to two hundred years old, and when made of old bayeta and native-dyed and woven yarn is exceedingly scarce and valuable.

This is one of the choicest old bayeta blankets of the Fred Harvey collection.

It should be noted, however, that there is such a demand for blankets of this type that some of the traders keep one or more of their best weavers continually at work making them. They are not quite as closely woven as the old ones, but after they have had twenty-five years or so of rough usage on the floor of a living room, or as couch-covers, or in any

* In color section.

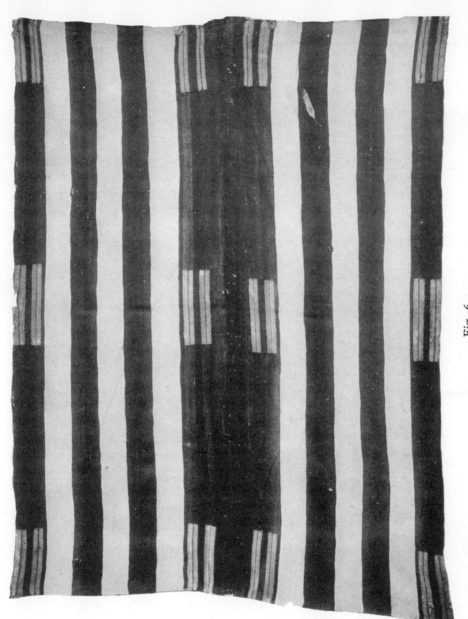

Fig. 6.

Bayeta "Chiefs" Blanket.

(In American Museum of Natural History.)

[Page 32]

place where there are a number of children, they begin to take upon themselves the appearance of age, and then they increase in value. It is a singular fact that the longer they are used and the more roughly they are treated, the more pleasing they become to the eye.

Another fine chief's blanket is in the Vroman collection, shown in Fig. 8.* The body bands are white and black, with the center band composed of red, blue, and black narrower stripes. In the center of this band is the blunt-pointed diamond figure, with the half of a similar figure at each end. The upper and lower edge of the blanket has the same narrower bands of red, blue, and black as the center band. This blanket is a fine old specimen, and its size is forty-seven by sixty-eight inches.

Perhaps one of the most pleasing of the small blankets of the Fred Harvey collection at Albuquerque is the old bayeta blanket, reproduced in Fig. 9.* In all my experiences among the Navahos I have seen very few blankets of this type, one of them being in my own collection and illustrated elsewhere. The red of the bayeta has toned down to a soft delicate rose madder, while the blue of the zigzags and the smaller figures of the designs are as rich and as deep undoubtedly as the day the yarn came from the dyeing vessel. The blue of the border stripes has softened down wonderfully until it is almost steel-like in appearance; on the other hand, the white has taken a tone until it is a delicate cream, and where this white has been interwoven, as it is in a number of the stripes and in some of the small figures of the design with the red bayeta, a most pleasing effect is produced.

This blanket is undoubtedly of the very earliest type and will go back fully one hundred and fifty to two hundred years, and although it has seen exceedingly rough usage, as all saddle blankets are subject to, it is almost as perfect today as when it left the hands of the original weaver.

Fig. 10.* is a fine specimen of a Navaho squaw dress, although only half of it is here presented. Generally these squaw dresses were woven in two halves, which were sewed together and then worn as shown in various pictures throughout the book in which Navaho women are represented. The body part of this is of black wool, very closely woven, the two ends being of red bayeta, with the design in very deep blue with small stripes of old-gold-green in the geometrical figures. This little tip of green materially enhances the beauty of the blanket, and age has improved it without the slightest marring of the rich perfect color of the bayeta. This is a blanket of the type that would undoubtedly hold water. The battening down has been done so thoroughly by the weaver that it is almost impossible to open a stitch of the weft to reveal the strands of the warp.

Blankets of this type are highly prized by the collector and are now

* In color section

never made. They therefore are seldom found or offered for sale at any price.

A beautiful specimen of an old bayeta saddle blanket is that shown in Fig. 11 from my own collection. The red is fairly harmonious through-out and has retained much of its original brilliancy, as have also the blue and old-gold-green of the design. It is thirty and a half by forty-two and a half inches in size, and its weight is nearly two pounds. It has no other colors than red, blue, and green, though there are a few touches and out-lines in white. The groundwork is red, while the zigzag of the larger design is in old-gold-green and blue, the former being outside. The inner designs alternate between green and blue, while some of them contain both colors with touches of white.

The brilliancy of the color of the blanket as a whole has deceived several into believing it was not an old bayeta, yet on careful examination there can be no question of its age. Fortunately, I know its history. It was purchased by an army officer who was in the Navaho country in the early fifties; hence it could not possibly be any other than an old bayeta, or a native-dyed, native-wool blanket, and the Navahos never made so brilliant a red with any of the dyes they were then accustomed to use.

Of greater age still, though entirely different in appearance, is Fig. 4. It is thirty by forty-eight inches in size, and the only colors are red and blue, with considerable of the design (about one-fourth) in white. The red has toned down to a soft and delightful shade of plum red, that is alluring and restful to the eye. It is of much finer weave, though of sim-pler design than Fig. 11.* I secured it in the following unromantic way: On one of my exploring trips in New Mexico I came to an old Mexican *jacal*. It was getting late at night, raining and cold. My horses were anxious to stop and so was I, so I asked permission to bring my blankets into the rude hut, and place my horses in the scant shelter of the corral. I slept on the floor, cooked my frugal breakfast in the morning, which I prevailed upon my host and hostess to share with me, and then went out into the wet and filthy corral to harness up. Here, kicking about in the dirt, and thick with the accumulated muck of the corral, superposed upon the horse-sweat of many long rides, was something that at first I took for a gunny sack. Preferring its dirt to axle-grease, I picked it up to take hold of the wagon-nut as I greased the axle of my buggy. To my surprise I found it to be a saddle-blanket. With the instinct of the collector always alert, I asked the old man if he would let me have it, and for how much. He laughed at my paying him anything for it; said he had used it as a saddle-blanket ever since he had been married; that it was worthless, and that, if I insisted upon paying for it, fifty cents would be far more than it was worth. I threw it into the conveyance and forgot all about

* In color section.

Fig. 12.
Rare Old Bayeta.
(In American Museum of Natural History.)   [Page 35]

Fig. 13.
Rare Old Bayeta.
(In Metropolitan Museum of Art.)   [Page 35]

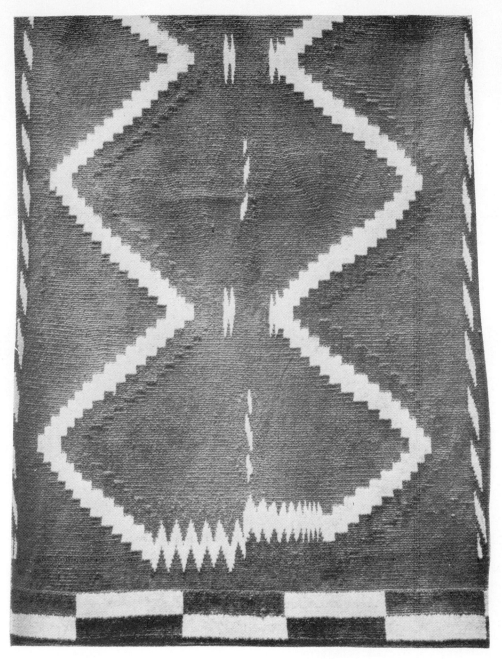

Fig. 14.
Portion of Center Panel of Fig. 13.

Fig. 15.
Fine Bayeta.
(In Metropolitan Museum of Art.)   [Page 35]

it, packing it up and sending it home with other "trash" as early as possible. Some weeks after, when I returned home, I soaked it in strong amole-suds for days, possibly two or three weeks, scrubbing, working, and rinsing it again and again. Slowly there emerged from the filthy water this blanket, and after a score or more of "cleanings," and a final rinse and hanging on the line to dry, my delight can be imagined when this exquisite specimen of the art came into full view. It has been badly abused, but is still in fair condition, and is a joy to all connoisseurs. When I realized its value, and saw my old Mexican friend again, I tried to give him further compensation, but, though poor, he was proud, and anyway, "had I not already paid him for it?" It required some diplomacy and tact to get him to accept even a parting present, but this was essential for the peace of my own mind. From what he and his wife said of it I can well believe that this must have been fully one hundred and fifty to two hundred years old. Its weight is nearly two pounds, and several times I have been offered in the neighborhood of three hundred dollars for it.

Fig. 12 is of a rare old bayeta, with body of red, with the design in white and old-gold-green. This is one of a collection of twenty-two of the finest bayetas procurable, sold by A. C. Vroman, of Pasadena, California, to the Metropolitan Museum of Art, and the American Museum of Natural History in New York. These were equally divided and there are eleven of them in each museum, Fig. 12 being in the latter.

Fig. 13 is of another bayeta of the Vroman collection. The main body of the blanket is in the shade known as old rose. The steps of the border are in white and black and the color effect is exquisite. Mr. Vroman regarded this as the finest blanket he was ever able to secure, and on one occasion he refused an offer of five hundred dollars for it. It is now hanging over the door of the Metropolitan Museum in New York.

Fig. 14 is a portion of the center panel of Fig. 13, clearly showing the perfection of the weave.

Another of the Vroman bayetas, now in the Metropolitan Museum, is Fig. 15. The body of this blanket is in soft rose red, the center of the diamond in the center panel, however, being of a rich bright red. The other colors of the diamond are red and old-gold-green. The waving lines at top and bottom are in white, with blue and green, while the two inner waving lines are of blue and green without the white.

Fig. 16*is of an exquisite and delicate bayeta, the property of Mr. Vroman. It is mainly of white, with stripes and connected-diamonds in red and deep blue, with a little rich old-gold-green here and there.

Fig. 17*is of a blanket in the Vroman collection about which experts differ. Some term it a bayeta and others say the body is made from red flannel, unraveled and rewoven without being respun. Red flannel and

* In color section.

red baize are merely two brands of the same thing, though of different qualities. Had the weave been finer and the yarn tighter this would have been bayeta. As it is, it is doubtless correct to call it flannel. The design is in dark blue and green, though in the zigzags in the center of each diamond a little yellow is introduced. The blanket is of good size, fifty-four by seventy-eight inches.

Another blanket of the same general characteristics is shown in Fig. 18. This is of the same "flannelly" texture, the main body being in red, with the waving-stepped-lines in black and white.

A blanket that has become world-famous in a rather remarkable way is that pictured in Fig. 19. Some years ago Mr. Vroman desired to present a novel set of playing-cards to the world. On the corner of each card he had a beautiful engraving of a western scene, and all the backs were adorned with a reproduction, in colors, of this design. It is a small but very fine bayeta, the body in red, and it was purchased by Mr. Vroman in New Mexico, at the little Mexican hamlet of San Rafael. It is now in the P. G. Gates collection.

Fig. 20 is of a *bayeta* blanket in the Matthews collection.* It is of the type designated by Father Berard, as *honalchodi,* and commonly referred to in the trade as a *Chief's blanket.* Elsewhere I have explained why these were woven broad size instead of long side on. The design of this blanket is antique and it is made entirely of native dyed wool and bayeta. It is six feet six inches by five feet three inches in size, and its colors are black, white, dark blue, and the red of the bayeta, and — in a portion of the stair-like figures — a pale blue.

Fig. 21 is of another Matthews blanket of a tufted character, "of a kind not common," he says, "having much the appearance of an Oriental rug"; it is made of shredded red flannel, with a few simple figures in yellow, dark blue, and green.

---

* This collection was made by Dr. Washington Matthews while he was stationed in New Mexico. His authoritative works on the Navaho are largely quoted from elsewhere in these pages.

Fig. 18.
A Flannel Blanket.
(Vroman Collection.)

Fig. 19.
The "Playing Card" Blanket.
(Collection of P. G. Gates)

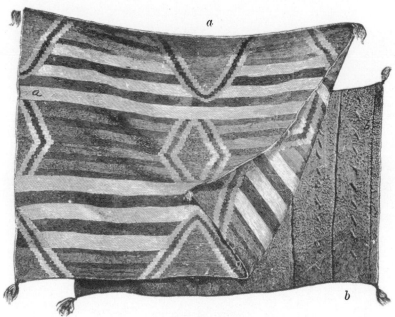

Fig. 20(a).
Bayeta Blanket.
(Matthews Collection)

Fig. 21(b).
Red Flannel Blanket.
(Matthews Collection.)

[Page 36]

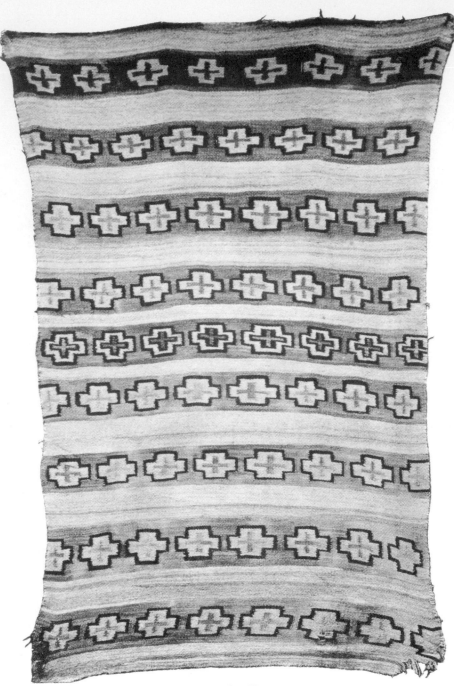

Fig. 22.
Old Style Native Blanket.

Fig. 23.
Old Style Native Wool Blanket.
(In American Museum of Natural History.)　　　[Page 37]

CHAPTER V

Old Style Native Wool Blankets

WHILE in the main all I shall say in a following chapter on the temporary deterioration of the art of weaving among the Navahos is correct, there were a few stalwart weavers who refused to lower their standard and who continued to do excellent work. It was from these weavers that the later bayeta, and the best of the earlier Germantown blankets came. At the same time a few of them began the weaving of a less closely spun yarn into a softer, and more clinging type of blanket, that was better adapted for use as a personal wrap or sleeping blanket than were the tightly spun, tightly woven fabrics.

From this date, or epoch, there comes to us, therefore, a rarely found soft, yielding, pliable blanket, of native wool and generally of native dyes, now and again mixed with a little soft woven Germantown yarn, and occasionally with an admixture of native yarn, dyed with aniline dyes, but all choice, beautiful, artistic, and highly desirable specimens.

Among the earliest of this class that I was able to secure is Fig. 22. I bought it some twenty-two years ago from an old man in New Mexico. It was in a somewhat dilapidated condition, and the owner said he had possessed it over sixty years. Consequently it is of native dye, wool warp, and native wool throughout.

Fig. 23 is of similar type, though far more ornate and beautiful in design and of much finer texture and weave. It is in the American Museum of Natural History, New York.

Another rare and beautiful specimen — indeed in color scheme it is one of the most charming blankets I have ever seen — is of double saddle-blanket size, which I secured several years ago, shown in Fig. 24.* The main body is red, with stepped diamond designs of which the outer lines are black and the inner ones a peculiar yellow. The bars are in grays of several shades, with a pale violet, doubtless secured from berry juice. The whole piece has toned down to a restful and attractive softness, and it is much admired by all who see it.

One of the best blankets of this type I think I have ever seen is Fig. 25.* This I purchased over twenty years ago on the reservation, and it was an old blanket then. It is of ordinary double saddle-blanket size, the body in red, while the lighter stripes, as shown in the engraving, are of a faded pink, or old rose, the dividing lines being in light green

* In color section.

37

and orange. The serrated diamonds are in red with the lines in old-gold-green and deep blue. The waving lines are in orange and green. The blanket weighs a little over two pounds and is a much-treasured specimen of a kind now very seldom seen, except in the collections of museums or connoisseurs.

Two other choice blankets in my own collection, made about this time are worthy of especial note. Fig. 26*is a beautiful, soft piece of weaving, six feet six inches by four feet six inches in size, the body of dark gray, the eight hourglass designs in black and red, and the serrated waves in white and black, outlined in red. The step designs at each end are in red and white. The dark gray of the major portion of the blanket makes a remarkably pleasing background and there is enough of color and design to lighten it up. The weave is rather coarse and not too tightly battened down, hence the blanket is one that can be used as a traveling rug or a bed cover with advantage. It has been in constant use as a lounge cover for several years.

Another blanket of similar soft quality and adaptability for real use *as a blanket* is Fig. 27. The color scheme, however, is entirely different. It is the same width, but about six inches shorter. The body is in white, with design in red and a pale green, so pale indeed, that it can only be called a shade or tone rather than a color.

A soft beautiful blanket is shown in Fig. 28. This is coarsely and loosely woven, but it has extra strong wool warp, and has a body of white. The stripe-colors are black and deep blue, red and old-gold-green, while the Greek key design is in red, with a filler of white and a light shade of brown. All the colors seem to be native dye, but the blanket has been washed several times, and from the Greek key of the upper and lower border, which is of a deeper red than elsewhere in the blanket, the color has "run" somewhat and slightly stained the surrounding white. Nowhere else has the color run, hence the assumption either that the wool for this red was colored with aniline dye, or a strong native red was used with insufficient, or not strong enough, mordant to hold the color.

It will be observed that the design is irregular, and the measurements of the upper and lower thirds of the blanket materially differ, yet, in spite of these facts, I have always been very appreciative of it, and for years have used it over the foot of my own bed. It makes an excellent traveling blanket, or steamboat rug.

In this type, as in all other Navaho types, the constant surprise of the careful observer is the great variety of color and design. Every collection is sure to contain specimens utterly unlike those gathered by other collectors of many years' experience, and the variety is the ever-increasing wonder of the student.

* In color section.

Fig. 27.
Another Soft-Weave Blanket.
(Author's Collection.)

Fig. 28.
An Excellent Traveling Blanket.
(Author's Collection.)   [Page 38]

CHAPTER VI

Navaho and Pueblo Squaw Dresses

IT IS natural to assume that the earliest products of the Navaho woman's loom were used for the clothing of herself and her children — especially the girls, who were more often left to her care, while the boys would go off hunting with the father.

The first squaw dresses that were woven were undoubtedly of the native wool of the sheep, undyed, hence must have been either white, black, brown, or gray. Tradition bears out this statement. The Pueblo Indians had been weaving their blankets for centuries, doubtless, from cotton, and still continued to do so, though they also introduced wool as soon as the Spaniards taught them its value. Hence it is quite possible that, for a time at least, the Pueblo and Navaho squaw dresses were somewhat similar in color and weave.

Then some one introduced variations of color in their most simple form, viz., by alternating bands of black and white, or black, white, and gray, which latter is an admixture of the two former. When dyes were introduced by the Mexicans or Spaniards among the Pueblo Indians, or became common, color began to appear even in Navaho weaving, and at about this time the Navaho squaw dress (perhaps as early as 250 years ago) took on the distinguishing and marked characteristics which it has borne up to the present. It is now, unfortunately, about to disappear from the world. For let me here anticipate somewhat and state that the strikingly individualistic, exquisitely well-woven, and attractive squaw dresses that for a century or more have delighted the eye of every white man who has ever carefully observed them, are no longer woven, no longer worn, and are absolutely not obtainable anywhere, at any price, save from the collectors and dealers who were fortunate enough to secure a few before they finally disappeared. They are now almost as rare as fine old bayetas, and less often seen, for there seems to be fewer of them, those that were woven having been worn until they fell to pieces.

The red bayeta was undoubtedly the first touch of color introduced into these dresses. It is a part of the romance of commercialism that the development of the art of dyeing and consequent enlargement of the artistic faculty in designing and weaving blankets of extraordinary patterns among the Navahos should have sprung from the introduction of a peculiarly woven and finished red cloth *(bayeta)* from the mills of the north of England.

When by theft, barter, or purchase the Navahos secured their first bayeta we do not know, and it would be interesting could we penetrate the secrets of the past and discover by what mental processes, or by what accident, the Navaho weaver was first led to *unravel* a piece of bayeta, respin it, and reweave it into her own fabric. This respinning was done for two purposes. Sometimes in unraveling the yarn became somewhat untwisted, and it was essential to respin it to give it proper strength for weaving. Again, the weaver desired a finer thread and a tighter texture than the piece of English woven "baize," hence she respun the yarn to give her the desired results.

In time a third idea sprang up. A *coarser* thread was sometimes desired, so the bayeta yarn was doubled, or even trebled, to produce the thicker yarn.

Now the Navaho woman was ready to introduce red — the symbolic color of the blessed sunshine — into her dresses. At first it is very possible this was done in alternate stripes. Indeed, by my side, on the floor in my library, as I now write, I have a squaw dress (of a later date, however), which is made of alternate stripes of red, black, and gray. And in the hall close by is another squaw dress, of Hopi weave, 63x44 inches in size (hence made for a very rotund-formed woman), of black, gray, red, and deep blue stripes of irregular width. And I also find in my collection of Navaho squaw dresses an old one of this very type.

Then the creating genius was found who designed, or accidentally hit upon the exact combination that took the Navaho fancy, so that it established a fashion which has met with but slight changes during a full century or more. Broadly speaking, this fortuitous combination is a body of black — the blacker the better — with a broad red band at top and bottom, into which some geometrical design in black or deepest blue is worked, the red border finally edged with a narrow strip of deepest blue or black.

Fig. 10 is of a rare old specimen of this character from the private collection of John Lorenzo Hubbell, of Ganado. He tells me that for a dozen years or more scarcely an old piece of this character has passed through his hands. It is beautifully woven and the red is a rich bayeta, dyed in the best fashion of the England of a century or more ago. It is fully described on page 33.

In my own collection I have many somewhat similar specimens, though not quite so fine, in which the design is a little different. This, and the difference in size are practically the only variants. These are all

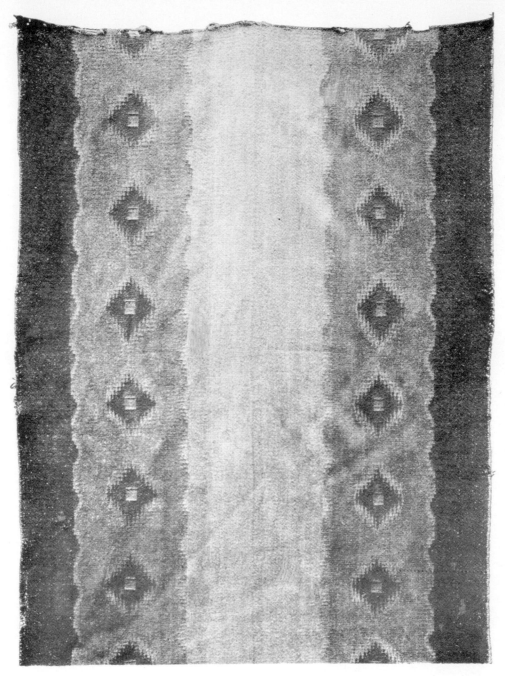

Fig. 31.
Zuni Squaw Dress, Fine Old Weave.
(Author's Collection.)   [Page 41]

woven in two pieces, which are then sewed together, and worn as elsewhere described and pictured.

A little later, however, a few weavers made their dresses in one piece, and I have several specimens of this type. In the last one I purchased, too, there was a variation in color. Instead of the body color being black, it was of a deep maroon, almost brown, and the red bands each contain a Greek key design in striking green, while the terminal border, much wider than in the usual type, is of deep blue, indented into the red with a step (or rain-cloud) design. (Fig. 29.)*

Of somewhat established type as the one I have described as so popular with the Navahos is the one prevalent among the Zunis, though there is much greater variation existing among the specimens made by this tribe than I have seen, or been able to secure.

Mrs. Matilda Coxe Stevenson says of the Zunis that "the men's shirts, ceremonial kilts, and breechcloths and women's dresses and wraps are woven of black or dark-blue native wool in diagonal style." Strange to say, that while this diagonal weave is often found in Navaho blankets of a very inferior quality, it is seldom, if ever, found in their squaw dresses. The Pueblo Indians, however, of many villages use it to good effect, and nearly always in their own garments.

Fig. 30* is a characteristic and typical specimen of an old Zuni squaw's dress, now exceedingly rare. The ground color is blue of different shades, this being undoubtedly the result of the use of wool of different periods of dyeing. It appears, however (with exception of one stripe of a dark color that comes four and one-half inches from the second red band), as if the differences in the color of the blues were made purposely. Even the blue band at the upper and lower ends of the blanket are of rich deep blue, while in the center the color has toned down to a steely blue, yet the color used in the zigzag of the two wide red bands and the small design of the two narrower red bands are of the same deep blue as of the outer bands.

The green is soft old-gold-green with many striking variations, which look as if they might have been caused deliberately by the introduction of short lengths of yarn, each of a different tone.

This blanket is not of straight, but is of the twill weave, fully described in the chapter on weaving. Blankets of this type were always used as squaw dresses, in which case they were brought around the person under the right arm and fastened over the left shoulder and then sewed down the left side, although they were occasionally worn by the older women, as shown in Fig. 139. Around the waist was worn a sash of the same kind of weave, as is clearly observable in the engraving.

Fig. 31 is of a Zuni squaw dress in my own collection, the borders

* In color section.

of which are in blue and of diagonal weave. The apparently curved line is in deep green and the band containing the serrated diamonds figure is in dark red, the diamonds being in blue, outlined with dark green, and the inside square of red. The corresponding band below is of the same colors. The lighter center band is of a lighter red. The general effect is beautiful and harmonious; the dyes native and unfading, and the weaving even, smooth, and good. The warp is of homespun wool and exceedingly strong. This blanket has been under my feet in my library for over a dozen years, and while showing wear at the ends is otherwise as good as the day it was made.

Careful study of its weave shows that the diamonds are worked out so that the warp threads are brought to the surface, as Mr. A. M. Stephen describes the weave of the Hopi belts in another chapter. This is a rare thing to see, and in the thousands of blankets and squaw dresses that in the last thirty years have passed under my observation, I do not suppose I have seen it more than half a dozen times.

A squaw dress of this type, and that is rarely seen today, is pictured in Fig. 32.* I purchased it at Laguna, N. M., some twenty or more years ago, and ever since it has charmed my eyes as it has hung on one of the doors of my library. The body is of black, while the deep border at each end is of red, with a stepped design in blue, and a four-inch-wide strip of diagonally woven blue. The red is of different times of dyeing, as it varies in color.

The Acoma Indians make a squaw dress quite as ornate and beautifully woven as do the Zunis, and Fig. 33 is a good specimen found in the Fred Harvey collection, at Albuquerque, N. M. The body of the dress is black, and the designs on the borders are embroidered in significant designs. These dresses are generally used now only in the ceremonial dances in which the women take an important and impressive part.

I have elsewhere referred to the idiosyncrasies one often meets with in dealing with the Indian. The squaw dresses of the Pueblos afford a fine illustration.

Though the Hopis are the nearest Pueblo neighbors the Navahos have, and though many of their men are weavers, they do not follow the universal Pueblo method of weaving squaw dresses, but either purchase or barter for those of Navaho weave, or make them after the style of the ordinary weave, as I will afterwards describe.

Fig. 34 is of a rare Hopi ceremonial squaw dress in the Fred Harvey collection. It is of extra large size, well and finely woven, of white cotton body with embroideries of red, white, and black, which form most effective borders.

The every-day squaw dresses of the Hopi referred to above are by

* In color section.

Fig. 33.
Acoma Squaw Dress.
(Fred Harvey Collection.)   [Page 42]

Fig. 34.

Rare Hopi Ceremonial Squaw Dress.

(Fred Harvey Collection.)

The embroideries of this dress are somewhat similar to those shown in Fig. 5.

[Page 42]

no means common, and it is almost impossible to tell where any given specimen was made, unless the purchaser gained that knowledge at the time it was secured from the Indian.

Fig. 35 is of a man-woven Hopi squaw dress, which, however, I purchased from a Navaho. The man who wove it was a dweller in Tewa, or Hano, the first village on the eastern mesa of the Hopis. Now, strange to say, though regarded as Hopis, and always spoken of as Hopis, the Tewas are a foreign people who came from the Rio Grande region in order to help the Hopis fight the Utes and Apaches. These had been attracted from the north and south by the flocks of sheep and other possessions that the Hopi had acquired, and many a sharp battle of defense was fought, though the Hopis were never daring enough to make expeditions of reprisal upon their thieving and murderous foes.

Mr. A. M. Stephen thus relates how the Tewas came to be established with the Hopis:

While the Tusayan were still in the dire straits as related, they sent to their distant kinsmen on the Rio Grande, beseeching them to come to their relief. The messengers went to the village of Teh-wa, which is now called Peña Blanca, lying upon the east side of the Rio Grande in New Mexico. The Teh-wa, or "Tcheh-e-wa," House people, as they call themselves, speak a different tongue from the Hopi, but are very similar to them in all other respects. The difference in language, probably results, as has been suggested, by a former long-continued separation; but they also differed from the Hopi in possessing courage enough to take the field against a foreign enemy. They came to the aid of the Hopi, probably in 1720, moving as a sort of military colony, of about fifty families, and afterwards reinforced by as many more. On the day preceding their arrival at Walpi, the Ute had driven off the last flock of sheep belonging to that village; the Walpi were too completely cowed to venture out, but the Teh-wa at once took the trail, and came up with the Ute, not many miles away. They had driven the flock up a steep mesa side, and when they saw the Teh-wa coming, they killed the sheep on a broad ledge, and piled the carcasses up as a defense, behind which they fought. They had a few firearms, while the Teh-wa had only clubs, stone-hatchets, and their bows and arrows, but they charged and drove the Ute before them, and on some following night surprised the Ute asleep. They killed all but two, who were spared to go to the Ute country and tell their people that the Teh-wa warriors had come. On their return from this successful expedition, the Teh-wa built the village, close to the gap on the east mesa, which they still occupy. They claim that their redoubtable presence caused the hostile forays to cease, but as the region had been very persistently despoiled, it is more than likely that this circumstance also influenced the depredators to desist.

To return now to the blanket which has caused this somewhat lengthy digression. It is woven broad side on, and is therefore wider than it is long. Its size is 53x44 inches, woven in five panels, three of which are red, with designs in greenish-blue, and two of which are alternate stripes of gray and black. Like all other squaw dresses, this was worn folded, the sides sewn together so as to have the upper portion of the seam resting *on* the left shoulder, while the folded crease rested under the right shoulder.

Another squaw dress of similar style and make, though a trifle more ornate in design, is shown in Fig. 36. This is 48x60 inches in size, of soft texture and, therefore, loose weave, in five panels. Three of these are red, with square-like designs in a pale violet, on the two outer ones, and square or Greek crosses on the center panel. The two other panels are made up of gray and black stripes. In the center panel of this dress a distinct variation of the color of the stripe in which the crosses occur is seen. This is a striking illustration of the results of using yarn dyed at different times (though supposedly of the same color), and it also shows what I have elsewhere explained, that the weavers do not always take their yarn directly across the fabric, though that would appear to be the natural and workmanlike procedure.

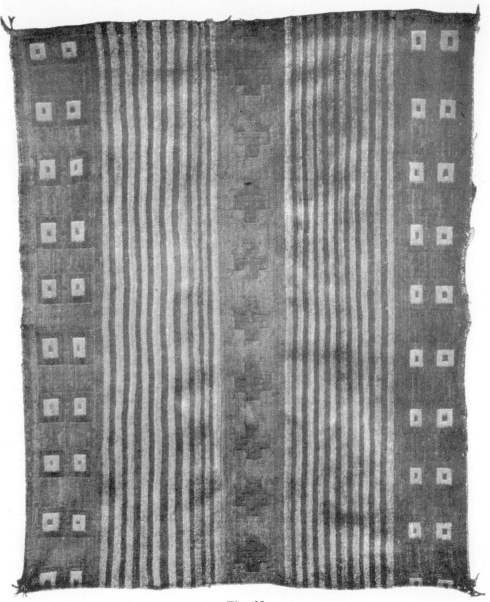

Fig. 35.
Man-Woven Hopi Squaw Dress.
(Author's Collection.) [Page 43]

Fig. 36.
Hopi Squaw Dress.
(Author's Collection.)
Somewhat unique.

[Page 44]

CHAPTER VII

The Song of Blessing of the Blanket

ONE of the most common chants or sacred songs of the Navaho is the *hozhóji,* or song of blessing or benediction. It is used on almost every occasion, in social and domestic life. One of these is on the setting up of the blanket before a newly erected *hogan.* Of course there are unbelieving and irreligious Navahos who care little or nothing for these ceremonies and chants that are very dear, sacred, and precious to the hearts of the truly religious; and the more industrious, skillful, and careful the weaver the more likely she is to be under the feeling of what to her are religious influences.

According to the mythology and beliefs of many Indian tribes, and among others, the near neighbors of the Navaho — the Hopi and Zuni — all prayers offered in the blessing of any particular object inhere to that object, hence the friendly races, combats, strivings, competitions, and strugglings to gain possession of these objects over which prayers have been offered, sacred songs sung, and rites performed. These are taken and used to make the cornfields more fruitful, to make the herds more prolific and to bring an abundance of good luck in every direction.

While, to most cultured Americans, there may seem to be nothing of good that can come from the prayers and songs of a barbaric Navaho, I am free to confess it does not lessen the value of a good blanket in my estimation to know that it is probable that songs of blessing and benediction and prayers of helpfulness have been sung and said over it. I like to feel that the Navaho woman thought of the beautiful poetic symbols of the first blanket when she made my blanket, and that before she began work upon it she prayed that only beautiful things should come in touch with it. Then I can see the ceremony of blessing the *hogan,* as it is elsewhere described in these pages. The doorway is an important spot in the *hogan.* It faces the rising sun. The sun is not a dead object of inanimate Nature to the Navaho, but a living, supreme, divine personality, whose eyes gaze upon the *innerness* of everything exposed to his gaze. The blanket that covers the doorway, therefore, is ever in his sight during the morning hours, and it, with all the rest of the *hogan,* is made the subject of the prayers of blessing.

45

CHAPTER VIII

The Temporary Deterioration of the Art of Navaho Blanket-Weaving

IT IS essential in studying aright the history of the Navaho blanket and its present condition to realize the causes that led to its deterioration, and, for a time, almost threatened its destruction. Fortunately, this condition was but temporary, and has been, in the main, bravely overcome.

As explained in an earlier chapter, up to about thirty-five or forty years ago the only Navaho blankets one could secure were bayetas, "native-wools" and "native dyes," with, now and again, a cheaper grade used as common blankets.

Four things were responsible for the rapid change and decline in the character of the Navaho weavers' work. These were: 1. The introduction of Germantown yarns. 2. The commercialization of the art. 3. The introduction of aniline dyes. 4. The introduction of cotton warps.

Let us consider these factors in their order and see how much influence each contributed to the temporary breakdown of the art.

1. The Introduction of Germantown Yarns

At the first, when Germantown yarn was introduced to the Navaho, fully forty years ago, the weaver took it upon herself to retwist the yarn to make it firmer and tighter. The result was that the earlier woven Germantowns are almost as good as those made from bayeta or native-dyed wools. The reason for this is clear. The earlier Germantown yarns were dyed, as were the English bayetas, from old vegetable and other dyes of tested quality, and the mordants were as carefully chosen as the dyes. Hence the colors were sure and reasonably free from liability to fade.

But there was a subtle, because almost imperceptible, injurious influence introduced when the weaver could purchase yarn ready-made instead of being compelled to engage in the labor of making it herself.

When, too, the Germantown yarns began to be dyed with aniline dyes they lost their old time charms, gave to the civilized world more gorgeous brilliant hues, dazzled its eyes as well as those of the Navaho weavers, and helped pervert the popular taste in regard to colors, just as

46

too much salt in a cooked dish destroys the subtler and finer flavors and essential essences of the dish itself.

Yet while the *general* effect of the introduction of Germantown yarns was to produce deterioration for a time, there were some weavers who now did their best work. The marvelous increase in colors and the ease with which they procured the yarn all ready for weaving seemed to stimulate these women to high endeavor. Hence, some exquisite specimens of Germantown blankets come to us from this period. Such a one is Fig. 37, from the Vroman collection. It is as gorgeous as a ballet in a Christmas pantomime, and though it fairly revels in riotous color, in design and weave it is a wonderfully superior piece of work. I doubt if a finer piece of Navaho weaving of Germantown yarn has ever been seen. It is as close and tight as felt and will carry water today, although it has been in constant use on the floor ever since it was purchased.

2. *The Commercialization of the Art*

Now came the serious step in the art's downfall. It appeared for a while as if it might be a frightful precipice over which it would fall forever. And yet, when the step was first taken, it was with the best of intention and without any thought of doing injury to the Navahos or their art. Indeed, it was with the desire to enlarge the Indians' productiveness. John Lorenzo Hubbell was already well established as an Indian trader among the Navahos at Ganado, Arizona. In the year 1884 C. N. Cotton joined him there in partnership.

Their whole purchase of blankets that year amounted to but between 300 and 400 pounds. These were of the common, straight-pattern type and were purchased or traded for at about $2.00 each. No saddle-blankets were either offered for sale or bought.

The following year Messrs. Hubbell and Cotton began to see possibilities in the blanket business. Why could they not get a market for these products of the Navahos' looms? While the finer quality of native-wool, native-dyed blankets, and also those of Germantown yarn were being made, practically none were being offered for sale or barter to the traders. Mr. Cotton began to urge upon the weavers that they bring in more blankets of the better qualities and also that they make more of the common grades. Little by little they built up a good business, and all seemed to be well. The Navahos were glad of the increase in their income, and the fact that Hubbell and Cotton purchased all the blankets the weavers brought in soon spread over the reservation, and added both to their fame, their ordinary business, and the stock of their blankets. This state of affairs continued, however, for but a short time.

Two new and disturbing elements were at hand. These were the introduction of aniline dyes and cotton warps.

3. The Introduction of Aniline Dyes

At this time, Mr. B. F. Hyatt, who was the post trader at Fort Defiance, introduced aniline dyes and taught the Navaho women with whom he traded how to use them. Mr. Cotton wished to do the same at Ganado, but Mr. Hubbell objected, foreseeing what afterwards actually occurred — the deterioration of the quality of the work. The Navahos already had indigo and most of the old blankets in which blue is the predominating color date from the early eighteen eighties. The indigo was purchased from the Mexicans, or later, from the traders.

In the winter of 1886-7, however, Mr. Cotton had his way and he succeeded in having one of the great dye manufacturers put up, ready for use, a quantity of aniline dyes. He instructed the weavers how to prepare them and then encouraged them in the making of various and individualistic designs. Those weavers who showed artistic and inventive skill he took particular pains with, as now did also Mr. Hubbell, and instead of buying the product of their looms by the pound, they were purchased by the piece — the price always being proportioned to the tightness and fineness of the yarn, the cleanliness of the wool, the color scheme, the individuality of the design, and the closeness of the weave.

Thus was begun the trade in the modern blanket, and to Mr. Hyatt is due the honor — and also the execration — that has followed the introduction of the aniline dye to the Navahos. For a time all seemed to go well. The demand for Navaho blankets increased rapidly. The traders could not secure enough to supply their customers.

4. The Introduction of Cotton Warp

To hasten on the manufacture of more blankets, therefore, the traders themselves introduced a cotton warp which they sold at a low price to the Indian. Thus relieved of the trouble and labor of making wool warps, blankets were made much easier, and therefore cheaper than before, and speedily a great demand was created for cheap blankets. Urged on to greater productiveness the Indians failed to clean the wool aright; they had neither the time properly to scour and wash it, remove the burrs, nor extract the dirt, dust, and grease. Such wool as this never takes the dye properly, hence the colors were uneven. Rushed to complete her task, for which she knew she would get a small price, the weaver

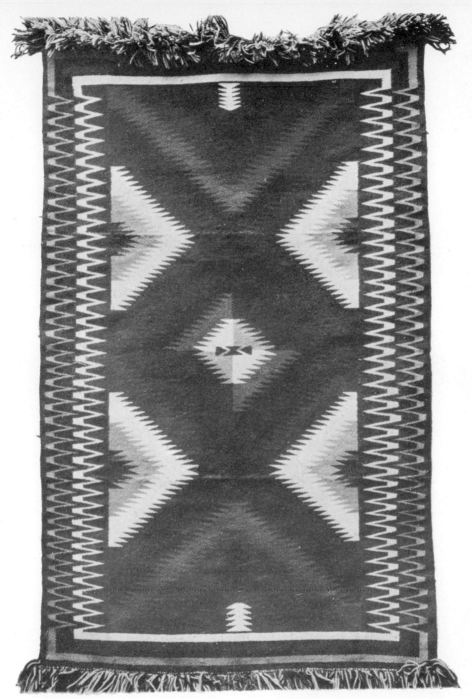

Fig. 37.
A Navaho Weave of Germantown Yarn.
(Vroman Collection.)
A fine specimen.

[Page 47]

spun her dirty, greasy, poorly-carded, imperfectly-dyed wool into the loosest, thickest, and coarsest kind of yarn, and then hastily and indifferently wove it — upon the cheap and flimsy cotton warp — in poor designs, with a loose stitch, the sooner to get it into the trader's hands and secure her pay.

Even in the case of the Germantown yarns, cotton warps were used, and though the designs were better than in the ordinary blankets the work was hastily done, not thoroughly battened down, and consequently soon exposed the flimsy warp to the wear and tear of daily use.

These were the factors that combined to pull down and degrade the weaver's art, but it did not take practical business sense long to assert itself and bring about a change. This was being done slowly, but surely, all the leading traders refusing to purchase at any price the badly cleaned, dyed, spun, and woven articles. Unable to sell them or even get rid of them in trade, the weavers were compelled to use them for their own purposes, and thus the most careless and indifferent were brought to see the necessity for improvement, when, by the irony of fate, a well-intentioned movement, inaugurated by two wealthy New York brothers brought back for a short time the evil conditions, and yet, in the end, made the improvement more certain. In about the year 1900 the Hyde Exploring Expedition was organized. Mr. B. T. Babbitt-Hyde and his brother were exceedingly desirous of thoroughly and scientifically exploring the little known and secret recesses of the Navaho reservation, and they became so interested in the Navahos and their weaving art that they determined to help enlarge their output of blankets by opening up large depots in American cities to dispose of all they would weave. A most laudable purpose and one which should have redounded to their credit. But, unfortunately, all their traders in the field were not imbued with their spirit and high purpose, and before they could stop it, the demand created for blankets was bringing in a flood of the wretchedly inferior work above described.

The results might have been foreseen. The public — or the more shrewd and discerning of it — refused to buy this inferior work, whether of the dirty, greasy, coarser native wools, or the poorer work of the expensive Germantown yarns. Yet the flood of poor quality, thick, coarse, loosely woven blankets, wretchedly dyed in hideous combinations of colors continued to pour into the market. As an *art,* Navaho weaving was doomed unless something speedily was done. While the conscientious traders had purchased few or none of this kind, selecting all the blankets offered with the greatest care and discernment, this other flood placed the Hyde Exploring Expedition in the anomalous position of offering for sale, at one and the same time, though through their different stores, the very highest specimens of the modern Navaho weaver's art, and the lowest—or pretty nearly so.

The very magnitude of this laudable and praiseworthy endeavor, the great advertising it secured, the immense number of the blankets purchased, the arousal of the public interest, the number of newspaper and magazine articles published about the Navaho Indian and his blanket, all had an educative effect, which had an ultimate reaction for positive good upon the art itself. Unable to cope with the situation, or determined to free themselves from the burden placed upon them by irresponsible men, the Hyde Exploring Expedition sold out to Mr. J. W. Benham and his associates, who speedily established the business upon a sound footing, on the lines indicated in the next chapter. The lesson has been well learned. The public, now, is too well-informed upon the Navaho blanket to tolerate any further playing with the business. It demands, and will have, good blankets, *or none,* and in that insistent demand the art finds its chief and surest safeguard.

CHAPTER IX

Improving the Art of Navaho Blanket-Weaving

NO STUDENT of the Navaho blanket will contend for one moment that the fine old weaves are not the most eagerly sought after, and oftentimes the most perfectly woven blankets known to the connoisseur. A blanket in which native dye was used, made of finely spun and closely woven native wool, which was thoroughly cleaned and scoured before being dyed, embellished with a design that attracts and pleases the eye is as eagerly sought as ever. So is one in which the retwisted red *bayeta* forms the main body of the blanket. Almost equally desirable are the earlier and better qualities made of Germantown yarn, where the warps were of wool, even though the colors and designs, originally, were of barbaric splendor. In time these colors tone down to exquisite harmonies that make the blankets pictures of beauty and charm.

Such blankets as these will ever be in demand, and are eagerly sought after today at prices that are constantly increasing.

Yet it cannot be denied that as good blankets are being made now as ever. As a rule when the white man has commercialized an aboriginal art it becomes degraded and debased so that one is compelled to look for the finest specimens among the oldest examples.

While this is true of the Navaho blanket, the finest old specimens being scarce and almost priceless, it is a remarkable fact that, in spite of the period of marked deterioration, fully explained in the preceding chapter, the Navaho weaver has reasserted herself, and is now making blankets that in general and specific terms equal those of the past in everything except age and the use of native dyes.

When blanket weaving reached its lowest stage and the public had begun to realize the cheap and almost worthless character of much of the work offered to them the sales dropped off woefully, for they refused to purchase more of such unworthy goods.

This worked like an electric shock upon the traders. They saw — not all at once — but with the speediness of shrewd business men, that in their haste to develop a trade they had made a grave mistake. Yet they had self-willed Indians to deal with, who neither understood nor cared anything for the white man's method of reasoning. If they refused to accept blankets in trade, however poor, the Indians would go off in a huff and do their trading elsewhere. The traders had no union or league so that they could pool their interests. They were too far apart to have the opportunity to meet with one another, save by accident; hence for a while blanket matters stood at a low ebb. Soon, however, it became apparent to the most indifferent and thoughtless that something must be done, or ruin stared them in the face. They could not continue to purchase poor quality blankets which they could not sell, no matter what the Navahos thought or did. As soon as this idea was fully developed in their minds things began to change for the better.

To four firms, more than any others, who stand in close relation to the purchasing public, is owing, undoubtedly, the rapid improvement of the art in late years. Fred Harvey, whose great Indian collections at Albuquerque, New Mexico, and at the Hopi House at the Grand Canyon, have been the delight and instruction of many thousands, and who has Indian stores at many of the leading depots along the line of the Santa Fé railway, set his face definitely and unalterably against all of the low-grade, common, and poorly made blankets. He would not handle them at any price. He demanded of his weavers throughout the reservation the best, and refused all others. Cotton warps, save in the few exceptional cases referred to, were positively debarred, and all yarn must be thoroughly cleansed, deodorized, dyed, and spun before it was woven, or it could not be disposed of to, or by, him. This naturally made the Fred Harvey blankets *seem* to be of a higher price than those offered by others. But it was and is only a seeming. The purchaser who is discriminating and wants only the good thing, does not always have the time or opportunity to study into the details of his purchases. He wishes to deal with a reliable house who will guarantee to him that he is purchasing the best. He is willing to pay a fair price for such expert advice, and such guaranteed protection, and from this standpoint Fred Harvey's blankets are as reasonable as those of any house in the trade. He also carries an immense stock, not only of the rare old type of blankets, but of the modern weaves, of every style and make.

In a similar manner The Benham Indian Trading Company stood between its customers and poor work. Mr. J. W. Benham, the founder of the company, and his father, Mr. A. M. Benham, were men of the most upright character, who thoroughly understood the business from beginning to end, and they built up a large trade by their integrity and conscientious treatment of their customers. The present head of the firm, by whose name the business is now known — The Burns Indian Trading Company — was practical manager of the older business for some years and is carrying on the business on the same high plane.

Messrs. Hubbell and Cotton also demanded the better work, and when the partnership between them was dissolved the former made arrangements with all the leading weavers of his part of the reservation, and for twenty-five years or more has kept them all busy making fine blankets that are standards of excellence throughout the trade.

About the beginning of this century Mr. J. B. Moore, who had a trading post on the reservation at a point afterwards named Crystal, New Mexico, made a further step in advance in the improvement of the art. Instead of allowing the Indians to card, scour, and dye their wool, he carefully selected the finest quality and longest staple of the wool he had purchased from the Navahos, and shipped it east in carload lots to the mills, where with modern machinery and by improved mechanical and chemical methods all the impurities, the grease, the attendant odor, were scientifically and certainly removed. Then the cleaned and purified wool was shipped back, and, under his own direction, carded, spun into yarn by the Navahos, and dyed with colors of his own choosing. Thus the dyes were more likely to be permanent, and none of the inharmonious colors were introduced.

Now the yarn was issued to those weavers who had proven their craftsmanship and artistic skill. Only enough was issued for one blanket at a time, and the size of it was to be carefully shown. The weaver was left to her own originality and creative power if she had shown her ability in the past, otherwise a blanket was placed before her and she was instructed to make her design as near to that as possible. To get her to copy a design exactly is almost impossible. Even with the least original of designers there seems to be the pride of the true artist who must originate and not copy.

This plan of Mr. Moore's worked well, for there are some weavers who have superior technical skill in the mere mechanical part of weaving but who lack the artistic and creative power to originate striking and pleasing designs. By this method they are given the suggestion for designs which they always deviate from and thus secure the touch of original personality, while at the same time the weaving is done with that superior skill that is their especial pride and boast.

By these means Mr. Moore secured blankets of superior uniformity of quality, whose points of superiority were perfect cleanliness of the wool, odorlessness, dyes of assured permanency, richness and harmoniousness of color scheme, fine and tightly spun woof threads, the same assured quality in the wool warp threads, novel and pleasing designs carefully executed, and that tightness or closeness of weave that alone assures durability.

Most of these blankets of Mr. Moore's were sold directly to the individual purchaser. He did a large mail order business, without allowing his goods to go into the hands of the dealer, and gained considerable note as well as a large financial return by this method of sale.

In 1911-12, however, he sold out to Mr. J. A. Molohon, who, at the same post, is carrying on the business in the same manner and has materially added to his staff of expert weavers.

One of the finest specimens extant of the best class of blanket which the superior and honest weavers of this epoch made is shown in Fig. 38.* These were generally made for *shamans* (medicine men), or those who were regarded as chiefs of their section of country; hence received all the care and attention that blankets for ceremonial and personal use were entitled to before the days of commercialism.

The body is in the plain straight stripes, mainly of black and blue with two relief bands, in which old-gold-green, and blue are included between two bands of red. The center of the blanket contains the conventionalized zigzag design, and the two ends are likewise finished with this conventionalized zigzag symbol.

This blanket has seen good service, and is today in good condition. Its use and old age have improved it. The weave is not too tight, although tight enough to be solid, but the blanket is soft and yielding. The one great charm of blankets of this kind is found in the subtle variations of tone that the colors take on during the lapse of time. Some of the black stripes take on a brownish tinge, while the blue varies in quality, and as one moves it and looks at it there is a play of color upon it that reminds one of the elusive though positive hues and tints that are found on the desert. This blanket possesses a rich iridescence, combined with that elusive quality. It is in the Fred Harvey collection.

It is freely conceded by all traders that the Navaho is a shrewd business man, and the women are as keen, intelligent, and self-reliant as the men. This in itself has been one of the strong reasons for the improvement in the blanket. As soon as the weaver realized that the cupidity of the trader had led him to overreach himself in urging the use of inferior material, etc., the wiser of the weavers took the matter into their own hands and began to remedy the evil. But the Navaho, being a keen trader, it was but natural, says one who knows him well, "if he saw he could get an equally good price for an inferior and poor article, than he could for one upon which he had expended much care, time, and labor, he would do just about what his palefaced brother would do."

Hence the education in some cases had to be *of the trader* rather than the weaver. The former had to learn that the public was growing more discriminating and would no longer be satisfied with a poor quality of work. The lesson is now pretty well learned by both Indian and

* In color section.

trader, hence the quality of blankets will continue to improve, even though the output increases and becomes four times what it now is.

The steps by which improvement has come are very simple. First, cotton warps were frowned upon, and some of the wiser traders refused to sell another pound of them. Those who dealt in aniline dyes made a careful choice of a few good colors, that experience had demonstrated were "faster" than others, and that were less glaring and fantastic when combined. Today only a few standard colors can be bought by the Navahos from their regular traders. If they wish the more startling colors they must go or send to some *civilized* city drug-store, for the traders have learned wisdom and refuse to carry them.

Then came the pressure put upon the Indians for the improvement of the native wools, even though they used the aniline dyes in their coloring. First the thorough cleaning and carding of the wool was demanded, with the extracting of all foreign substances and the elimination of matted and greasy clumps. Then they saw to it that the wool was thoroughly scoured and deodorized, so that none of the "sheepy" smell adhered to it. Now it was fit to be dyed, and, being clean and sweet, took the color perfectly and satisfactorily. It next became a matter of persuasion by offering larger pay to get the weavers, first, to spin their yarn, both for warp and woof, tighter and finer. In this way it was soon made equal and even superior, when thoroughly and tightly spun, to the Germantown. Second, to invent and weave more artistic, pleasing, striking, and original designs; and, third, to weave them tighter, closer, and more carefully, so that the critical eye and hand had less faults to find than formerly.

Some traders went so far as to offer prizes for the best blankets offered by their weavers. A few of the more intelligent traders, who every year had been giving the Indians of the surrounding country a "feast," now used these gatherings for the purpose of creating rivalry in blanket weaving. All the best blankets of their stock were exhibited in a booth, and competitions thus freely and openly made soon aroused the desire for improvement — even for mastery.

The result of these efforts is seen in that the Navahos are now weaving few blankets of any kind that have a cotton warp, except the small and cheap pillow covers, which do not have the same strain of wear and tear that the larger blankets are subject to. Of the Germantown yarn blankets there are not five per cent. made of the number that were manufactured ten or fifteen years ago. Yet this is not because the Germantown yarn is not good.

It is rather that the Navahos have learned that, if they would preserve their profitable industry, they must themselves make a yarn that, in every sense of the word, is equal to the Germantown. This they are now doing, as all the experts who have watched recent developments freely testify.

Of such yarn is that used in Fig. 39, which represents a modern blanket made by one of Fred Harvey's weavers at Albuquerque, New Mexico. This is a perfect illustration of the assertion that I have so often made in these pages that the weavers of today are making just as good blankets as any that have ever been made. While the yarn of this blanket is not quite as fine as that of an old bayeta, it is even more closely woven. Such a blanket as this is so stiff from the firmness of the battening down process that it cannot be used as a wrap or a cover for the body. It is almost as stiff as cardboard. This fine quality, however, renders it perfect as a rug and there is no such thing as wearing out a blanket of such texture and weave as this. The design is simple but pleasing, the main body being in native grays of different tinges and shades. The border is of native black — not dyed — wool. There are also lines of a deeper brown in the square stepped figures, and these also are of undyed wool. The color effect is exceedingly pleasant, while a touch of red adds sufficient life to attract and please the eye.

There are also other powerful factors at work which tend directly to the improvement of the art of the Navaho weaver.

In the early days the Navaho knew nothing of scientific breeding or care of his sheep. In 1851 Dr. Letherman wrote:

The males are permitted to run with the herds at all seasons, and the young, consequently, are born in the winter as well as in the spring and autumn, and many die. For this reason their flocks do not increase with the rapidity generally believed by those not much acquainted with these people. It is a great mistake to suppose there is anything peculiar about Navaho sheep, for such is not the case.

At that time he estimated the number of the sheep to be about two hundred thousand, and he declared that the "wool is coarse and is never shorn. The sheep are in all respects similar to those raised by the Mexicans, occasionally one being seen having four horns."

He also refers to the fact that conditions were very adverse to sheep raising, as, for instance, in the winter of 1855, the Navahos were compelled to abandon the country north of Fort Defiance on account of the cold and depth of the snow, which prevented their sheep from grazing.

Some of these conditions still remain, but the general improvement of the life of the Navahos has resulted in better quarters for the sheep in bad weather, and, in special cases of entire lack of grazing material, hay is purchased for their sustenance.

Another grave and serious difficulty the Navahos have had to contend

Fig. 39.
Modern Native Wool Navaho, Best Quality.
(Fred Harvey Collection.)

The weave and material in this blanket are as good as in some of the older ones. The quantity of this grade now produced is comparatively limited.

[Page 56]

with for many years has been, during the hot summer months, that they have had a poor supply of water.   As Dr. G. H. Pepper once wrote:

This scarcity of water is the all-absorbing topic of whites as well as natives in the great Southwest.   There are spring and autumn rains or showers, as a rule, but at times almost a year will pass without enough water falling to fill the pockets in the rocks; at such times the Indian endeavors by songs and dances to propitiate the rain-gods and cause them to let fall the precious liquid that they are withholding; when their sheep and horses are dying from thirst they will dance continuously for weeks and then, in despair, make a forced drive across the fiery, alkaline plains to the mountains, where the streams will furnish what the gods of the plains will not; but in such a drive their flocks are so decimated that it hardly pays to make the effort.

Both these neglected conditions are now being taken hold of by the Government, through the Indian Department, in a most effective manner.   Its report for 1911 shows that "at the last dipping the Indians of Pueblo Bonita, New Mexico, had one hundred and twenty-three thousand sheep and goats," and that those of the Navaho Agency own "well in excess of five hundred thousand sheep."   It was also "roughly estimated that within one hundred miles of the Superintendency at Keams Canyon, Arizona, four hundred thousand dollars' worth of Navaho blankets were sold in the year" (1910).

The report then continues:

A plan has been outlined for improving the breed of sheep belonging to these Indians by the introduction from time to time of a limited number of high-grade Rambouillet and Cotswold rams into their flocks, with the hope that the improvement in the native sheep may be so apparent that the Indians of these reservations will, of their own volition, adopt methods of improving their flocks.   The aim is not only to increase the size of these animals so as to make them more desirable for mutton, but to improve the quality and amount of the wool so that the present clip of three or four pounds per animal may be increased to at least double that amount.

On February 7, 8, and 9, 1912, a conference of all the officials of the Indian Department on the Navaho Agencies was held at Fort Defiance, Arizona, for the purpose of discussing and considering various subjects and problems connected with the welfare of the Navaho.   It was there estimated by the men most competent to judge that there were then 1,429,821 sheep, valued at $2,924,960, and 318,955 goats, valued at $497,910, owned by the Navahos.   The wool clipped from the native sheep amounted to 3,375,000 pounds, valued at $429,375, and from the graded merino sheep 293,463 pounds, valued at $35,664.   Not all of this wool is woven by the Navahos into blankets.   Vast quantities are bought by the traders and shipped to the white man's woolen mills, but the Department estimated that in 1912, 843,750 pounds of native wool was woven into blankets. The output of blankets for the year was estimated to be, from native wool, $675,000, and from Germantown yarn, $36,000.

As far as the water supply is concerned, the situation is rapidly being changed. The Hyde Exploring Expedition, when it began its work in Arizona, relied for two years upon the surface water just as did the Navahos, but the third year, writes Dr. G. H. Pepper in 1902:

> In digging a reservoir to catch the seep from an arroyo, a water-bearing stratum was reached; below this there was a layer of quicksand; a foot deeper we came to water-bearing gravel that furnished water for our stock, and also for all the Indian stock in the vicinity. The supply seems inexhaustible and on feast occasions from 200 to 300 head of stock have been watered there in a single day. Navahos travel for miles to fill their kegs from this pure source and none were more surprised than they when it was first discovered; this is not an isolated case, for another well, sunk by our party about thirty miles distant from the one mentioned, only twenty-five feet deep, supplied enough to tide over a very dry season — a simple illustration that serves to show what the government might do to help the Navahos.

This suggestion was carried out, and in the year 1910 water experts went over the major part of the reservation making careful observations and surveys, and the year following the work of putting in wells was actually begun. The result is that now (spring of 1914), as one travels through the Navaho country he sees, every now and again, the surprising spectacle of skeleton steel towers, tanks, and pumps, with watering troughs, around which horses, cattle, and sheep daily congregate, when other water supply fails.

The intention of the Government is to continue this work in all parts of the reservation until enough wells are bored to insure the Navahos against future scarcity of water.

No chapter dealing with the improvement of the art of Navaho blanket weaving would be complete without especial reference to the work of one man. This is Mr. W. T. Shelton, the founder and present superintendent of the San Juan Agency at Shiprock, New Mexico. Mr. Shelton has shown a greater grasp of the situation, it appears to me, than any other man in the whole history of the Indian Service. To him has been largely owing the furtherance of the plan for providing water for the Indians' flocks and also the improvement of the breed of their stock. He has personally purchased several high-bred rams, and has been tireless in his determination to inculcate a desire for, and interest the Indians in, improving the breed of their animals.

But far more than this, in 1909 he conceived the idea of holding a fair at the San Juan Agency at Shiprock and invited not only the Indians but also the Indian traders of the district to make as extensive exhibits as possible of every department of Navaho industry. To attract the Indians he offered general prizes for foot-races, horse-races, and a variety of other native games. He also let it be known that there would be no objections to the Indians indulging in some of their own sacred dances, and at his own expense he secured the services of several of the leading *chanters,* as the head medicine-men or dance-directors are known.

This fair was a great success, although it only foreshadowed what its possibilities might be. Among the exhibits there were two hundred and thirty blankets of native wool and twenty-five Germantown blankets.

In October, 1912, the fourth fair was held, and four times as many blankets were displayed and the improvement in their quality was remarkable. Thirteen Indian traders were represented, but all of these allowed the weavers in their districts to make their own exhibits, so that the Indians themselves received full credit in person as well as the prizes which were awarded for the best blankets.

Personally I was unable to be present at this fourth Navaho fair, but I arrived at the Agency a few weeks afterwards. I saw the prize blankets, and they confirmed Father Berard's statement that as fine blankets are being made today as ever in the history of the Navaho. In a large four-square enclosure, substantial wooden booths were erected with abundant space for the hanging up of the different blankets, and he who saw such a display as this for the first time must have fully realized that under such fostering conditions there was little possibility of the further deterioration of the art.

It is impossible to estimate the beneficial effect of these fairs, and now that Mr. Shelton has demonstrated that they can be conducted successfully, it is to be hoped that they will be started in other parts of the reservation so that every weaver thereon may have the benefit of these opportunities for comparison and suggestion.

CHAPTER X

The Significance and Symbolism of Color in the Navaho Blanket

I T was to be expected that as primitive man developed the weaving art, the introduction of color into his textiles would suggest itself. Surrounded on every hand by vivid brilliancies of color — in the gorgeous and glowing sunrises and sunsets, in the dazzling brilliancy of the sunshine upon the variegated colorings of the desert, in the equally impressive color-attractions of his corn-fields, the wild flowers, the birds, reptiles, and animals with which he daily came in contact — he could scarcely ignore their insistent intrusion.

How it was that color ultimately came to have a distinct symbolism in the Indian mind is a most interesting question, and one upon which, doubtless, knowing experts of the white race would have great and wide diversity of opinion.

On this question, however, W. S. Blatchley, State Geologist of Indiana, writes some interesting and important things. To the thinking reader it will appear remarkable that a modern scientist should reason things out and come to the same *kind* of conclusions, even though not exactly the *same* conclusions, that were reached centuries ago by the so-called savages of our Western Wilds. Professor Blatchley says:

The " Symbols of Nature's Hues," is a theme which to a painter's brush or a poet's pen should yield inspiration noble. Green stands for youth, for cells rich in protoplasm and chlorophyll, strong in the power of storing energy, potent in the factor of growth. For that reason green is ever welcome, for it is the hue of promise, of hope, of growth, and work, of life yet to be, of crops of the future. It is the garb of springtime, the garb in which Mother Earth delights to clothe herself after her winter's sleep.

Yellow and blue, orange, and red, represent maturity, the harvest time. Growth has ceased. Energy is stored. Cells are full of starch and protein, of food and power. These hues should also stand for peace and content, for happiness if it is ever to be — for these years which are the crowning glory of a life well spent.

Brown and gray are sombre colors, hues of death and decay. Too often they follow the green of youth with none of the brighter tints intervening. The crop is harvested before full maturity. The seed shrivels and shrinks. Life is a failure, a succession of years of longing for that which never comes, which never can be.

Black is for mourning, for despair, for grief over brown and gray, for the shroud to cover their faces, hide their faults. It is a hue seldom seen in Nature for her days and years are full of promise, too precious to be wasted in long spent grief. Green and the hues of perfect maturity are those in which she most delights.

Browns and grays and blacks are for her waste places, her deserts and mountain tops, her late autumns and winters; greens for her oases, valleys, and prairies.

White is for innocence, for purity, for the first hours of the new born plant and animal, for the mantle which shall hide the black despair of deepest winter, but which shall be uplifted to disclose the first glimpse of the garb of green which follows the great awakening.*

Thus reasons a modern scientist. Let us look at and compare this with the reasoning of the Navaho Indians. To the older Indians, who had not yet become sophisticated by contact with the white man, color was sacred—a gift of the best of their gods, and it was also symbolic. Every color meant something; it was not a mere haphazard, a chance, an accident. Red is the color of the sunshine, hence its glorification in so many Navaho blankets. In the early days one could scarcely find a blanket which did not contain red—red, red, more red, much red. For sunshine was the medium in which the Navaho lived, moved, and had his being. Sunshine was his life. Take him away from it and he speedily pined away and died. It was his daily blessing, his stimulation, the source of his exhilaration, his joy. Do you wonder, then, that he used it abundantly in his blanket, that he wanted to wrap himself up in it on the days when the dark clouds hid the real sun, sleep on it during the darkness of the night, cover his children with it when they were cold, or when they slept?

When one realizes this fact he sees that the Indian's love for red is not a mere vagary, a whim, a fancy of the eye, a barbaric taste in the wildly gorgeous, a flaunting of his inability to appreciate color, but a keen and grateful recognition of one of the greatest gifts of the gods to men— the warming, vivifying, fructifying, life-giving sun, and in the use of the color of the sunshine he pays a subtle compliment to the gods.

Red, however, is but one of the colors, and the Navaho appreciates others, and the reason is evident when one understands the working of his mind.

He sees in the East the white light of the morning, hence white is always symbolic of the East. The cloudless South is generally blue, hence blue always symbolizes South. The sunset in the West is so often characterized by yellow that that color always symbolizes West, while from the North come the dark, black clouds, hence black always symbolizes North.

Then, by a symbolism of sex, color comes also to have a sexual significance. On this subject Dr. Matthews writes:†

Of two things which are nearly alike, or otherwise comparable, it is common among the Navahos to speak of or symbolize the one which is the coarser, rougher,

---

* *Woodland Idyls*, pp. 47-48, by W. S. Blatchley; The Nature Publishing Co., Indianapolis.

† *The Night Chant*, Memoirs of American Museum of Natural History, Vol. VI, p. 6.

stronger, or more violent as the male, and that which is the finer, weaker, or more gentle as the female.   Thus: a shower accompanied by thunder and lightning is called *ni'ltsabaka* or he-rain, while a shower without electrical display is called *ni'ltsabaad* or she-rain; the turbulent San Juan River is called *To'baka* or Male Water, while the more Placid Rio Grande is known as *To'baad* or Female Water. Other instances of this kind might be cited from the vegetable kingdom and other sources.   As an instance of this principle the south, and the color of the south, blue, belong to the female; the north, and the color of the north, black, belong to the male.   The north is assigned to the male because it is to the Navahos a rough and rigorous land.   Not only do inclement and violent winds come from the north, but the country north of Navaho-land is rugged and mountainous, and within it rise the great snow-covered peaks of Colorado.   The south is assigned to the female because gentle and warm breezes come from there, and because the landscape south of the Navaho country is tame compared to that of the north.

Hence in the preparation of his Plumed Wands to be used by a shaman, or medicine man, in certain ceremonials, those which are to represent the male are painted black — the color of the North — and these are used in the masculine region, the North, while those of the female are painted blue — the color of the South — and are used for the South.

Here are some of the methods invariably followed by the shamans to denote certain specific objects and thoughts, in which color and design have distinct meaning:

Red on a black or dark background suggests sunlight on the back of a cloud, and on some of the masks used in sacred dances borders are made of the feathers of red-tailed woodpeckers to represent rays of sunlight streaming out at the edge of a cloud.

On many of the masks used in their ceremonies there is a yellow streak at the chin, crossed with black lines, to symbolize rain and the evening sky.   Rain is commonly represented by eight vertical lines, painted black.

The rainbow is a hard symbol to produce in any textile material owing to the geometrical necessities of weaving, but the attempt is often made, generally in four colors.

In the sand-paintings rainbows are symbolized in two different ways, for they are regarded as of two different origins and entities.   Sometimes they are the trails, the paths of the gods in the heavens, and at other times they are the gods themselves.   When it is desired to represent them as symbols of the former they are supposedly made in five lines of color, though generally only red and blue are used, with dividing and border lines of white — thus making the five.

As a deity the rainbow is regarded as female for the reasons explained in the references to the symbolism of sex.   And as there are five colors (to the Navaho) in the rainbow, some of their medicine-men affirm that each color represents a different individual. Hence, according to this theory, there are five rainbow goddesses.

They say the bows are covered with feathers, which give the colors. In the dry-paintings, the rainbow is usually depicted with a head at one end, and legs and feet at the other. The head is always square, to show that it is a female. Three colors only have been seen in the body of the bow, which is red and blue, bordered with white. In some sweat-house decorations, the rainbow symbol is shown with a head at each end, indicating that each separate band of color represents a separate goddess.

In many of the sand-paintings, where the gods are represented and their legs are drawn (some are covered with skirts so they cannot be drawn), they are girded with rainbow garters. These are invariably the parallel lines of color, supposedly five, though generally red and blue are used, separated and also banded on the outside with white, thus forming the five lines.

It may be interesting to note that you will never see a Navaho point to a rainbow, or a rainbow symbol, with his finger. To do this would be unlucky and be sure to result in the coming of a felon on the offending member. He always points at it with his thumb.

In making the prayer-sticks, hundreds of which sometimes are used in a single Navaho ceremony, this symbolism of color comes into play. Those that are to be placed to the East are made of mountain mahogany (*Cercocarpus parvifolius*); those to be South of a shrub called coyote-corn (*Forestiera neomexicana*); those to the West of juniper (*Juniperus occidentalis*); and those to the North of cherry (*Prunus demissa*). Dr. Matthews says of these:

Mountain mahogany is probably selected for the east, because its abundant plumose white styles give the shrub a whitish aspect and white is the color of the east. *Forestiera* may be chosen for the south because its small olive-shaped fruit is blue, the color of the south. Juniper is perhaps taken for the west because its outer branchlets and leaves have, in the arid region, a tone of yellow, which is the color of the west. Cherry seems to be adopted for the north because the fruit of *Prunus demissa,* the common wild cherry of New Mexico, ripens black, and black is the color of the north.*

Those who have observed the ceremonies of the Navahos doubtless have been struck with the frequency of the appearance and use of the long cotton-string. It is used on the prayer-sticks, attached to the prayer-plumes, the sacred cigarettes, etc. The white cotton string represents the *biké-hozoni,* the beautiful or happy trail of life, so often mentioned in the Navahos' songs and prayers, which the devotee hopes, with the aid of the gods, to travel. "With all around me beautiful, may I walk,"

* *The Night Chant.*

say the prayers, and for this reason the string passes through beautiful beads, which, by their colors, symbolize the four cardinal points of the compass. "With beauty above me, may I walk," "With beauty below me, may I walk," are again the words of the prayers; so the string includes feather and hair of the turkey, a bird of the earth, and of the eagle, a bird of the sky. "My voice restore for me," "Make beautiful my voice," are expressions of the prayers and to typify these sentiments the string includes feathers of warbling birds whose voices "flow in gladness" as the Navaho song says.

Hence it will be seen that color has a definite symbolism to the Navaho and that everything connected with it is sacred and significant.

CHAPTER XI

Dyeing With Native and Aniline Dyes

IN Chapter IV, dealing with the Bayeta Blanket, I deemed it advisable to introduce, ahead of this chapter, considerable information about the dyeing of bayetas and pellons. It will be well, therefore, for the reader who wishes a full grasp of this part of the subject to turn again to that chapter.

That dyeing is a primitive art the earliest books clearly reveal. In the Book of Exodus, 25:4, 5, we are told that Moses was instructed to require the children of Israel to bring certain gifts for the erection of a tabernacle, and among them are enumerated "rams' skins dyed red," together with blue, purple, and scarlet, and fine linen. Isaiah cries out (Is. 63:1): "Who is this that cometh from Edom, with dyed garments from Bozrah?" and in the next verse suggests how the art of dyeing may have had its origin: "Wherefore are thou red in thine apparel, and thy garments like him that treadeth in the winefat?" Just so soon as garments began to be worn, aye, even before then, the stain upon body and fleece, skin, hair, or texture must have suggested the idea of ability to change color by staining with fruit juices, the juices of nuts, skins, plants, leaves, etc. And the *idea* once in the mind of the primitive man or woman it would not require much experience to fix it permanently for the future benefit of the race.

The Tinnehs of Alaska, of which family the Navahos are a branch, have used a few dyes from time immemorial, as their colored buckskins, blankets, and baskets clearly show. Hence it may be assumed that a crude and simple knowledge of the art was possessed by the first Navahos who settled where they are now found. Then contact with the Pueblos, and, later, with the Mexicans, stimulated their knowledge, and when they once began to weave after the Pueblo fashion their improvement in the art of dyeing was assured.

There is a general cry of regret today that the art as followed by the Navahos of as late as fifty years ago, or, in a few isolated cases, even twenty years ago, has been lost, and that aniline dyes are substituted for the native ones.

But the question of native Navaho dyes *versus* aniline or some form of modern dyes is settled forever by laws over which the purchaser practically has no control.   I say "practically," for undoubtedly were the purchasers of Navaho blankets to "arise in their might" and as one man demand no other than native dyes they would get them.   But it is impractical, impossible, to get them to make such a demand, and therefore by the very force of simple acquiescence in a fact that cannot be helped the native dye is disappearing — nay, has already practically disappeared.

Yet, in spite of this affirmation that, in the main, the question of native *versus* modern dyes is forever settled, efforts are being made by white friends of the Navaho to materially improve his present methods of dyeing.   Col. J. S. Lockwood, president of the Indian Industries League, of Boston, Massachusetts, is seeking to interest the Indian Department in the putting up of modern, scientific, and well-equipped wool-scouring and dyeing plants on the Navaho reservation, where the wool of the native sheep may be thoroughly washed, cleaned, deodorized, and then dyed with superior and reliable dyes and mordants.   I believe this would be a decided step in advance and of material benefit to the art and to the Navahos.   There will naturally be opposition on the part of the Indians, and it will take patience and wisdom to overcome this. Navahos are conservative to a high degree, though, as I have shown in Chapter IX; they are beginning to be reasonably alert to all plans that seek their material advancement and increased prosperity.

Colonel Lockwood urges also that when blankets are woven with yarns thus properly prepared, the Indian Department should place seals upon them as guarantees both to traders and private purchasers.

In regard to the old native dyes there are, perhaps, half a dozen weavers on the whole reservation today — perhaps more, possibly less — who retain all the secrets and are willing to go to the trouble to dye the wool with them and thus produce a "native wool, native dyed, native woven" blanket.

Fortunately, however, the methods were observed by intelligent and recording white men in time to save the art from being lost, and from their writings the following account is compiled.   The name of each author, unless otherwise stated, is placed in brackets at the end of each quotation:

In preparing the wool for dyeing, it is picked apart and the tangled masses are loosened, but, as a rule, there is no washing done.   To most students of weaving, especially those who have become interested in the art of dyeing, it would seem that, in omitting the washing of the wool one of the essentials had been overlooked.   In fact, many dyers insist that upon the quality of the water used depends the success of the work, and they, therefore, use nothing but soft water.   The scarcity of water in the Navaho country is responsible for this seeming negligence on the part of the blanket maker. But, in judging these worthy people we must remember that the wool of the Navaho sheep is not greasy as is that of the merinos and many other sheep and therefore does not require the elaborate washing and scouring that must be undergone ere the ordinary wool is workable. The Navaho herdsmen are particularly careful about keeping their sheep from crossing with the merinos of the Mexicans, as they realize that the merino wool cannot be washed or bleached and that the use of the wool in its natural state causes unsightly streaks in their blankets. These streaks not only detract from the aesthetic appearance of their productions but cause a depreciation in value.

For making native dyes the Navaho dyer needs the vegetable and mineral ingredients required for the specific dyes; a pot in which to make the decoction of barks, flowers, twigs or roots, for which their own native pots are preferred, probably because the acid of the mordants will not act chemically upon earthen vessels as it will upon tin or iron; a skillet, or frying pan, to prepare certain of the ingredients, and a few thin, slender sticks to immerse the wool with, or take it out of the dye, and to spread it out to dry.

Each dye consists of at least two ingredients, a coloring matter and a mordant, usually some acid substance to fix the color fast.— [Berard.]

The black dye is made of the leaves and twigs of the aromatic sumac (*Rhus aromatica*), a native yellow ochre, and the gum of the pinion (*Pinus edulus*). The process of preparing it is as follows: They put into a pot of water some of the leaves of the sumac and as many of the branchlets as can be crowded in without much breaking or crushing, and the water is allowed to boil for five or six hours until a strong decoction is made. While the water is boiling they attend to other parts of the process. The ochre is reduced to a fine powder between two stones, and then slowly roasted over the fire in an earthen or metal vessel until it assumes a light-brown color; it is then taken from the fire and combined with about an equal quantity in size of pinion gum; again the mixture is put on the fire and constantly stirred. At first the gum melts and the whole mass assumes a mushy consistence; but as the roasting progresses it gradually becomes drier and darker until it is at last reduced to a fine black powder. This is removed from the fire, and when it has cooled somewhat it is thrown into the decoction of sumac, with which it instantly forms a rich, blue-black fluid. This dye is essentially an ink, the tannic acid of the sumac combining with the sesquioxide of iron in the roasted ochre, the whole enriched by the carbon of the calcined gum.

There are, the Indians tell me, three different processes for dyeing yellow; two of these I have witnessed. The first process is thus conducted: The flowering tops of *Bigelovia graveolens* are boiled for about six hours until a decoction of deep yellow color is produced. When the dyer thinks the decoction strong enough, she heats over the fire in a pan or earthen vessel some native almogen (an impure native alum), until it is reduced to a somewhat pasty consistency; this she adds gradually to the decoction and then puts the wool in the dye to boil. From time to time a portion of the wool is taken out and inspected until (in about half an hour from the time it is first immersed) it is seen to have assumed the proper color. The work is then done. The tint produced is nearly that of lemon yellow. In the second process they use the large fleshy root of a plant which, as I have never yet seen it in fruit or flower, I am unable to determine. The fresh root is crushed to a soft paste on the *metate*, and, for a mordant, the almogen is added while the grinding is going on. The cold paste is then rubbed between the hands into the wool. If the wool does not seem to take the color readily a little water is dashed on the mixture of wool and paste, and the whole is very slightly warmed. The whole process does not occupy over an hour, and the result is a color much like that now known as " old gold."

The reddish dye is made of the bark of *Alnus incana var. virescens* (Watson), and the bark of the root of *Cercocarpus parvifolius;* the mordant being fine juniper ashes. On buckskin this makes a brilliant tan color; but applied to wool it produces a much paler tint. — [*Matthews.*]

Father Berard's descriptions are as follows:

Black. — To make this dye the twigs, with leaves and berries of *tsilchin,* or *ki,* are gathered and crumpled together into small bunches. A pot of water is put over the fire and as many of the bunches as possible crowded into it. This is brought to boil and allowed to continue so for from five to six, or more hours, when a strong decoction is obtained.

While the twigs, leaves and berries are boiling some pinion gum *(je)* is put into a skillet and allowed to melt over a slow fire. When melted it is strained to remove dirt and other impurities, replaced in the skillet, and brought to a high degree of heat. Then some native ochre *(tsekho),* which has been powdered between two stones, and roasted to a light brown color, is slowly added to the hot gum. The pasty mass which results from this mixture must be constantly stirred, since it will be spoiled if allowed to burn. Great care must also be taken that the mass does not catch fire, since the pinion gum or pitch is inflammable, for that would spoil the whole mass, and the work would have to be begun anew. While thus seething and being stirred over the fire the pasty mass gradually yields up its moisture, becomes dryer and dryer, until finally a fine black powder remains. This powder, after cooling off somewhat, is thrown into the decoction of sumac, with which it readily combines, and forms a rich blue-black fluid. This continues to boil for about a half-hour when the wool is immersed in it, allowed to boil a short time, and then taken out. The color produced by this dye is a jet black, and is still used for dyeing yarn, buckskin and women's dresses. It is a very fast color and never fades.

Yellow. — The flowering tops of *kiltsoi,* gold rod, *Bigelovia,* of which several species grow in the Navaho country, are boiled for about six hours, until a decoction of a deep yellow is produced. When the dyer thinks the decoction is strong enough she heats over a fire, in a pan or earthen vessel, some native almogen called *tse dokozh,* saline rock, a kind of native alum or salt rock, until it is reduced to a somewhat pasty consistency. This she adds from time to time to the decoction, and then puts the wool in the dye to boil. Ever and anon she inspects the wool, until in about one half hour from the time it was first immersed it is seen to have assumed the proper color. The tint produced is nearly that of lemon color.

Another process of making a yellow is a decoction of the root of a plant called *chantini,* or *jatini,* with *tse dokozh,* native alum or salt rock. *Chatini* is a plant, or rather a weed, belonging to the *Pogonaceae, or buckwheat family,* of the species *Rumex hymenosepalum,* and Dr. G. H. Pepper says it " is commonly known as *canaigre.*"

The process is then described almost in the exact words of Dr. Matthews quoted above.

Red.—This is a purely vegetable dye, all the ingredients being plants or parts of plants. To make this dye the woman first burns some twigs of the juniper tree,

(Juniperus occidentalis), called *gad.* The roots of *tseesdazi, (Cercocarpus parvifolius),* a kind of mountain mahogany, are crushed and boiled. To this is added the juniper ashes and the powdered bark of the black alder, *(Alnus incana var. virescens)* known as *kish,* together with a plant called *nibadlad,* a moss which acts as a mordant. After the mixture has boiled until it is thought to be right it is strained and the wool or yarn is soaked in it over night. The result is a fine red color.

The dull reddish dye is made of the powdered bark of *kish* and the root bark of *tseesdazi,* which makes a fine tan color on buckskin, but produces a rather pale shade on wool.

In former years the Navaho had a native blue made of *adishtlish,* a kind of blue clay which was pulverized and boiled with sumac *(ki)* leaves to obtain a mordant. Later this was entirely superseded by indigo *(beediltish)* obtained from Mexicans. Urine, preserved in large Zuni pots, was used as a mordant into which the indigo was poured and the wool dipped. This was then allowed to stand from five to ten days, after which it was removed from the vessel and after drying was ready for use.

Here are Dr. G. H. Pepper's descriptions:

The native yellow dye, *Kay-el-soey Bay-toh,* in common use when the traders entered the Navaho country, was made from the flowering tops of the Rabbit weed or bush, *Kay-el-soey, (Bigelovia graveolens).* This plant is a member of the aster family and grows on the open prairies. It has a slender stalk which is crowned by a mass of yellow blossoms. It grows in clumps, as a rule, and there are three or four varieties in the Southwest. The flower-clusters are gathered and placed in a large pot containing water. This is allowed to boil from four to six hours. During the boiling the squaw places native alum, *Say-doh-kans,* almogen, in a frying pan and heats it until it is reduced to a pasty consistency. When the boiling has extracted the juices from the weed, the alum, which is to act as a mordant, is added. The liquid is now ready for the reception of the wool.

In dyeing the wool with the yellow decoction, it is placed in the pot of boiling liquid and allowed to boil for fifteen or twenty minutes, after which it is tested every few minutes until it has assumed the color desired. The tints obtained from this dye range from a canary yellow to an old gold, and even an olive green may be produced.

The only native dyes that are used by the Navahos at the present time are the red and black. These are used for dyeing the buckskin uppers of their moccasins. Machine-made shoes of the white man are being used to such an extent, however, that a few years will suffice to stamp out the last vestiges of a once popular and worthy industry.

In preparing the red dye for moccasins or any other article of buckskin, the process is as follows:

First a large rock is dusted and on it a fire is built. The sticks used for the fire are branches of the Juniper tree *(Juniperus occidentalis),* called by the Navahos, *Kot.* Branches of this material are added from time to time until enough ashes have accumulated. The fire is then allowed to burn out. All of the ashes, *Kot Deed-lit,* are collected and placed in a cloth which is rolled up and put aside. The squaw now attends to the preparation of the other ingredients.

Roots of the Mountain mahogany, *Say-es-tozzie Bay-heck-klohl, (Cercocarpus parvifolius),* are gathered and stripped of their bark by a pounding process. For this work a flat stone and a hand hammer-stone are used. The root-bark, *Say-es-tozzie*

Bay-heck-klohl Bo-coggy is loosened by continued pounding and is then rolled from the roots. The bark is the only part retained, the roots themselves being devoid of color-bearing matter. When a sufficient quantity of the root-bark has been prepared it is placed in a kettle of water and allowed to boil for several hours.

While the root-bark is boiling the squaw brings forth from her bundles of household goods a number of pieces of the Black Alder, *Kish, (Alnus incana var. virescens.)* In many parts of the reservation this material must be brought from a distance and, as it is one of the principal ingredients, it is carefully prepared. A large buckskin is spread upon the floor of the *hogan* and upon it a stone slab is placed. The squaw now assumes a kneeling posture and, with a combination hammer and grinding stone, proceeds to reduce the bark to a powder. The first step is to break the bark into small pieces. This is done by means of a gentle pounding with the hammer end of the stone. As the bark is very brittle, care must be taken, as the pieces are to be kept from flying beyond the limits of the buckskin, hence the hammer strokes are short ones and are more in the form of a crushing movement than of a blow. When the bark has been reduced to small pieces, the hammer end of the stone is again brought into play, this time as a pulverizer. The accumulated pieces of bark are made still smaller and then the hand-stone is reversed. The flat side is thus brought into use and the last process, that of grinding, is begun. The bark is reduced to a powder in the same manner as corn is made into meal, the work being done, at times, on a regular meal metate. The powdered bark is now swept into a pile and transferred from the buckskin to a piece of cloth and placed beside the juniper ashes.

When the root-bark decoction *Say-es-tozzie Bay-toh* is ready for use, the small ash-twigs that have retained their shape are separated from the fine ashes and placed in a can into which some of the liquid from the boiled root-bark has been poured. These are allowed to remain about ten minutes, then the pieces that have not dissolved are removed.

Everything in the way of preparation having been attended to, the work of dyeing is begun by placing the piece of buckskin that is to be treated, upon a smooth surface of the sandy floor. The juniper ashes are the first to be applied. They are sprinkled upon the surface and rubbed in with the hands. Small pinches of this material are added from time to time until the entire surface has been uniformly prepared. The mahogany-root-bark-liquid is now poured upon the skin and worked into it with the fingers. The surface of the skin is also roughened with the nails. This rubbing and scratching continues until enough liquid has been applied to almost saturate the skin. The powdered alder bark is the next to be applied. It is put on in the form of a thick layer and the skin is kneaded and patted until the bark combines with the liquid. A thin layer of bark is now sprinkled upon the skin and upon this is poured the liquid obtained by mixing the juniper ashes with the mahogany root-bark extracts. A final patting and rubbing ensues and the buckskin is then rolled up and, in an absolutely saturated condition, is put aside to dry.

The color resulting from this process is a dull red. It gives a very satisfactory color when applied to the buckskin, but it cannot be used to dye wool. It has been tried, but the resulting color is too light a red to be used for blanket work.

The black dye, *Eel-gee Bay-toh,* is used for both buckskin and wool. In preparing this dye a fire of greasewood branches is started and upon it a pot of water is placed. While this is heating, twigs and leaves of the Aromatic Sumac, *Key (Rhus aromatica)*, are twisted into bunches. These bunches average about six inches in length and with them the pot is filled. They are allowed to boil from five to six hours. During this time a second fire is built. Yellow ochre *Tset Koomph,* is powdered by grinding and is then roasted in a frying pan. The roasting turns the ochre to a dull red color. A portion of pinion gum, *Jay,* the gum of the *Pinus edulis,* equal in quantity to that of the ochre, is added. The mass soon assumes a pasty form, but it is stirred constantly until the gum carbonizes and combines with the ochre, thereby forming a black powder. The bundles of twigs are taken from the pot and the contents of the frying pan are dumped into the dark colored extract of the sumac, *Key Bay-toh.* The pot is allowed to remain on the fire, and after the powder is added, the boiling continues for fully half an hour. The wool is then introduced, allowed to boil, and the dyeing is complete.

As the Navahos have the natural black wool it is generally used for the black designs of blankets. It is tinged with red, however, and is therefore almost always dyed before being used.

CHAPTER XII

The Origin and Symbolism of Navaho Blanket Designs

FROM what has been presented in earlier chapters it will be evident to the casual reader that the Navahos are a very symbol-loving people. As we have seen, they have a symbolism of color, a symbolism of sex, symbolism in the adornment of the representations of their gods, and symbols for almost every natural object connected with weather and meteorological phenomena. Hence it may not be altogether too great an assumption that in their blanketry the older weavers followed this tribal law or custom, and, while inserting certain symbols in their blankets, attached thereto certain personal meanings or interpretations.

Father Berard, however, does not think so. He says:

> There is no system as to the use of the different figures; that is, they are not arranged into any kind of hieroglyphic order by which a woman could weave her life's history, or any other history or story, into the blanket, as has been asserted by some writers. The Navaho blanket, therefore, is a *human document* only in so far as it shows the untiring patience and diligence, the exquisite taste and deftness, of a semi-barbaric people, and the high art and quality of their work, wrought with such simple tools and materials.

As applied to the modern blanket, I have no doubt but that this dictum is correct. The Navahos design in accordance with the known wishes of the trader, and often make alterations and combinations of design to please him. It necessarily follows, therefore, that designs thus tampered or played with cannot have any especial significance or interpretation to the weaver, except that so much work, so well done, in so many days, will mean the receipt of so much cash, or groceries, or other commodities. In other words, it is a purely commercial proposition.

Yet as this subject is of far deeper significance than most students comprehend, I feel that I owe the readers of this volume a very clear statement as to my position upon it. For what I have written upon the symbolism of designs in the *baskets* of the Indian tribes of the Southwest has not only been much misquoted, distorted, and falsified, but I have been made responsible for much misinformation, and the ostensible authority for deliberate and wilful misrepresentation. For instance, because I have asserted, and demonstrated, that *some* baskets are "human documents," in that the weaver has put into the design her hopes, ambitions, religion, etc., irresponsible and dishonest traders have conjured up wild and fantastic, though interesting and romantic, stories about the designs of the baskets they had for sale, and have given them to their patrons, quoting me as their authority that *all* baskets contain such stories.

Here is exactly what I did say in my book, *Indian Basketry,* the first edition of which was published in 1900:

The only reliable method of determining the meaning of a basketry design is to obtain a clear explanation from its maker. And this must be done cautiously. With her habitual reserve and fear of being laughed at by the whites, the Indian woman is exceedingly susceptible to suggestion. If you ask her whether her design does not mean this or that, you may with certainty rely upon what the answer will be before it is given. She will respond with a grunt or word of affirmation, and, at the same time, laugh within herself at the folly of the questioner. For, of course, she is "smart" enough to know that if you make the suggestion that the design means so and so, she will be safe if she accept your suggestion.

If the basket is an old one and the maker is dead, one must be content to receive such explanation as the older members of the tribe can give as to the interpretation of its design. Yet it must not be overlooked that the observations of experienced ethnologists insist that these explanations cannot be relied upon. On this subject Farrand says: " It should be noted that most of the designs show variants and also that what were originally representations of very dissimilar objects have converged in their evolution until the same figure does duty for both — conditions which result in uncertainty and difference of opinion among native connoisseurs, and consequently, in the conclusions of the ethnologist. Nevertheless, the great majority of the patterns are well recognized under specific names. There are, of course, geometric designs which, so far as all obtainable information goes, are used simply for the decorative value of their lines and angles; but such patterns are usually of great age, and it is quite possible that their representative meaning is lost in antiquity or has only baffled the diligence of the inquirer. The well-known conservatism of the Indian insures the relative permanence of a design, even when its meaning is not recognized."

Hence it will be seen that I carefully guarded my statement by showing that no person living can determine what the meaning of the design of any given basket is — provided it has a meaning — save the weaver herself. And I am fully satisfied that the same caution must be observed in determining the meaning of any design upon a Navaho blanket. Personally I am not yet prepared to accept Father Berard's belief that it has no meaning, or, rather, that in *the earlier days of the art* the weaver attached no significance to her design. I am perfectly aware that in this commercialized era the Navaho's art has suffered, and, as I have stated in other chapters, designs are handed out to the weavers with instructions to reproduce them, as near as may be, in the blankets that are to be woven. Here, then, is evidence sufficient that in many modern blankets there is no pretense of significance to be attached to the symbol or design used.

Yet, even granting all this, it cannot fail to be highly interesting, and instructive also, to trace out, as far as may be, the origin and history of many of the designs common to the Navaho weaver.

Whence did she gain her designs?

Some have claimed that they were stolen bodily from the Pueblo Indians — who were supposed to have taught the Navahos how to weave — others that they took them from the Mexican serapes, and still others that they have originated them from a careful observation of Nature.

I am inclined to the belief that none of these claims is altogether justified, though there may be some truth in each of them when applied to individual cases; but to suppose that all the Navaho designs came from the Pueblos, or from the Mexicans, or from Nature alone are suppositions not borne out by the facts.

An understanding of the origin of Navaho designs cannot be had without a fairly comprehensive knowledge of the Navaho himself, racially, socially, religiously considered. His whole life and mental attitude must be understood before the secret of his use of design will be revealed. Hence the pains taken to present in these pages as full pictures as possible of the Navaho on his reservation, in his native environment, in his home, and in his mental and religious attitude toward things.

To one unacquainted with the religious thought of the Navaho weaver it might seem absurd to affirm that there is a close connection between her religious observances and many of the designs introduced into her blankets. Yet I think it can clearly be shown that there is an intimate connection between the two. Indeed, I doubt whether the subject will ever be clearly understood until we have gained a much larger knowledge than we now possess of the *sacred sand-paintings* used by the shamans in their religious ceremonials. Far more complex than the sand-paintings of the Hopis, the Zunis, or any other of the Pueblo tribes, those of the Navaho are marvelous in their symbolism, remarkable in their invention, and fascinating in their weird picturesqueness. No adequate work has ever been published upon this subject, because no ethnologist has yet been found to devote himself enough to the Navahos to gain the requisite knowledge. Enough was done, however, by James Stevenson and Washington Matthews, both formerly connected with the Bureau of American Ethnology, to give one a clue to the mental processes of the inventive Navaho, and my own studies of Navaho ceremonials in which the sand-paintings are used have shown clearly how much they have influenced the Navaho weaver in her work. Mrs. John Wetherill, of Kayenta, Arizona, whose husband is a Navaho Indian trader, with a keen appreciation of the value of a series of studies of these sand-paintings, is now engaged in making a collection of them from the few remaining old medicine-men chanters of the tribe, and it is to be hoped that her valuable illustrations and descriptive manuscript will be given ere long to the scientific world.

Of these sand-paintings, or dry-paintings, as he prefers to call them, Dr. Matthews thus writes:

The excellence to which the Navahos have carried the art of dry-painting is as remarkable as that to which they have brought the art of weaving. Unlike the neighboring Pueblos, they make no graven images of their divinities. They do not decorate robes and skins with moist colors as do the Indians of the plains. They make little pottery and this little is neither artistically nor symbolically decorated. Their petroglyphs are rare and crude; the best rock inscriptions, which abound in the Southwest, are believed to be the work of Cliff Dwellers and Pueblo Indians, or their ancestors. Seeing no evidence of symbolic art among them, one might readily suppose they had none. Such was the opinion of white men (some of whom had lived fifteen years or more among the Navahos), with whom the author conversed when first he went to the Navaho country, and such was the opinion of all ethnographers before his time. The symbolic art of the Navahos is to be studied in the medicine-lodge. The Pueblo Indians — those of Zuni and Moki — and some of the wilder tribes — Apaches and Cheyennes — understand the art of dry-painting; but none seem to have such numerous and elaborate designs as the Navahos.

The pigments are five in number; they are: white, made of white sandstone; yellow, of yellow sandstone; red, of red sandstone; black, of charcoal, mixed with a small proportion of powdered red sandstone to give it weight and stability; "blue," made of black and white mixed. These are ground into fine powder, between two stones, as the Indians grind corn. The so-called blue is, of course, gray; but it is the only inexpensive representative of the blue tint they can obtain and, combined with other colors, on the sandy floor, it looks like a real blue. These colored powders, prepared before the picture is begun, are kept on improvised trays of pine-bark. To apply them, the artist picks up a little between his first and second finger and his opposed thumb, and allows it to flow out slowly as he moves his hand. When he takes up his pinch of powder he blows on his fingers to remove aberrant particles and keep them from falling on the picture, out of place. When he makes a mistake he does not brush away the color; he obliterates it by pouring sand on it and then draws the corrected design on the new surface.

The dry-paintings of the largest size, which are drawn on the floor of the medicine-lodge, are often ten to twelve feet in diameter. They are sometimes so large that the fire in the center of the lodge must be moved to one side to accommodate them. They are made as near to the west side of the lodge as practicable. The lodge is poorly lighted, and on a short winter day the artists must often begin their work before sunrise if they would finish before nightfall, which it is essential they should do.

To prepare the ground work for a picture in the lodge, several young men go forth and bring in a quantity of dry sand in blankets; this is thrown on the floor and spread out over a surface of sufficient size, to the depth of about three inches; it is leveled and made smooth by means of the broad oaken battens used in weaving.

The drawings are begun as much toward the center as the design will permit, due regard being paid to the precedence of the points of the compass; the figure in the east being first, that in the south second, that in the west third, and that in the north fourth. The figures in the periphery come after these. The reason for thus working from within, outward is practical; it is that the operators may not have to step over and thus risk the safety of their finished work.

The pictures are drawn according to an exact system, except in certain well defined cases, where the limner is allowed to indulge his fancy. This is the case with the embroidered pouches the gods carry at the waist. Within reasonable limits the artist may give his god as handsome a pouch as he wishes. On the other hand, some parts are measured by palms and spans and not a line of the sacred design may be varied in them. Straight and parallel lines are drawn with the aid of a tightened cord. The naked bodies of the mythical figures are first drawn and then the clothing is put on.

The shamans declare that these pictures are transmitted unaltered from year to year and from generation to generation. It may be doubted if such is strictly the case. No permanent design is anywhere preserved by them and there is no final authority in the tribe. The pictures are carried from winter to winter in the fallible memories of men. They may not be drawn in the summer. The custom of destroying these pictures at the close of the ceremonies and preserving no permanent copies of them arose, no doubt, largely from a desire to preserve the secrets of the lodge from the uninitiated; but it had also perhaps a more practical reason for its existence. The Navahos had no way of drawing permanent designs in color. When it became known to the shamans (and no attempt was ever made to hide the fact from them) that the author kept water-color drawings of the sacred pictures in his possession, these men, at the proper season, when about to perform a ceremony, often brought their assistants to look at the drawings, and then and there would lecture the young men and call their attention to special features in the pictures, thus, no doubt, saving themselves much trouble afterwards in the medicine-lodge. These water-colors were never shown to the uninitiated among the Indians and never to any Indian during the forbidden season.

Owing to the large place the dry-paintings have in the sacred or ceremonial life of the Navaho, I have included among the pictures a plate of the dry-painting representing the *Place and Vision of the Whirling Logs* (Fig. 40). The myth or legend connected with this would take up many pages even to outline, hence I must refer those who are interested to the great work of Dr. Matthews, *The Night Chant,* published by the American Museum of Natural History, from which both the illustration and text are taken.

The chief character in the story is Bitahatini, or the Visionary, who, whenever he went out by himself, heard, or thought he heard, the songs of spirits sung to him. His three brothers had no faith in him and said: "When you return from your solitary walks and tell us you have seen strange things and heard strange songs you are mistaken; you only imagine you hear these songs and you see nothing unusual."

In one of Bitahatini's journeys he had marvelous and wonderful experiences with the gods which are now regarded as of the utmost importance and are introduced into the nine-days' and nights' ceremonies of "The Night Chant." In these experiences he was taught certain things by the *yei,* or gods, of the Navaho, and in the legend there is

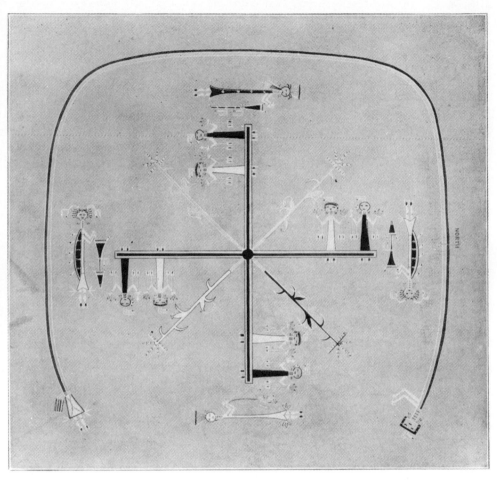

Fig. 40.
Dry-Painting Representing the Place and Vision of the
Whirling Logs.
(Courtesy of American Museum of Natural History.)   [Page 76]

a hint of an idea that it may, at one time, have been woven into a blanket of cotton, for the old medicine man who related the story said:

The *yei* did not draw this picture upon the sand as we do now; they had it on a sheet of some substance called *nesha*. We do not know now what this substance was; it may have been cotton. They unfolded this sheet whenever they wanted to look at the picture. The *yei* who unfolded it to show to the prophet (or Visionary) said: "We will not give you this picture; men are not as good as we; they might quarrel over the picture and tear it, and that would bring misfortune; the black cloud would not come again, the rain would not fall, the corn would not grow; but you may paint it on the ground with colors of the earth."

The picture, therefore, is painted by the medicine man with the greatest care and represents the vision of the prophet at the lake To'nihilin.

The bowl of water in the center, sprinkled with charcoal, symbolizes the lake. The black cross represents the spruce logs crossing one another. The colors edging the cross show the white foam on the waters, the yellow water-pollen, the blue and red rainbow tints.

Four stalks of corn are depicted as growing on the shores of the lake; each has three roots and two ears. The white stalk of corn, according to its color, belongs to the east; the blue, to the south; the yellow to the west, and the black to the north; but the conditions of the picture require that these stalks should be directed to intermediate points. Each stalk is bordered with a contrasting color.

Eight *yei* or divine characters — four male and four female — are shown seated on the floating logs. The legs of the four gods in the periphery of the picture are depicted; this is to indicate that they are standing; but the legs of the eight gods on the cross are not depicted; this is done to indicate that they are sitting; the feet seem hanging below the logs. The four outer *yei,* on the cross, dressed in black, are males. The sex is indicated: (1) by the round head representing the cap-like or helmet-like mask which a personator of a male divinity wears; (2) by showing attached to the mask the two eagle-plumes and the tuft of owl-feathers worn by each male dancer in the dance of the last night; (3) by the symbol of a spruce twig in the left hand and of a gourd rattle painted white in the right — such implements are carried by the male dancers. The four inner *yei,* dressed in white are females. The sex is indicated: (1) by the rectangular mask or domino; (2) by the yellow arms and chests — females were created of yellow corn and males of white corn, according to the myths — and (3) by a symbol of a spruce wand in each hand, for such wands does the female dancer carry in the dance the last night.

The figures in the north and south represent *Ganaskidi* or humpbacks as they appear in the rites. These are Mountain Sheep or Bighorn Gods, which figure so prominently in the myth of the Visionary. The blue male mask, the headdress with its zigzag line for white lightning, the radiating scarlet feathers to represent sunbeams, the blue imitation horns of the mountain sheep, the black sack of plenty on the back, and the *gis* or staff on which the laden god leans, are all symbolized or depicted in the picture.

The white figure in the east is that of *Hastseyalti,* the Talking God. He is thus represented: He wears the white mask which the personator of this character always wears in the ceremonies, with its eagle-plumes tipped with breath-feathers, its tuft of yellow owl-feathers, its ornament of fox-skin under the right ear, and its peculiar mouth-symbol and ear-symbols, but without the corn-symbol on the nose. He carries a pouch made of the gray skin of Abert's squirrel *(Sciurus Aberti)*, which is depicted with care. The general gray of the squirrel is shown by the gray or so-called blue color of the body. The fact that the hairs of the animal are tipped with white is indicated by making a white margin and by sprinkling white powder lightly over the blue — the latter device is very imperfectly shown in the illustration. The black tips on ears, nose, and feet, as well as the chestnut spot on the back, are indicated — the latter by a short red marginal line interrupting the white.

The black figure in the west is that of *Hastsehogan*. He is shown in this manner: He wears a beautifully ornamented black dress and a blue mask, decorated with eagle-plumes and owl-feathers. The ornament under his right ear consists of strips of otter-skin with porcupine quills. He carries in his hand a black wand colored with charcoal of four different plants, ornamented with a single whorl of turkey-feathers, with two eagle-feathers tied on the cotton string, with a white ring at the base of the whorl, and with the skins of two bluebirds.

The two *Ganaskidi* and *Hastsehogan* are supposed to be punching the logs and causing them to whirl with their staves, while Hastseyalti scatters pollen from his pouch.

Surrounding the picture on three sides, appears the anthropomorphic rainbow, or rainbow goddess, wearing the rectangular female mask and carrying at the waist an embroidered pouch, tied on with four strings. The hands of all the other divinities are shown occupied, but the hands of the rainbow are shown empty; this is that they may be ready to receive the cup of medicine which is placed on them after the picture is finished.

The rainbow and the eight divinities on the cross are represented with breath-feathers tied on the tops of the heads by means of white cotton strings, and the horns of the *Ganaskidi* are similarly decked. All the gods are shown with garnished moccasins, tied with white strings. All of those showing their legs have rainbow garters. Five have ornamented fringes on their kilts or loincloths. The bodies of all are fringed with red to represent sunlight; the Navaho artist does not confine the halo to the head of his holy subject. All have ear-pendants of turquois and coral. The eight central figures are represented with strips of fox-skin — blue and yellow — hanging from elbows and wrists and garnished at their ends. Such adornments, it is said, were once used in the dance, but are now obsolete; they, in turn, represented beams of light. The yellow horizontal line at the bottom of each pictured mask represents a band at the bottom of the actual mask worn by the actor, and this band in turn symbolizes the yellow evening light.

All have the neck depicted in the same manner. The blue is generally conceded by the shamans to symbolize the collar of spruce twigs; but opinion is divided with regard to the meaning of the transverse red lines. The original significance of these is perhaps forgotten. Some say they represent the rings of the trachea; but those shamans whose opinion the writer most values say they represent an obsolete neck ornament called *tsitse'yo,* or cherry-beads, which was made neither of cherries or corals.

It is well now to consider a few Nature symbols that are extensively used by the Navahos *today* in their religious ceremonials. As corn is one of the most important foods of the Navaho, it plays a great part in all their ceremonies. Its symbol is used continually, both on dry-paintings and sacred masks. On many of these it is represented as an irregular upright stem with waving leaves on either side and the corn branching out higher up the stalk, with the pollen-laden flower above. (See Fig. 41.)

FIG. 41

The sign or symbol for the eye is found on the sacred masks used in the dances and other ceremonials. The mouth is similarly represented on these masks.

On the sand-paintings sunbeams are made of radiating scarlet feathers, but when drawn are represented by straight lines parallel, and, if possible, in some scarlet or red color.

On the masks they are shown by ten quills of the red-shafted woodpecker, radiating from the edge of the crown, which is painted black to represent the storm-cloud. They then symbolize sunbeams streaming out of the edge of a dark cloud.

Another design is that called the queue symbol, which represents the scalps of their enemies. It is painted on the body of the representative of their god Tobadzistsini, or Child of the Water. The Navahos and many other tribes of the Southwest wear the hair done up in a queue, which is not allowed to dangle, as does that of the Chinese, but is tied up close to the occiput; hence the symbol of a queue is also that of a scalp. Sometimes the symbols are closed, and at other times open, as shown in the diagram.

FIGS. 42, 43, 44

The open symbol has a different significance from the closed symbol. (See Figs. 42, 43, 44.)

A design that is often found on the blanket is the "bow" (Fig. 45). These are placed upon the body of the personator of the god Nayenezgani, are always made with five different lines drawn from the above downward and in an established order from which no deviation is allowed, as that would destroy the effect desired. When a bow is to be represented as unstrung, the upper end of the cord is unattached, as shown in Fig. 46.

FIGS. 45, 46

Zigzag lines generally represent lightning, and in the Navaho myths the gods are said to carry on their persons strings of real lightning, which they use as ropes.

Whenever zigzag lines are painted in white on a black background they symbolize lightning on the face of a cloud.

In the foregoing is a wealth of proof that the Navaho is essentially a religious being; that he symbolizes almost everything; that he regards these symbols as more than mere decorative designs; in fact, that they speak to him in no uncertain terms of sacred and mysterious things that he must regard and remember.

Is it then an irrational assumption that in the earlier day, before the commercial spirit of our money-mad civilization had entirely driven out their ancient reverence from many of the Navahos, the simple-hearted, reverent, and religious weavers put into their blankets the thoughts that moved them, the ambitions and aspirations that inspired them, the hopes that sustained them, and the religious ideas that guided them in their somewhat rude and rough pathway through life? That, in fact, their blankets *were* human documents, though pathetically inadequate, when compared with the white race's literature.

While from the foregoing enough has been presented to show that the Navaho has taken many of his symbols or designs from Nature, it must not be forgotten that his nearest neighbors, the Pueblo Indians, especially the Hopis, decorated their pottery with a wealth of design that will be the surprise and admiration of the modern designer when he observes it for the first time.

The importance of this close proximity to the Pueblos and of the marvelous art development these sedentary people had attained in the decoration of their pottery, cannot be over estimated. Like produces like; we are the product of our heredity and environment; we develop along the lines of least resistance — these are axiomatic propositions that help us understand the development of the Navaho weavers as creators of artistic and striking designs.

Neither should it be overlooked that the Pueblo weavers were using colors and incorporating similar designs into their textiles that they were placing upon their pottery long prior to the coming of the Spaniards into New Mexico (1540). Indeed in the American Museum of Natural History in New York there is a fine specimen of weaving in colors, taken from a prehistoric Cliff Dwelling, in which the design is closely similar to some of the pottery designs herein presented.

It is to an elaborate and beautifully illustrated monograph by Dr. J. Walter Fewkes, published by the Bureau of American Ethnology, that we owe our knowledge of these designs, and to Dr. Fewkes, and Dr. F. W. Hodge, Chief of the Bureau, we are indebted for the privilege of reproducing them here.

After showing the human figure, the whorls in which the hair of the Hopi maiden is dressed, mythic personages, the human hand, quadrupeds, reptiles, tadpoles, butterflies, moths, dragon flies, birds, feathers, vegetables, etc., Dr. Fewkes finally comes to a consideration of geometrical figures.

In regard to the interpretation of these figures he frankly says:

Two extreme views are current in regard to the significance of these designs. To one school everything is symbolic of something or some religious conception; to the other the majority are meaningless save as decorations. I find the middle path the more conservative, and while regarding many of the designs as highly conventionalized symbols, believe that there are also many where the decorator had no thought of symbolism.

It must be clearly remembered that in giving his explanations of these symbols, Dr. Fewkes is working *with prehistoric material,* purely guessing at the significance, for he has no possible means of *knowing* the mind of the decorator. Hence, his words must be taken at the value he himself places upon them as far as definite knowledge of the symbolism involved is concerned. But the symbols or designs are themselves of superlative value, as demonstrating the artistic and inventive genius of the ancient aboriginal potters, and revealing how prolific and creative they were.

Might not the Navaho weavers have been the same? If they were not, then the fact should not be overlooked that they had this wealth of design in the old pottery constantly before them to copy, or from which they might receive suggestions.

After explaining the presence and meaning of crosses, swastikas, terraced figures, the crook, the germinative symbol, and broken lines, Dr. Fewkes proceeds:

The simplest form of decoration on the exterior of a food bowl is a band encircling it. This line may be complete or it may be broken at one point. The next more complicated geometric decoration is a double or multiple band. The breaking up of this multiple band into parallel bars is shown in Fig. 47. These bars generally have a quadruple arrangement, and are horizontal, vertical, or, as in the illustration, inclined at an angle. They are often found on the lips of the bowls and in

FIG. 47—Oblique parallel line decoration

a similar position on jars, dippers, and vases. The parallel lines shown in Fig. 48 are seven in number, and do not encircle the bowl. They are joined by a broad

FIG. 48—Parallel lines fused at one point

connecting band near one extremity. The number of parallel bands in this decoration is highly suggestive.

Four parallel bands encircle the bowl shown in Fig. 49, but they are so modified in their course as to form a number of trapezoidal figures placed with alternating sides parallel. This interesting pattern is found only on one vessel.

FIG. 49—Parallel lines with zigzag arrangement

The use of simple parallel bars, arranged at equal intervals on the outside of food bowls, is not confined to these vessels, for they occur on the margin of vases, cups and dippers. They likewise occur on ladle handles, where they are arranged in alternate tranverse and longitudinal clusters.

The combination of two vertical bands connected by a horizontal band, forming the letter H, is an ornamental design frequently occurring on the finest Hopi ware. Fig. 50 shows such an H form, which is ordinarily repeated four times about the bowl.

FIG. 50—
Parallel lines
connected
with middle
bar

The interval between the parallel bands around the vessel may be very much reduced in size, and some of the bands may be of different width or otherwise modified. Such a deviation is seen in Fig. 51, which has three bands, one of which is broad with straight edges, the other with serrate margin and hook-like appendages.

In Fig. 52 eight bands are shown, the marginal broad with edges entire, and the medium pair serrated, the long teeth fitting each other in such a way as to impart a zigzag effect to the space which separates them. The remaining four lines,

FIG. 51—Parallel lines of different width ; serrate margin

two on each side, appear as black bands on a white ground. It will be noticed that an attempt was made to relieve the monotony of the middle band of Fig. 52 by the

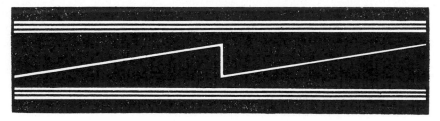

FIG. 52—Parallel lines of different width ; median serrate

introduction of a white line in zigzag form. A similar result was accomplished in the design in Fig. 53 by rectangles and dots.

The modification of the multiple bands in Fig. 53 has produced a very different decorative form. This design is composed of five bands, the marginal on each side

FIG. 53—Parallel lines of different width ; marginal serrate

serrate, and the middle band relatively very broad, with diagonals, each containing four round dots regularly arranged. In Fig. 54 there are many parallel, non-continuous bands of different breadth, arranged in groups separated by triangles with

FIG. 54—Parallel lines and triangles

sides parallel, and the whole united by bounding lines. This is the most complicated form of design where straight lines are used.

We have thus far considered modifications brought about by fusion and other changes in simple parallel lines. They may be confined to one side of the food bowl,

FIG. 55—Line with alternate triangles

may repeat each other at intervals, or surround the whole vessel. Ordinarily, however, they are confined to one side of the bowls from Sikyatki.

Returning to the single encircling band, it is found, in Fig. 55, broken up into alternating equilateral triangles, each pair united at their right angles. This

FIG. 56—Single line with alternate spurs

modification is carried still further in Fig. 56, where the triangles on each side of the single line are prolonged into oblique spurs, the pairs separated a short distance from each other. In Fig. 57 there is shown still another arrangement of these triangular decorations, the pairs forming hourglass-shape figures connected by an

Fig. 57—Single line with hourglass figures

encircling line passing through their points of junction. In Fig. 58 the double triangles, one on each side of the encircling band, are so placed that their line of separation is lost, and a single triangle replaces the pair. These are connected by the line surrounding the bowl and there is a dot at the smallest angle. In Fig.

Fig. 58—Single lines with triangles

59 there is a similar design, except that alternating with each triangle, which bears more decoration than that shown in Fig. 58, there are hourglass figures composed of ovals and triangles. The dots at the apex of that design are replaced by short parallel lines of varying width. The triangles and ovals last considered are arranged

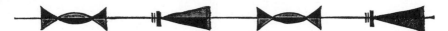

Fig. 59—Single line with alternate triangles and ovals

symmetrically in relation to a simple band. By a reduction in the intervening spaces these triangles may be brought together and the line disappears. I have found no specimen of design illustrating the simplest form of the resultant motive, but that shown in Fig. 60 is a new combination comparable with it.

Fig. 60—Triangles and quadrilaterals

The simple triangular decorative design reaches a high degree of complication in Fig. 60, where a connecting line is absent, and two triangles having their smallest angles facing each other are separated by a lozenge-shape figure made up of many parallel lines placed obliquely to the axis of the design. The central part is composed of seven parallel lines, the marginal of which, on two opposite sides, is minutely dentate. The median band is very broad and is relieved by two wavy lines. The axis of the design on each side is continued into two triangular spurs, rising from a rectangle in the middle of each triangle. This complicated design is the highest development reached by the use of simple triangles. In Fig. 61, however, we have a simpler form of decoration, in which no element other than the rectangle is employed. In the chaste decoration seen in Fig. 62 the use of the

FIG. 61—Triangle with spurs

rectangle is shown combined with the triangle on a simple encircling band. This design is reducible to that shown in Fig. 60, but it is simpler, yet not less effective.

FIG. 62—Rectangle with single line

In Fig. 63 there is an aberrant form of design in which the triangle is used in combination with parallel and oblique bands. This form, while one of the sim-

FIG. 63—Double triangle; multiple lines

plest in its elements, is effective and characteristic. The triangle predominates in Fig. 64, but the details are worked out in rectangular patterns, producing the terraced designs so common in all Pueblo decorations. Rectangular figures are more

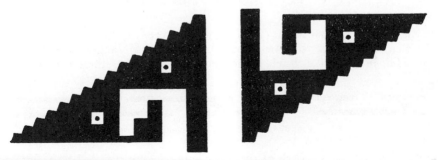

FIG. 64—Double triangle; terraced edges

commonly used than the triangular in the decoration of the exterior of bowls, and their many combinations are often very perplexing to analyze.

In Fig. 65, starting with the simple encircling band, it is found divided into alternating rectangles. The line is continuous, and hence one side of each rectangle

FIG. 65—Single line; closed fret

is not complete. Both this design and its modification in Fig. 66 consist of an unbroken line of equal breadth throughout. In the latter figure, however, the openings in the sides are larger or the approach to a straight line closer. The forms

FIG. 66—Single line; open fret

are strictly rectangular, with no additional elements. Fig. 67 introduces an important modification of the rectangular motive, consisting of a succession of lines broken at intervals, but when joined always arranged at right angles.

FIG. 67—Single line; broken fret

Possibly the least complex form of rectangular ornamentation, next to a simple bar or square, is the combination shown in Fig. 68, a type in which many changes are made in interior as well as in exterior decoration of Pueblo ware. One of these

FIG. 68—Single line; parts displaced

is shown in Fig. 69, where the figure about the vessel is continuous. An analysis of the elements in Fig. 70 shows squares united at their angles, like the last, but that in addition to parallel bands connecting adjacent figures there are two marginal

FIG. 69—Open fret; attachment displaced

bands uniting the series. Each of the inner parallel lines is bound to a marginal on the opposite side by a band at right angles to it. The marginal lines are unbroken through the length of the figure. Like the last, this motive also may be regarded as developed from a single line.

Figs. 71 and 72 are even simpler than the design shown in Fig. 69, with appended square key patterns, all preserving rectangular forms and destitute of all

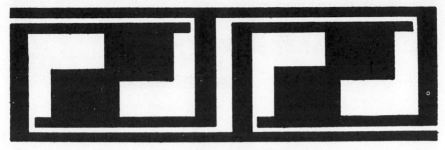

FIG. 70—Simple rectangular design

others. They are of S-form, and differ more especially in the character of their appendages.

FIG. 71—Rectangular reversed S-form

FIG. 72—Rectangular S-form with crooks

While the same rectangular idea predominates in Fig. 73, it is worked out with the introduction of triangles and quadrilateral designs. This fairly compound pattern, however, is still classified among rectangular forms. A combination of rectangular and triangular geometric designs, in which, however, the former

FIG. 73—Rectangular S-form with triangles

predominate, is shown in Fig. 74, which can readily be reduced to certain of those forms already mentioned. The triangles appear to be subordinated to the rectangles, and even they are fringed on their longer sides with terraced forms. It may be said that there but two elements involved, the rectangle and the triangle.

FIG. 74—Rectangular S-form with terraced triangles

The decoration in Fig. 75 consists of rectangular and triangular figures, the latter so closely approximated as to leave zigzag lines in white. These lines are simply highly modified breaks in bands which join in other designs, and lead by comparison to the so-called "line of life" which many of these figures illustrate.

FIG. 75—S-form with interdigitating spurs

The distinctive feature of Fig. 76 is the square, with rectangular designs appended to diagonally opposite angles and small triangles at intermediate corners. These designs have a distant resemblance to figures later referred to as highly conventionalized birds, although they may be merely simple geometrical patterns which have lost their symbolic meaning.

FIG. 76—Square with rectangles and parallel lines

Fig. 77 shows a complicated design, introducing at least two elements in addition to rectangles and triangles. One of these is a curved crook etched on a black ground. In no other exterior decoration have curved lines been found except in the form of circles, and it is worthy of note how large a proportion of the figures are drawn in straight lines. The circular figures with three parallel lines extending from them are found so constantly in exterior decorations, and are so strikingly like some of the figures elsewhere discussed, that I have ventured a suggestion in regard to their meaning. I believe they represent feathers, because the tail feathers of certain birds are symbolized in that manner, and their number corresponds with those generally depicted in the highly conventionalized tails of birds.

FIG. 77—Rectangles, triangles, stars, and feathers

In Fig. 78 a number of these parallel lines are represented, and the general character of the design is rectangular. In Fig. 79 is shown a combination of

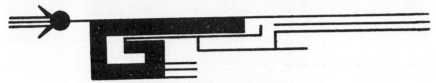

FIG. 78—Crook, feathers, and parallel lines

rectangular and triangular figures with three tapering points and circles with lines at their tips radiating instead of parallel. Another modification is shown in Fig.

FIG. 79—Crooks and feathers

80 in which the triangle predominates, and Fig. 81 evidently represents one-half of a similar device with modifications.

FIG. 80—Rectangle, triangles, and feathers

One of the most common designs on ancient pottery is the stepped figure, a rectangular ornamentation, modifications of which are shown in Figs. 82, 83, and 84. This is a very common design on the interior of food vessels, where it is commonly interpreted as a rain-cloud symbol.

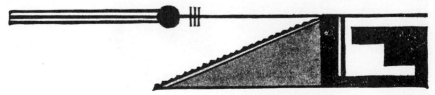

FIG. 81—Terraced crook, triangle, and feather

Of all patterns on ancient Tusayan ware, that of the terrace figures most closely resemble the geometrical ornamentation of cliff-house pottery, and there seems every reason to suppose that this form of design admits of a like interpretation. The evolution of this pattern from plaited basketry has been ably discussed by Holmes and Nordenskiöld. The terraced forms from the exterior of the food bowls here considered are highly aberrant; they may be forms of survivals, motives of decoration which have persisted from very early times. Whatever the origin of the stepped figure in Pueblo art was, it is well to remember, as shown by Holmes,

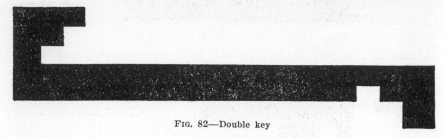

FIG. 82—Double key

that it is "impossible to show that any particular design of the highly constituted kind was desired through a certain identifiable series of progressive steps."

For some unknown reason the majority of the simple designs on the exterior of food bowls from Tusayan are rectangular, triangular, or linear in their charac-

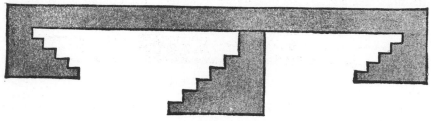

FIG. 83—Triangular terrace

ter. Many can be reduced to simple or multiple lines. Others were suggested by plaited ware.

In Fig. 82 is found one of the simplest of rectangular designs, a simple band, key pattern in form, at one end, with a re-entrant square depression at the opposite

FIG. 84—Crook, serrate end

extremity. In Fig. 83 is an equally simple terrace pattern with stepped figures at the ends and in the middle. These forms are common decorative elements on the exterior of jars and vases, where they occur in many combinations, all of which are reducible to these types. The simplest form of the key pattern is shown in Fig. 84,

and in Fig. 85 there is a second modification of the same design a little more complicated. This becomes somewhat changed in Fig. 86, not only by the modifications
of the two extremities, but also by the addition of a median geometric figure.

FIG. 85—Key pattern; rectangle and triangles

FIG. 86—Rectangle and crook

The design in Fig. 87 is rectangular, showing a key pattern at one end, with
two long feathers at the opposite extremity. The five bodies on the same end of the
figure are unique and comparable with conventionalized star emblems. The series
of designs in the upper left-hand end of this figure are unlike any which have yet
been found on the exterior of food bowls, but are similar to designs which have
elsewhere been interpreted as feathers. On the hypothesis that these two parts of
the figure are tail-feathers, we find in the crook the analogue of the head of a bird.
The five dentate bodies on the lower left-hand end of the figure also tell in favor of
the avian character of the design, for the following reason: These bodies are often
found accompanying figures of conventionalized birds. They are regarded as modified crosses of equal arms, which are all but universally present in combinations with
birds and feathers, from the fact that in a line of crosses depicted on a bowl one

FIG. 87—Crook and tail feathers

of the crosses is replaced by a design of similar character. The arms of the cross
are represented; their intersection is left in white. The interpretation of Fig. 87
as a highly conventionalized bird design is also in accord with the same interpretation of a number of similar, although less complicated, figures which appear with
crosses. Fig. 88 may be compared with Fig. 87.

Numerous modifications of a key pattern, often assuming a double triangular form, but with rectangular elements, are found on the exterior of many food bowls.

FIG. 88—Rectangle, triangle, and serrate spurs

These are variations of a pattern, the simplest form of which is shown in Fig. 89. Resolving this figure into two parts by drawing a median line, we find the arrangement is bilaterally symmetrical, the two sides exactly corresponding. Each side consists of a simple key pattern with the shank inclined to the rim of the bowl and a bird emblem at its junction with the other member.

FIG. 89—W-pattern; terminal crooks

In Fig. 90 there is a greater development of this pattern by an elaboration of the key, which is continued in a line resembling a square spiral. There are also dentations on a section of the edge of the lines.

FIG. 90—W-pattern; terminal rectangles

In Fig. 91 there is a still further development of the same design and a lack of symmetry on the two sides. The square spirals are replaced on the left by three

FIG. 91—W-pattern, terminal terraces, and crooks

stepped figures, and white spaces with parallel lines are introduced in the arms of a W-shape figure.

In Fig. 92 the same design is again somewhat changed by modification of the spirals into three triangles rimmed on one side with a row of dots, which are also found on the outer lines surrounding the lower part of the design.

FIG. 92—W-pattern ; terminal spurs

In Fig. 93 the same W-shape design is preserved, but the space in the lower re-entrant angle is occupied by a symmetrical figure resembling two tail feathers and the extremity of the body of a bird. The median figure is replaced in Fig. 94 by

FIG. 93—W-pattern ; bird form

a triangular ornament. In this design the two wings are not symmetrical, but no new decorative element is introduced. It will be noticed, however, that there is a want of symmetry on the two sides of a vertical line in the figure last mentioned.

FIG. 94—W-pattern ; median triangle

The right-hand upper side is continued into five pointed projections, which fail on the left-hand side. There is likewise a difference in the arrangement of the terraced figures in the two parts. The sides of the median triangles are formed of alternating black and white blocks, and the quadrate figure which it incloses is etched with a diagonal and cross.

The decoration in Fig. 95 consists of two triangles side by side, each having marginal serrations, and a median square key pattern. One side of these triangles

FIG. 95—Double triangle; two breath feathers

is continued into a line from which hang two breath feathers, while the other end of the same line ends in a round dot with four radiating straight lines. The triangles recall the butterfly symbol, the key pattern representing the head.

FIG. 96—W-triangle; median trapezoid

In Fig. 96 there is a still more aberrant form of the W-shape design. The wings are folded, ending in triangles, and prolonged at their angles into projections to which are appended round dots with three parallel lines. The median portion,

FIG. 97—Double triangle; median rectangle

or that in the re-entrant angle of the W, is a four-sided figure in which the triangle predominates with notched edges. Fig. 97 shows the same design with the median portion replaced by a rectangle, and in which the key pattern has wholly disap-

FIG. 98—Double compound triangle; median rectangle

peared from the wings. In Fig. 98 there are still greater modifications, but the symmetry about a median axis remains. The ends of the wings, instead of being folded are expanded, and the three triangles formerly inclosed are now free and extended. The simple median rectangle is ornamented with a terrace pattern on its lower angles.

FIG. 99—Double triangle; median triangle

Fig. 99 shows a design in which the extended triangles are even more regular and simple, with triangular terraced figures on their inner edges. The median figure is a triangle instead of a rectangle.

FIG. 100—Double compound triangle

Fig. 100 shows the same design with modification in the position of the median figure, and a slight curvature in two of its sides.

FIG. 101—Double rectangle; median rectangle

Somewhat similar designs, readily reduced to the same type as the last three or four which have been mentioned, are shown in Figs. 101 and 102. The resemblances are so close that I need not refer to them in detail. The W form is wholly lost,

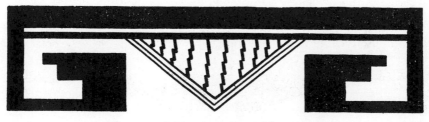

FIG. 102—Double rectangle; median triangle

and there is no resemblance to a bird, even in its most highly conventionalized forms. The median design in Fig. 101 consists of a rectangle and two triangles so arranged as to leave a rectangular white space between them. In Fig. 102 the median triangle is crossed by parallel and vertical zigzag lines.

In the design represented in Fig. 103 there are two triangular figures, one on each side of a median line, in relation to which they are symmetrical. Each triangle has a simple key pattern in the middle, and the line from which they appear to

FIG. 103—Double triangle with crooks

hang is blocked off with alternating black and white rectangles. At either extremity of this line there is a circular dot from which extend four parallel lines.

A somewhat simpler form of the same design is found in Fig. 104, showing a straight line above terminating with dots, from which extend parallel lines, and

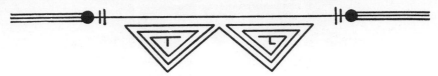

FIG. 104—W-shaped figure; single line with feathers

two triangular figures below, symmetrically placed in reference to an hypothetical upright line between them.

Fig. 105 bears a similarity to the last mentioned only so far as the lower half of the design is concerned. The upper part is not symmetrical, but no new dec-

FIG. 105—Compound rectangle, triangles, and feathers

orative element is introduced. Triangles, frets, and terraced figures are inserted between two parallel lines which terminate in round dots with parallel lines.

The design in Fig. 106 is likewise unsymmetrical, but it has two lateral tri-angles with incurved terrace and dentate patterns. The same general form is

FIG. 106—Double triangle

exhibited in Fig. 107, with the introduction of two pointed appendages facing the hypothetical middle line. From the general form of these pointed designs, each of which is double, they have been interpreted as feathers. They closely resemble the tail-feathers of bird figures on several bowls in the collection, as will be seen in several of the illustrations.

FIG. 107—Double triangle and feathers

Fig. 108 is composed of two triangular designs fused at the greatest angles. The regularity of these triangles is broken by a square space at the fusion. At each of the acute angles of the two triangles there are circular designs with radiating

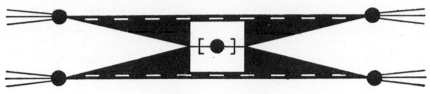

FIG. 108—Twin triangles

lines, a common motive on the exterior of food bowls. Although no new elements appear in Fig. 108, with the exception of the bracket marks, one on each side of a circle, the arrangement of the two parts about a line parallel with the rim of the bowl imparts to the design a unique form. The motive in Fig. 109 is reducible to

FIG. 109—Triangle with terraced appendages

triangular and rectangular forms, and while exceptional as to their arrangement, no new decorative feature is introduced.

The specimen represented in Fig. 110 has as its decorative elements, rectangles, triangles, parallel lines, and birds' tails, to which may be added star and crosshatch

FIG. 110—Mosaic pattern

motives. It is, therefore, the most complicated of all the exterior decorations which have thus far been considered. There is no symmetry in the arrangement of figures about a central axis, but rather a repetition of similar designs.

The use of crosshatching is very common on the most ancient Pueblo ware, and is very common in designs on cliff-house pottery. This style of decoration is only sparingly used on Sikyatki ware. The crosshatching is provisionally interpreted as a mosaic pattern, and reminds one of the beautiful forms of turquoise mosaic on shell, bone, or wood, found in ancient pueblos, and best known in modern times in the square ear pendants of Hopi women. Fig. 110 is one of the few designs

FIG. 111—Rectangles, stars, crooks, and parallel lines

having terraced figures with short parallel lines descending from them. These figures vividly recall the rain-cloud symbol with falling rain represented by the parallel lines. Fig. 111 is a perfectly symmetrical design with figures of stars, rectangles, and parallel lines. It may be compared with that shown in Fig. 110 in order to demonstrate how wide the difference in design may become by the absence of symmetrical relationship. It has been shown in some of the previous motives that the crook sometimes represents a bird's head, and parallel lines appended to it the tail-feathers. Possibly the same interpretation may be given to these designs in the

FIG. 112—Continuous crooks

following figures, and the presence of stars adjacent to them lends weight to this hypothesis.

An indefinite repetition of the same pattern of rectangular design is shown in Fig. 112. This highly decorative motive may be varied indefinitely by extension or concentration, and while it is modified in that manner in many of the decorations of vases, it is not so changed on the exterior of food bowls.

There are a number of forms which I am unable to classify with the foregoing, none of which show any new decorative design. All possible changes have been made

FIG. 113—Rectangular terrace pattern

in them without abandoning the elemental ornamental motives already considered. The tendency to step or terrace patterns predominates, as exemplified in simple form in Fig. 113. In Fig. 114 there is a different arrangement of the same terrace pattern, and the design is helped out with parallel bands of different length at the ends of a rectangular figure. A variation in the depth of color of these lines adds to the effectiveness of the design. This style of ornamentation is successfully used in the designs rep-

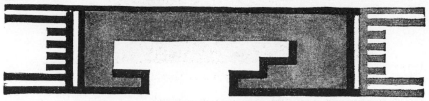

FIG. 114—Terrace pattern with parallel lines

resented in Figs. 115 and 116, in the body of which a crescentic figure in the black serves to add variety to a design otherwise monotonous. The two appendages to the

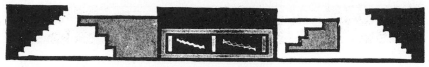

FIG. 115—Terrace pattern

right of Fig. 116 are interpreted as feathers, although their forms depart widely from that usually assumed by these designs. The terraced patterns are replaced by dentate

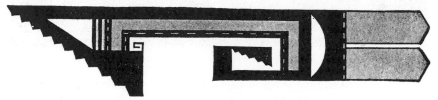

FIG. 116—Triangular pattern with feathers

margins in this figure, and there is a successful use of most of the rectangular and triangular designs.

FIG. 117—S-pattern

In the specimens represented in Figs. 117 and 118 marginal dentations are used. I have called the design referred to an S-form, which, however, owing to its elongation is somewhat masked. The oblique bar in the middle of the figure represents the body of the letter, the two extremities taking the forms of triangles.

So far as the decorative elements are concerned, the design in Fig. 119 can be compared with some of those preceding, but it differs from them in combination. The

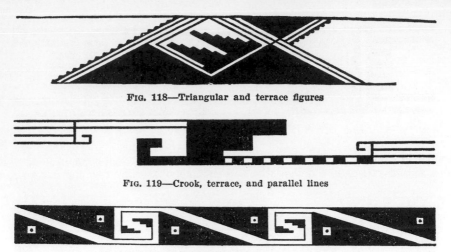

FIG. 118—Triangular and terrace figures

FIG. 119—Crook, terrace, and parallel lines

FIG. 120—Triangles, squares, and terraces

motive in Fig. 120 is not unlike the ornamentation of certain oriental vases, except from the presence of the terraced figures. In Fig. 121 there are two designs separated by

FIG. 121—Bifurcated rectangular design

an inclined break the edge of which is dentate. This figure is introduced to show the method of treatment of alternating triangles of varying depth of color and the breaks

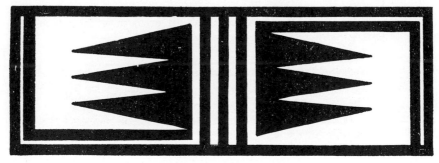

FIG. 122—Infolded triangles

in the marginal bands or "lines of life." One of the simplest combinations of triangular and rectangular figures is shown in Fig. 122, proving how effectually the original design may be obscured by concentration.

In the foregoing descriptions I have endeavored to demonstrate that, notwith-standing the great variety of designs considered, the types used are very limited in number. The geometrical forms are rarely curved lines, and it may be said that spirals, which appear so constantly on pottery from other (and possibly equally ancient or older) pueblos than Sikyatki, are absent in the external decorations of specimens found in the ruins of the latter village.

Every student of ancient and modern pueblo pottery has been impressed by the predominance of terraced figures in its ornamentation, and the meaning of these ter-races has elsewhere been spoken of at some length. It would, I believe, be going too far to say that these step designs always represent clouds, as in some instances they

FIG. 123—Human hand

are produced by such an arrangement of rectangular figures that no other forms could result.

The material at hand adds nothing new to the theory of the evolution of the ter-raced ornament from basketry or textile productions, so ably discussed by Holmes, Nordenskiöld, and others. When the Sikyatki potters decorated their ware the orna-mentation of pottery had reached a high development, and figures both simple and com-plicated were used contemporaneously. While, therefore, we can so arrange them as to make a series, tracing modifications from simple to complex designs, thus forming a supposed line of evolution, it is evident that there is no proof that the simplest figures are the oldest. The great number of terraced figures and their use in the representa-

FIG. 124—Animal paw, limb and triangle

tion of animals seem to me to indicate that they antedate all others, and I see no reason why they should not have been derived from basketry patterns. We must, however, look to pottery with decorations less highly developed for evidence bearing on this point. The Sikyatki artists had advanced beyond simple geometric figures, and had so highly modified these that it is impossible to determine the primitive form.

The human hand also is used as a decorative element in the ornamentation of the interior of several food bowls. It is likewise in one instance chosen to adorn the exterior. It is the only part of the human limbs thus used. Figure 123 shows the hand with marks on the palm probably intended to represent the lines which are used in the measurement of the length of *pahos* or prayer-sticks.

The limb of an animal with a paw, or possibly a human arm and hand, appears as a decoration on the outside of another food bowl, where it is combined with the ever-constant stepped figure, as shown in Fig. 124.

To summarize the subject, then, is it not apparent that, with such a wealth of suggestive material around her on every hand, the Navaho weaver could scarcely avoid becoming a master in the art of design? With this extraordinary environment of art suggestions and the instinctive individuality of the weaver asserting itself, it was to be expected that a remarkable variety of new designs would be invented or created, and that old designs would take on new forms by mutation, and would be placed together in new, unique, striking, and attractive combinations. Here, therefore, I think we find the fullest and most satisfactory explanation of the remarkable wealth of design found in Navaho blanketry.

Fig. 125.
Navaho Weaver at Her Open-Air Loom.
(Copyright by George R. King. Used by permission.)

CHAPTER XIII

A Navaho Weaver at Work

ONE of the first great surprises to a white visitor to the Navaho reservation is that he sees so few Indians or their dwellings. Mile after mile he drives over the roads through the heart of what seems to be an entirely unpeopled country, save for the occasional teams he may meet, or the solitary Navaho horseman who now and again passes with a word, or in silence. He thinks the barren and waterless nature of the country may have to do with this absence of population, and in this he is largely correct. It is only where water is to be found — at least not too far away — that the Navaho establishes his residence. There must also be a patch of arable land within reasonable proximity to supply him with the corn that is his daily food. Here, then, he builds his *hogan;* if for summer use, a temporary structure of brush, a rude lean-to against the wall of a canyon or an excavated bank, or a mere circular shelter of green boughs, made in half an hour by a couple of men skilled in the use of the axe. If it is a permanent winter *hogan* it is built with the solemn and serious earnestness which characterizes all the important features of a Navaho's life.

No sooner is the household "settled" than a framework is erected outside, merely covered with brush, arrow-weed, or tules to keep off the sun's rays, and under this the loom is set up. Some *hogans* are built large enough to accommodate the loom, but in summer it is always in the open, merely placed so that during the working hours of the day it is in the shade.

Not infrequently the loom is set up in the open, the weaver so placing it that the sun's rays will not disturb her at the time she expects to work. Such a loom is pictured in Fig. 125, made from a copyright photograph by George R. King, of Pasadena.

The Navaho loom is a remarkable exhibition of primitive ingenuity and effectiveness. While there are diversities in details, in the main practically they are all alike. The accompanying illustration, Fig. 126, is from Dr. Matthews's admirable monograph on "Navaho Weavers," which appears in the *Third Annual Report of the Bureau of American Ethnology,* and a large portion of the description is in the author's own words. Two upright posts set firmly in the ground, wide enough (*a a*) apart to accommodate the full width of the blanket to be woven, are braced together top and bottom by equally strong cross pieces (*b c*). Trunks of small growing trees are occasionally used as the necessary uprights. This may be called the frame in which the loom is to be lashed. The loom proper has its lower beam (*k*) and upper beam (*d*). On neither of these, however, is the warp wound. The warp is tied at the top to a border cord (*h*), and also at the bottom. This border cord (*h h*) is lashed or tied with rope coils (*e e*) to the upper and lower loom beams and the warp is thus securely placed. But before weaving can be done

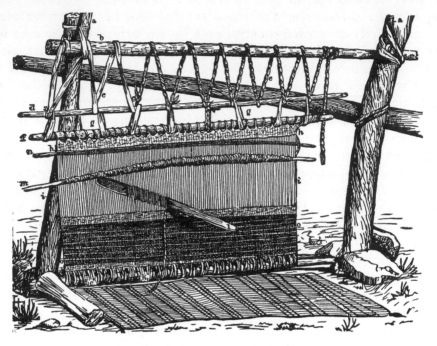

FIG. 126—Ordinary Navaho blanket loom

this warp must be fixed firmly in the frame and stretched tightly, as the work demands. This is done by first of all lashing the lower beam (*k*) to the lower brace (*c*) of the frame. Then a new stout brace or beam is introduced at the top of the loom, which Dr. Matthews appropriately terms a "supplementary yarn-beam." This is firmly and securely lashed to the upper yarn-beam (*f*), and then, with a strong rawhide, which is wrapped spirally or tied (*g g*) around the upper brace of the loom-frame, the warp (*i i*) is made as taut as the weaver desires.

This supplementary beam also serves another purpose. The blanket is woven from the bottom. The weaver squats in front of her work, and as soon as weaving is done as high as her arms find it convenient she loosens the rawhide lashing of the supplementary yarn-beam and folds the woven part of her blanket, securely sewing the upper part of the fold to the lower beam. The rawhide lashings are again pulled tight, and this is sometimes done so thoroughly that the marks of the sewing remain in the blanket for years, sometimes even as long as the blanket itself lasts.

A loose flat stick, sharpened on one side, and some two feet long, and, say, three inches broad is the *batten stick* (*l*). This is loose and inserted by the weaver whenever and wherever desired to "batten," or beat down, the weft snug into place.

A long slender circular stick serves as a *heald-rod*. The healds are made of cord or yarn fastened to a rod (*m*), and are tied to alternate threads of the warp. This heald-rod (*m*) serves, when pulled forward, to open the shed for the insertion of the shuttle. The upper shed is kept patent by a stout rod which has no healds attached, and called by Matthews the shed-rod (*n*). A small several-toothed wooden fork serves the purpose of the reed in our looms, and is used by the weaver to press in

FIG. 127—Diagram showing formation of warp

place the weft where it is irregularly woven, or does not go completely across the warp where it can be wedged home with the batten stick.

Now let us see the weaver actually at her work. We will assume that all prior processes are completed. The weaver has washed, spun, and dyed the wool, she has decided upon the size of her blanket, and formulated in her active and imaginative brain the design that she intends to materialize. She is now ready, therefore, for the preparing or constructing of the warp. Dr. Matthews thus clearly and graphically describes the process:

A frame of four sticks is made, not unlike the frame of the loom, but lying on or near the ground, instead of standing erect. The two sticks forming the sides of the frame are rough saplings or rails; the two forming the top and bottom are smooth, rounded poles — often the poles which afterwards serve as the beams of the loom; these are placed parallel to one another, their distance apart depending on the length of the projected blanket.

On these poles the warp is laid in a continuous string. It is first firmly tied to one of the poles, which I call No. 1 (Fig. 127); then is passed over the other pole, No. 2, brought back under No. 2 and over No. 1, forward again under No. 1 and over No. 2, and so on to the end. Thus the first, third, fifth, etc., turns of the cord cross in the middle, the second, fourth, sixth, etc., forming a series of elongated figures 8, as shown in the following diagram — and making, in the very beginning of the process, the two sheds, which are kept distinct throughout the whole work.

When sufficient string has been laid the end is tied to pole No. 2, and a rod is placed in each shed to keep it open, the rods being afterwards tied together at the ends to prevent them from falling out.

This done, the weaver takes three strings (which are afterwards twilled into one, as will appear) and ties them together at one end. She now sits outside of one of the poles, looking toward the center of the frame, and proceeds thus: (1) She secures the triple cord to the pole immediately to the left of the warp; (2) then she takes one of the threads (or strands, as they now become) and passes it under the first turn of the warp; (3) next she takes a second strand, and twilling it once, or oftener, with the other strands, includes with it the second bend of the warp; (4) this done, she takes the third strand and, twilling it as before, passes it under the third bend of the warp, and thus she goes on until the entire warp in one place is secured between the strands of the cord; (5) then she pulls the string to its fullest extent, and in doing so separates the threads of the warp from one another: (6) a similar three stranded cord is applied to the other end of the warp, along the outside of the other pole.

At this stage of the work these stout cords lie along the outer surfaces of the poles, parallel with the axes of the latter, but when the warp is taken off the poles and applied to the beams by the spiral thread, as above described, and as depicted in Fig. 126, and all is ready for weaving, the cords appear on the inner sides of the beams, i. e., one at the lower side of the yarn-beam, the other at the upper side of the cloth-beam, and when the blanket is finished they form the stout end margins of the web. In the coarser grade of blankets the cords are removed and the ends of the warp tied in pairs and made to form a fringe.

When the warp is transferred to the loom the rod which was placed in the upper shed remains there, or another rod, straighter and smoother, is substituted for it; but with the lower shed, healds are applied to anterior threads, and the rod is withdrawn.

The mode of applying the healds is simple: (1) the weaver sits facing the loom in the position for weaving; (2) she lays at the right (her right) side of the loom a ball of string which she knows contains more than sufficient material to make the healds; (3) she takes the end of this string and passes it to the left through the shed, leaving the ball in its original position; (4) she ties a loop at the end of the string large enough to admit the heald-rod; (5) she holds horizontally in her left hand a straightish, slender rod, which is to become the heald-rod — its right extremity touching the left edge of the warp — and passes the rod through the loop until the point of the stick is even with the third (second anterior from the left) thread of the warp; (6) she puts her finger through the space between the first and third threads and draws out a fold of the heald-string; (7) she twists this once around, so as to form a loop, and pushes the point of the heald-rod on to the right through this loop; (8) she puts her finger into the next space and forms another loop; (9) and so on she continues to advance her rod and form her loops from left to right until each of the anterior (alternate) warp-threads of the lower shed is included in a loop of the heald; (10) when the last loop is made she ties the string firmly to the rod near its right end.

When the weaving is nearly done and it becomes necessary to remove the healds, the rod is drawn out of the loops, a slight pull is made at the thread, the loops fall in an instant, and the straightened string is drawn out of the shed.

The weaver is now ready to proceed with the actual weaving — the insertion of the weft. As before stated, she has no shuttle; small balls

Fig. 128.
Navaho Weaver at Work.
Showing batten stick horizontally placed ready to beat down the weft.

Fig. 129.

**Batten Stick in Position to Allow
Weft to Pass Through.**

Fig. 130.

Novel Arrangement of the Loom.
(From a painting by Cassidy Davis, owned by
J. L. Hubbell, Ganado, Ariz.)

of colored, and larger balls of white, black, or gray yarn being used as shuttles, though occasionally a thread may be wrapped around the end of a stick for more convenient handling.

Squatted upon a sheep skin or a folded blanket before the warp, she decides to begin by weaving in the lower shed. She draws a portion of the healds towards her, and with them the anterior threads of the shed; by this motion she opens the shed about 1 inch, which is not sufficient for the easy passage of the woof. She inserts her batten edgewise into this opening and then turns it half around on its long axis, so that its broad surface lies horizontally; in this way the shed is opened to the extent of the width of the batten — about three inches; next the weft is passed through. In Fig. 126 the batten is shown lying edgewise (its broad surfaces vertical), as it appears when just inserted into the shed, and the weft, which has been passed through only a portion of the shed, is seen hanging out with its end on the ground. In Fig. 129, the batten is shown in the second position described, with the shed open to the fullest extent necessary, and it is while in this position the weaver passes the shuttle through. When the weft is in, it is shoved down to its proper position by means of the reed-fork, and then the batten, restored to its first position (edgewise), is brought down with firm blows on the weft. It is by the vigorous use of the batten that the Navaho serapes are rendered waterproof. In Fig. 128, the weaver is seen bringing down this instrument "in the manner and for the purpose described," as the letters patent say.

When the lower shed has received its thread of weft the weaver opens the upper shed. This is done by releasing the healds and shoving the shed-rod down until it comes in contact with the healds; this opens the upper shed down to the web. Then the weft is inserted and the batten and reed-fork used as before. Thus she goes on with each shed alternately until the web is finished.

It is, of course, desirable, at least in handsome blankets of intricate pattern, to have both ends uniform even if the figure be a little faulty in the center. To accomplish this, some of the weavers depend on a careful estimate of the length of each figure before they begin, and weave continuously in one direction; but the majority weave a little portion of the upper end before they finish the middle. Sometimes this is done by weaving from above downwards; at other times it is done by turning the loom upside down and working from below upwards in the ordinary manner.

The ends of the blanket are bordered with a stout three-ply string applied to the folds of the warp. The lateral edges of the blanket are similarly protected by stout cords applied to the weft. The way in which these are woven in, next demands our attention. Two stout worsted cords, tied together, are firmly attached to each end of the cloth-beam just outside the warp; they are then carried upwards and loosely tied to the yarn-beam or the supplementary yarn-beam. Every time the weft is turned at the edge these two strings are twisted together and the weft is passed through the twist; thus one thread or strand of this border is always on the outside. As it is constantly twisted in one direction, it is evident that, after a while, a counter twist must form which would render the passage of the weft between the cords difficult, if the cords could not be untwisted again. These cords are tied loosely to one of the upper beams for this purpose. From time to time the cords are untied and the unwoven portion straightened as the work progresses. The coarse blankets do not have them.

Yet, while this is the rule for all weaving, it is not always followed. There seems to be a great deal of self-will, of individuality, of refusal to be tied down to rules, among these Navaho weavers, and it is no uncommon thing to find a weaver doing as is illustrated in Fig. 128, where, without any apparent reason, the woof-threads are not taken across the whole width of the blanket. In Figs. 143-4-5, which are of blankets that would be called of *standard* grade (see page 149), the zigzag pattern of the design of both blankets is clearly worked without any regard to the ordinary demands of woof-weaving, viz., that the threads go straight across the blanket to allow of them being battened down evenly. Even in the illustrations, if a glass is used, I have no doubt the oblique character of the threads can be seen, and expert weavers on the white man's machines, to whom I have shown these specimens, express surprise at the perfection of the work, and also their inability to understand how it is done. This remarkable facility in doing the unusual thing, in finding a way to do something that has never been done before, is ever and anon cropping up in Navaho work, and necessarily makes the study that much the more interesting.

Another interesting variation in Navaho weaving is shown in Fig. 130, which is from an excellent painting by Cassidy Davis, in the collection of John Lorenzo Hubbell, of Granado, Arizona. For some reason the weaver did not wish her loom to stand too high. Her warp, therefore, was brought over the upper beam of her loom-frame and lashed to an extra beam, securely fastened to the uprights at about half their height. In all my thirty years of travel among Navaho weavers I have seen this method followed not more than three or four times.

Before weaving can be begun, however, the yarn must be prepared. The processes of dyeing have already been explained, but not those that are gone through from gathering the wool to spinning it ready for the dye pot.

Shearing is done in the spring and fall. The Navahos are expert at the work, but are neither as rapid, skilful, nor as careful as the Indian shearers of California. The fall shearing is begun as early as possible to avoid the cold of winter, and in spring it is postponed as long as is safe, so as to avoid the sudden storms of that period.

Just before lambing time the herds are removed to the mountains, where there is generally plenty of good pasturage and water. Here corrals for their protection are easily constructed, and here they are kept —the whole Navaho family often remaining until the lambs are strong enough to travel.

Up to a few years ago the sheep were seldom washed either before or after shearing, but now the Government has provided in several places on the reservation places for dipping and washing. This keeps the animals more healthful, and also materially aids in cleansing the fleece. When shearing time comes the men do the larger part of the work, though the women render constant and effective assistance, often catching the animals, turning them upon their backs, and completing the shearing themselves. American clippers have entirely supplanted the rude flint knives that alone were used in the earlier days.

When the fleece is removed and the wool is to be used for weaving, it is first thoroughly tossed, shaken, or beaten against a tree, a wagon wheel, upon the rocks or hard ground to remove the sand and as much loose and foreign material as can be shaken out. Then it is thrown over some object and all the burrs and lumps or matted wool carefully picked out.

Now it is ready to be washed. Bowls are prepared full of the clearest water obtainable, and if it is possible to be near a stream or spring advantage is taken of this close proximity. From the weaver's household stores several pieces of the root of the amole are taken. *Yucca glauca, Y. baccata, Y. angustifolia, Y. radiosa,* and *Y. elata* are all used for this purpose, though the second named seems to contain the largest and richest saponine. These roots are beaten between rocks until reduced to a mass of fibres, and are then splashed up and down in a bowl of water until the latter becomes covered with a rich and soft, foamy lather. In these suds the wool is soaked and more or less thoroughly washed, according to the habit of the weaver. If she be conscientious and desirous of doing first-class work, she well knows the washing must be well done, or the dye will not "take" satisfactorily.

In the case of white wool, which is to be used, without dyeing, also of black, brown, and native gray, the careful weaver is extra particular to see that the wool is thoroughly washed. The fleeces are then spread out on whatever shrubs are nearest at hand to dry. This does not require long, as a rule, in the hot sunshine of the Arizona or New Mexico country, and the wool is then ready for carding.

In the olden days teasels were used. These are still found growing wild on the reservation. Of late years, however, the traders have supplied the weavers with the simple and somewhat primitive old-fashioned wire-toothed cards, such as our great-grandmothers used to use, and that remind us somewhat of a horse's curry-comb. With these — generally one in each hand — the wool is carded out until the staple is smooth and uniform and the wool made into a long loose roll.

Both in their loom and distaff the Navahos are rigidly conservative. For many years the Mexicans of the Southwest have been using the spinning wheel, and later, when the Mormons settled on the very edge of

Navaho territory, they also brought the wheel and endeavored to prevail upon the Navahos to adopt it. As yet, however, all efforts to lead them away from the primitive distaff have failed. They will neither buy, make, nor receive a gift of a spinning wheel.

The distaff, or spindle, held in the hand of the woman illustrated in Fig. 131 consists of a smooth round stick, about two feet long, pointed at both ends, and of a wheel or disk of flat wood some four or five inches in diameter, through the center of which is a small hole, made to hold the stick, at about a distance of five or six inches from the butt end of the stick.

When everything is ready for the spinning—carded-wool on a blanket on the ground, distaff in the right hand—the spinner squats down, Turkish or tailor fashion, and picks up a little of the wool in her left hand, into which she sticks the tip of the spindle. With a few dexterous turns the wool is soon caught fast, and now the distaff is kept spinning by a swift motion of the fingers of the right hand, while with the left the wool is drawn out to arms' length to the required thickness. While this operation is going on the end of the distaff rests upon the ground, and the wool is held so that it is on about a straight line with it. As soon as the strand is as long, and twisted as much, as the woman desires, she tilts the distaff so that it and the wool-strand are almost at acute angles, and, the spindle still kept twirling, the wool is wound up and down the upper portion of the stick. This is repeated until the stick will hold no more, when the stranded-wool is unwound from the spindle, wrapped into balls and laid aside. As soon as all the wool is spun, or so much as the weaver thinks she may need, it is all respun, once or twice, or even more, according to the thickness and tightness of the yarn needed. The second twisting is generally enough for the making of the wool warps, but the third twisting gives a tight, strong, bristly cord about as thick as ordinary binding twine. For the extra fine blankets the yarn is both fine and extra tightly woven.

Practically all Navaho blankets are "single-ply"—that is, the pattern or design is the same on both sides, no matter how elaborate or complex this may be.

To produce their variegated patterns they have a separate skein, shuttle, or thread for each component of the pattern. Take, for instance, the blanket depicted in Fig. 132. Across this blanket, between the points *a-b*, we have two serrated borders, two white spaces, a small diamond in the center, and twenty-four serrated stripes, making in all twenty-nine component parts of the pattern. Now, when the weaver was working in this place, twenty-nine different threads of weft might have been seen hanging from the face of the web at one time. When the web is so nearly finished that the batten can no longer be inserted in the warp, slender rods are placed in the shed, while the weft is passed with increased difficulty on the end of a delicate splinter

Fig. 131.
Navaho Method of Using Distaff or Spindle.
(By permission of the Bureau of American Ethnology.)

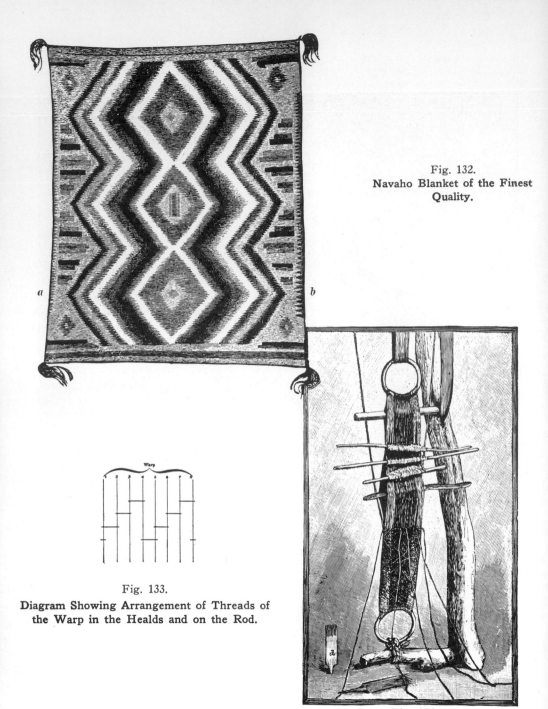

Fig. 132.
Navaho Blanket of the Finest
Quality.

Fig. 133.
Diagram Showing Arrangement of Threads of
the Warp in the Healds and on the Rod.

Fig. 134.
Weaving of Saddle Girth.

and the reed-fork alone presses the warp home. Later it becomes necessary to remove even the rod and the shed; then the alternate threads are separated by a slender stick worked in tediously between them, and two threads of woof are inserted — one above and the other below the stick. The very last thread is sometimes put in with a darning needle. The weaving of the last three inches requires more labor than any foot of the previous work. [Matthews.]

While the great majority of blankets are woven in this simple "single-ply" style, the Navaho weaver, by deft manipulation and digital dexterity gained by years of practice, is able to weave blankets, dresses, shirts, etc., in six different styles. Each of these has a separate name, (according to Father Berard), and the processes are as follows:

1.   *Yistlo.* — This is the simple straight method already described, in which the woof-strands are drawn horizontally through the warp and rammed tight with the batten-stick. Two healds are used in this mode of weaving.

2.   *Yishbizh.* — This word means braided, but is used in connection with blankets to designate a peculiar figure or run of the web, which runs diagonally across the blanket, giving it the appearance as if it were begun in one corner and woven to the opposite corner. The position of the loom and of the weaver is the same as in No. 1, but more healds are used.

3.   *Iimas.* — This is the diagonal weave, and Dr. Matthews thus describes the process:

"For making diagonals, the warp is divided into four sheds; the uppermost one of these is provided with a shed-rod, the others are supplied with healds. I will number the healds and sheds from below upwards. The diagram, Fig. 133, shows how the threads of the warp are arranged in the healds and on the rod.

"When the weaver wishes the diagonal ridges to run upwards from right to left, she opens the sheds in regular order from below upwards, thus: First, second, third, fourth, first, second, third, fourth, etc. When she wishes the ridges to trend in the contrary direction she opens the sheds in the inverse order. I found it convenient to take my illustrations of this mode of weaving from a girth. In Figs. 134 and 135 the mechanism is plainly shown. The lowest (first) shed is opened and the first set of healds drawn forward. The rings of the girth take the place of the beams of the loom.

"There is a variety of diagonal weaving practiced by the Navahos which produces diamond figures; for this the mechanism is the same as that just described, except that the healds are arranged differently on the warp. The diagram, Fig. 136, will explain this arrangement.

"To make the most approved series of diamonds the sheds are opened twice in the direct order (i. e., from below upwards) and twice in the inverse order, thus: First, second, third, fourth, first, second, third, fourth, third, second, first, fourth, third, second, first, fourth, and so on. If this order is departed from, the figures become irregular. If the weaver continues more than twice consecutively in either order, a row of V-shaped figures is formed, thus: VVVV. Fig. 137 shows a portion of a blanket which is part plain diagonal and part diamond."

4. *Diyugi,* or *Diyogi.* — This is really not a special style of weave, since it is the same as No. 1, only that soft, loose yarn is used, which makes the blanket look thick, soft and fluffy, and that is expressed by the word *diyugi,* or *diyogi.*

5. *Ditsosi.* — This word, meaning fuzzy, or downy, is applied to a species of blankets or rugs the one side of which looks very much like a long-haired sheep pelt, with the wool in small tufts. When the woman weaves this sort of blanket she has a quantity of long-haired wool near at hand. She first weaves about an inch, then, taking pinches of the long-haired wool, inserts them between the warp on the top of the woven part, leaving a tuft of about two inches out in front. When the whole row is thus tufted she rams it down with the batten-stick, weaves another course of about an inch, inserts another row of tufts, and thus continues until the blanket is finished. When finished it has the appearance of a shaggy pelt.

6. *Alneestloni.* — This is a double or two-ply weave, which shows a different design on either side. In weaving in this style as many as eight healds are used. By manipulating them in the right way, the desired result is obtained. In order to understand just how it is done, one would have to see a woman at work, and pay close attention to the manner of weaving, and to the arrangement and use of the healds.

That indefatigable student and observer, Dr. Matthews, found a blanket of this double or two-ply weave, and after gaining all the information he could upon the subject wrote the following article in the *American Anthropologist.* The whole of it is so interesting that it is quoted without abridgment:

As the American Indians are generally believed to be neither imitative nor inventive, it is well to consider a remarkable instance of their aptness in learning, and, added thereto, an example of their inventive advancement.

The whole art of weaving among the Navahos is worthy of close study for many reasons, but not least for a psychological reason. We have fair evidence from the early Spanish explorers that they knew nothing of loom-weaving three hundred years ago. The Navaho traditions (and the evidence of these is not without value) corroborate such statements. They tell us many times that the early Athabascan intruders in New Mexico and Arizona dressed themselves in rude mats or garments made of juniper bark, which must have been woven by the fingers without mechanical appliances. But we have also the evidence of travelers of a still earlier date that the sedentary Indians who were neighbors of the Navahos used the loom and wove fabrics of cotton and other materials. We have archæological evidence that the Pueblos and cliff-dwellers wove, with the assistance of a mechanism, webs of cotton, yucca-fiber, feathers, and hair, and that they knitted with wooden needles leggins of human hair; for this purpose, it is thought, they saved their combings.

Three hundred years ago, then, the Navahos knew nothing of the loom; but in the meantime they have become a race of expert loom-weavers, and they have accomplished this without coercion or any such formal methods of instruction as we employ;

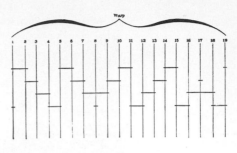

Fig. 136.

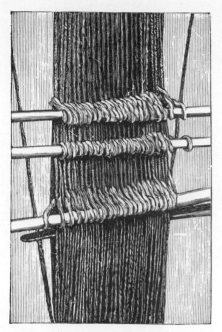

Fig. 135.

Fig. 135 is an enlarged section of Fig. 134, showing the manipulation of the healds for weaving in diagonals. Fig. 136 shows the arrangement of the healds for weaving diamonds, and Fig. 137 shows a blanket, part of which is diagonal and part diamond weave.

Fig. 137.

Fig. 138.
Two Sides of the Navaho Blanket, Each Side Being Different.
(Courtesy of the American Anthropologist.)

they having "picked it up." True, they had their instructors near at hand — the sedentary Indians with whom they have traded and intermarried — but other wild tribes of the southwest had the same opportunities to learn and never profited by them. All had an equal chance to steal sheep from the Mexicans; but all did not become shepherds. The weaving of wool was, of course, unknown in America before the Spaniards introduced sheep in the sixteenth century; but the Indians were not obliged to change their old looms when the new staple was introduced.

Within the time to which I allude, not only have the Navahos learned from their neighbors, the sedentary Indians, the art of weaving, but they have come to excel their teachers. Although blankets are still woven in Zuni today, if an inhabitant of that pueblo desires a specially fine serape, he purchases it from a Navaho.

While living in New Mexico during the years 1880-84, in daily contact with members of the Navaho tribe, I made a careful study of the Navaho art of weaving and wrote a treatise on the subject which appeared in the *Third Annual Report of the Bureau of Ethnology* (Washington, 1885). In that article I described all the important forms of Navaho blankets I had ever seen; but I had not seen a two-faced blanket, and, up to the date of writing, had not even heard of it; there is, therefore, no allusion to it in my treatise. I was absent from New Mexico, except during two short visits, for six years. Sometime after I returned to it, in 1890, for another sojourn of four years, I saw, for the first time, one of those two-faced blankets. Thus I may safely say that after I left New Mexico, in 1884, the process of making this blanket was invented by a Navaho Indian, and probably, though not necessarily, by a Navaho woman.

During my second sojourn in New Mexico I tried to find a woman who wove this peculiar blanket in order that I might induce her by liberal pecuniary promises, as I had done on previous occasions with other weavers of special fabrics, to come to my residence and work under my observation; but I never succeeded. I was told that the blankets were made in a distant part of the Navaho country; my informants knew not where. If there were more than one maker, I never learned; but from what I know of the Navahos I think it probable that the inventor has made no secret of the process and that now, at least, there are many weavers of the two-faced blankets.

Someone may question if this art did not exist during my first sojourn in the Navaho country previous to 1884, and if I might not have failed to observe it. This is by no means probable. Everyone in the Navaho country then believed that the distinguishing feature of the Indian blanket was that, no matter how richly figured, its two surfaces were always exactly alike in all respects. Mr. Thomas V. Keam, of Keam's Canyon, Arizona, is the Indian trader who has been longest established among the Navahos, and is their most popular trader; he has dealt and dwelt with them, I think, for about thirty years, and he is an educated, intelligent, and observant man. Had such blankets been even occasionally seen among these Indians prior to 1884, some of them would have been brought to him to trade and he would not have failed to observe their unusual appearance. In 1896 I wrote requesting Mr. Keam to get for me a two-faced blanket from his part of the country and asking him what he knew of the origin of the new blanket. In his reply, dated January 27, 1897, he says:

"As you suppose, it is only about three years since I first saw this work, and to date there are only a few who understand this weaving. The diamond or diagonal twill is undoubtedly copied by them from the Hopi, but the double or reversible weaving I believe to be of their own [Navaho] invention, as I know of no other tribe that does such weaving."

Thus we see that it was not until about the year 1893 that the oldest trader in the Navaho land saw a two-faced blanket.

As I have said, the Navaho loom is a machine, and a rather elaborate machine, too. The step from a tool to a machine marks a wide advance in human evolution. I have described accurately, in the paper already quoted, the mechanism of the Navaho loom (as it existed in the last decade, at least) and have analyzed its component elements, which are essentially those of our own household loom. There is no doubt that the ordinary Navaho loom is an aboriginal invention which has not been modified since pre-Columbian days. In the weaving of belts, hair-bands, and garters, the Zuni women employ a harness or heald which seems to be derived from the Old World; but the Navaho heald is a rude, aboriginal device.

I cannot say what particular modification has been made in the loom (or perhaps I would better say in the application or management of the loom) to produce the new style of web, but it would greatly interest me to know. I trust that some of the many scientific explorers who have recently taken to visiting the Navaho land may find time to determine this and to describe it in technical terms. If the step from a tool to a machine is long, so is the step from one form or application of a machine to another which can produce such unusual results as we see in the specimen here illustrated.

Another thing worthy of notice in this blanket is that we have here a diagonal cloth. There is considerable difference between the Navaho loom which produces this web and the machine which produces a plain surface. The difference is shown in the essay to which I have referred. As one might suppose, the loom that produces the twilled or diagonal surface is the more elaborate, and its manipulation requires the greater skill and care. This specimen shows that it is the more elaborate loom which the inventor has seen fit to modify for the new form.

But the specimen is not only a blanket partly woven (Fig. 138); it is a loom, and a nearly complete loom, lacking only two movable parts (reed-fork and batten) which are common to all looms. Where is the secret, then? Why may not I, by merely examining the loom, tell how the change is made? I answer that I cannot do so without seeing the mechanism in operation. I might invent a plausible explanation and deliver it with an air of certainty which would impress you as the truth and yet be far astray. I should have to see the weaver at work, and even then might find it difficult to analyze the process. This I know from experience. There are writers who can reconstruct looms and processes by merely examining the webs or the impression left by these webs on plastic clay; but, unfortunately, this is beyond my ability.

I know of no fabric made by civilized man that is quite like this. I have asked experts in the dry-goods line if they knew of any and have been told that they did not. The modern golf-cloth, which is perfectly plain on one side and figured on the other, is somewhat similar in character, but not quite. I have no doubt that, were such an end desired, the American inventor would have little difficulty in producing a loom that would weave a two-faced fabric; but so far he has not done so. I merely mention these facts to show that the Navaho inventor has received no suggestion from either an European fabric or a civilized artisan.

There are baskets made by certain Indians of the Pacific Coast in which the figures woven on the outside are quite different from those woven directly behind them on the inside. They are two-faced fabrics, but the work is done altogether by hand and so offers little comparison with the Navaho blanket-work which is done by machinery. I have never seen any of these two-faced baskets among the Navahos, and am certain they do not know how to make them; but I cannot deny that they may have seen them and have obtained at least an art suggestion from them.

During my many years of association with the Navaho I have been able to buy a few of these double-faced blankets, but have never seen the weaver of them at work, hence can add nothing to Dr. Matthews's description.

While, as a rule, among the Navahos, modern blankets are woven by women, there have always been men who have engaged in the art, and in describing some of the blankets herein pictured it will be observed that the masculine pronoun has been used, designating a man weaver. Dr. Matthews used to assert in his day that the best weaver on the reservation was a man, but it would be a rash statement to make today in the light of the excellent specimens constantly coming from the expert fingers of women. As some of the designs herein show, they are works of genius, which two or more generations of careful fostering have called into being.

It is a remarkable fact that while the Navahos have a wonderful variety of chants or songs which they sing in their ceremonies, the Navaho women seldom, if ever, sing at their work. In this regard they are different from their sisters of the Pueblo race. These Indians have many songs which they sing while grinding the flour at the *metate*, when attending their flocks, or out in the cornfield. But the Navaho women do not sing, except ceremonially, and there is little in the high-pitched, almost screeching, forced, and strenuously vociferous singing of the dances, to lead one to attempt it while engaged in the thoughtful, quiet, and sedentary occupation of weaving.

Yet it should not be thought from this that the songless Navaho woman is sad and forlorn. On the contrary, I know of no race of women in the world that are so physically self-reliant, so vigorous, strong, robust, and able as they; and mentally within their scope they are equally alert. And though they do not talk much (especially in the presence of white strangers) they are by no means a subdued, timid, and "put-upon" sex. They are self-assertive in a high degree and are given a much higher place in the social economy than most women. When they marry they retain their own property, and all children born belong to the mother. A woman can divorce a man as well and as easily as a man a woman, and while there is always a gift of ten or twelve horses from the bridegroom or his family to the parents of the bride, this is, as Berard says, not "the price paid for the girl, but a gift sanctioned by tradition, as the Navaho do not sell their children."

It should be noted, too, that the women are often the owners of the flocks of sheep, and in such case that the husband will not dare to sell even a single animal without the consent of his wife. And when the blanket is woven it is the wife, as a rule, who sells it and receives the money or goods that she barters in exchange for it.

One of the most peculiar taboos known is that of a Navaho man against sight of his mother-in-law. After the marriage ceremony he must never see her, officially. It is regarded as bad taste for a man to show any familiarity to the mother of the maiden he wishes to marry, possibly to prevent any feeling of jealousy between mother and daughter, and this may be the explanation of the taboo. The mother, after marriage, becomes *do-zo-ini*—"she who may not be seen." On several occasions I have done my utmost, played every kind of a trick imaginable, and exercised my inventive faculties to the utmost to bring mother-in-law and son-in-law together, but always in vain.

This undoubtedly is a good taboo. While it does not prevent a mother from visiting her married daughter, the fact that the visit is made in the husband's absence conduces to domestic peace, in that her suggestions for the conducting of her daughter's household are not made in the husband's presence and cannot, therefore, be construed into criticisms of him or his methods.

It should not be implied from the existence of this taboo that there is any personal aversion existing on the part of the husband against his mother-in-law. He may have been the best of friends with her, and still entertain the same kind of feeling. It is merely a fixed Navaho custom to which he must adhere whether he likes it or not, as evil is bound to come to him and his family if he dares to violate so long established a taboo.

General U. S. Hollister thinks that,

as the Navaho is polygamous, it is possible that this singular custom originated in a theory of protection for the husband. A man with half a dozen wives would have as many mothers-in-law, and, according to beliefs prevalent among white people, would also have a pretty hard time if all of them exercised influence over his household. Therefore, such a custom may be a very grave necessity in Navaho land.

The Navahos have special names for all the different kinds of blankets and Berard thus classifies them:

One of the very earliest and commonest forms was the *nakhai bicliidi,* which, as its name implies, is the Mexican rug or pelt. This style was a pattern borrowed from the Mexicans. The center was woven in a belt of blue, flanked by narrow strips of black, the remainder of the blanket alternating in belts of white, black, and blue, interspersed at optional intervals. The design was a very plain one and made for the Mexican trade.

This type of blanket, even by experts, will generally be called an "old Chimayó," for it is the same style of blanket made up to twenty-five years ago by the Chimayó and other Mexican weavers of New and Old Mexico. I have several old specimens of the Chimayó weave which were purchased from their weavers, and one of them is pictured in Fig. 249. I also possess, however, a Navaho blanket of almost similar type, and though I have shown it to several experts not one has recognized it as a Navaho, but all alike have denominated it Chimayó. Personally I can see no difference, and had I not purchased this latter blanket from an old Navaho, who herself wove it, I should have deemed it a Chimayó. (See p. 169.)

Nago nodozi, horizontally striped, a blanket woven in alternating stripes of black and white, with an occasional narrow strip of red added in the center, and the end belts of black. Red tassels decorated each corner.

A similar blanket, and one much in demand by the Utes, was known as *alni naijini,* or the blanket with the black (streak) belt in center. While the body of the blanket was laced with strips of white and black, the center was mounted with a wide black belt, with additional red and blue strips woven in between. Similar belts were woven in equi-distant intervals between the center belt and the ends, though they were narrower than the center belt. The corners were decorated with black tassels, making a very attractive blanket.

The *hanolchade,* or carded blanket, which is now designated as the *chief's blanket,* is probably the chief of blankets, though it can hardly be said to have been worn by the chiefs exclusively. Here, too, the idea of alternating stripes of black and white is retained in the body of the blanket, though as a distinctive feature three zigzag diamonds made of small cubes of blue, red, and black yarn are set in the center of a wide belt of black. The interior of each diamond is a perfect white surmounted by a red cross in the center. The top and bottom of the blanket is finished in similar half diamonds. — [Berard.]

When this type is found in the old bayeta or native-wool, native-dyed blankets they are regarded as almost priceless by collectors. Fig. 7 is a good representation of one of these blankets in the Fred Harvey collection. Some twenty-five years ago I purchased a modern blanket of this type from one of John Lorenzo Hubbell's weavers at Ganado. It has been in continuous use since that time, mainly on the floor of Dr. W. L. Judson's art studio at Garvanza (Art Department of the University of Southern California, Los Angeles), and is a far more desirable blanket today than when it was first purchased. It has toned down somewhat and taken on some of the dignity of age, and while there can be no danger of mistaking it for a bayeta it is so good a blanket, so well dyed and woven, that its value will be enhanced as the years go by. Mr. Hubbell still has several of his most expert and careful weavers who prefer to weave nothing but this kind of blanket, and he keeps them busy all the time, as there is always a larger demand for this type (when well woven) than can be supplied.   Fred Harvey also has several of his best weavers at work on this especial type.

Bil, woman's dress, was originally woven in black and blue.   The black color, which is a fast jet black, was made from a mixture of sumac, pitch, and native ochre, called *tsekho je ki,* while the blue was indigo, *bediltlish,* obtained from the Mexicans. The top and bottom of the blanket alternated in four lines of blue and three of black, with the body of the blanket, or its center, *alni,* a plain jet black.   The whole was bordered, *banati,* and tasseled, *bijanil,* in blue.

With the introduction of bayeta, red was substituted for the blue in the body of the blanket, though the blue border and tassels were retained (*dotlish bequaolo,* the weave runs out in blue).   The solid black center, too, was retained, and gradually various designs of red and blue were woven with the black, *lizhin bildestlo,* at each side of the center belt. — [Berard.]

Specimens of this earlier type of woman's dress are very scarce.   Only a few are to be found in the museums.   The only one I was ever able to secure from the Navahos was one that was made and worn for years by the wife of the great warrior chief Manuelito (see Fig. 139).   As it was the last of its kind, and was very worn and much repaired, she had carefully washed it and put it away amongst her treasures, from whence she drew it forth to show to me.   When I expressed my desire to purchase it she refused to let me have it, on account of its dilapidated condition. But as later we became good friends she finally insisted upon my taking it as a gift.

During an Indian fiesta held in Los Angeles I loaned this rare dress, with a score or more of other of my blanket treasures, and when I came to make up an accounting of the "returns" this was missing, and I have never since been able to trace it, to my extreme regret.

Of the later type, showing the bayeta, I have a number of fine specimens.   The older types are almost worth their weight in gold.   Fig. 10 shows one of the earlier ones in the Hubbell collection.   They are now neither woven nor worn and one may wander over the reservation for a year and not find one in any condition.   Hence those that are now in collections are highly treasured.

Ba dotlizhi, or *bil baba dotlizhi,* blue borders.   This was a woman's shawl, and owes its name to the two borders of blue which flanked the center of black.   While the bil, or woman's dress, was of two pieces, which were sewed at the top and sides, leaving an opening for the head and arms only, the shawls were made in a single pattern and used after the manner of a shawl or wrap, much as the men use the blanket.

Bil lagai, white shawl, was so called from the alternating white and red color which was woven horizontally in narrow strips throughout.   The border and tassels were blue.   It was the only woman's garment in which white was used, and therefore was appropriately designated.   The woman's dress and the shawls are not used today. — [Berard.]

Fig. 140.

Navaho Shirt of Very Early Weave.

(Collection of J. L. Hubbell.)

Fig. 139.

Manuelito's Widow Wearing Squaw Dress in Old Navaho
Fashion.

These were undoubtedly suggested by the white cotton shawls or garments of the Hopi women, as pictured elsewhere. There are none of these made by the Navahos today, though the Hopis still make them of cotton, finely embroidering them.

Baghaitloni, slit-weave. No special design seems to have been assigned to this blanket, but any blanket might be woven so as to leave a slit about four fingers wide in the center of the blanket, which was afterwards laced with blue yarn. It is generally stated that this weave had to be occasionally resorted to in order to avoid overdoing weaving. Yet it has also been advanced that this blanket was worn by the men just as the women used the *bil,* or woman's dress, and that to avoid ridicule, the above version of overdoing the weaving has been attached to the "slit-weave." But this seems rather far-fetched.—[Berard.]

Another shirt which, like the preceding, was originally borrowed from the Pueblo, was still in vogue not so very many years ago. It was woven of wool yarn in the shape of a woman's dress, but provided with a longitudinal slit in the center for the purpose of passing it over the head. Fig. 140. It was entirely black in color and the only decoration was a tassel in each corner. When too filthy it would be washed and redyed, and from its varied use in wearing it either side out, or turning the front to rear at will, it was called *ae nahotali,* or *bil lizhin ae nahotali,* "the black dress shirt which may be worn either side up." As the surface of the shirt was very rough, *ditsid,* which it was impossible to obviate even by a loose weave, *ilzholigo istlo,* a fur collar made of wildcat skin, *noshdui bakhagi,* was added and tied with buckskin thongs. The front sides of the shirt were folded inwardly and overlapped by the rear, in which fashion it was held close to the body by means of a cord tied around the waist. Despite this precaution the wind had free access to it, wherefore the more humorous dubbed it *ae akidanalki,* or "the shirt which flaps in the wind." It was worn in addition to and over the ordinary wool or calico shirt, and some did not despise to store it away, *indasistsos,* for festive occasions. At present it has disappeared entirely.

CHAPTER XIV

The Designs on Modern Navaho Blankets

IN CHAPTER XII the studious reader will find sufficient material for thought as to the origin and symbolism of designs in those days of the art when creative impulses were strong, men and women were contented with simple, natural, and beautiful things, and the feverish desire for the mere accumulation of wealth had not demoralized the simpler primitive instincts.

But in speaking of the designs woven into the modern products of the Navahos' loom we are upon different ground. In the main we can agree with Father Berard when he says:

> As for designs in modern blankets which by some are interpreted as replete with religious symbolism, such interpretations merely attach an undue idealism and importance to the design which it does not contain. A glance at the names for some of the designs will bear out this point and show that these names designate figures found on paper, cloth or anything else. Then, too, it will be remembered that Navaho women are devout and faithful clients of their religion, possibly more so than the men, and would scarcely trifle with religious symbols, many of which may be viewed in effigy in the course of certain rites, and at certain seasons of the year only. This conservatism is presumably responsible for the taboo placed upon the following and similar designs: thunder, zigzag lightning, the water, ox, the water horse, a horned monster, a monster eagle, a monster fish, a tortoise, the turtle, the coyote, the dog, the frog, the horned toad, the bull or blow snake, the track snake and snakes in general, in a word, anything harmful.
>
> On the other hand, designs of the rainbow, big stars, sheet lightning, the arrow, evening twilight, celestial blue, darkness, or of the sacred mountains, or anything of a beneficial character, may be designed with impunity.

It cannot be too often affirmed or too clearly understood that, while the exigencies of modern commercialism have led to the making of blankets of special designs *to order,* the natural impulse of the Navaho weaver is never to copy and never to repeat herself in her designs. The result is a wealth of designs, a bewilderment of figures, and combinations of figures that, could they be all massed together in one great exhibit, would be regarded as one of the wonders of the world. Hence, had I photographed a thousand blankets for reproduction in the pages of this book, they would have served but as suggestions to many other thousands that might, with equal reason and acceptability, have been chosen for that purpose.

Unless she intends to weave a design from one of the traders' diagrams, the Navaho woman begins her work without any outward representation, either upon paper, buckskin, or in the sand, of what she intends to produce. The plan may be carefully mapped out in her own busy brain—main figures, their sizes, with all the connecting details. But, as I shall show later, this is not always the case.

It will be noted by the careful observer that there are no circles, arches, or round corners in Navaho weaving. The reason for this may be traced to the development of the art from basketry, where the splints are less flexible and pliable and all the corners must be sharp-pointed, and the lines straight, oblique, zigzag, serrated, etc.

There are practically no set or tribal designs—that is, blankets that are all woven alike. The figures, mainly geometrical, are common to all, but the method of their introduction into individual blankets is the concern of the weaver alone, unless she be weaving a chosen design at the request of the trader.

There are many weavers, however, that no amount of pressure or persuasion can induce to weave any other than a blanket of her own designing, and some of these will never duplicate a design. Mr. Hubbell has several such weavers, and so has Fred Harvey. These are women of remarkable ability; the geniuses of their tribe, who rank as artists of the first class. Such an one is Elle, of Ganado, who has been steadily engaged at weaving by Fred Harvey for over a dozen years. Scores of thousands have seen her, seated at the loom, in the Fred Harvey Indian rooms at Albuquerque, New Mexico, at various fairs, and in the Land Shows and other exhibits at Chicago, etc. (See Fig. 141.) Her little daughter, when but five years old, began to weave, and now, though still a mere child, executes the most striking designs of her own creation. Here is one of the wonderful evidences of inheritance of creative ability and artistic skill. Before she could possibly know anything of her remarkable power, she was an artist in her own right. Another child, Tuli, and her partially woven blanket are represented in Fig. 142. This is another child wonder in the weaving world, found by Fred Harvey, and now regularly engaged at his blanket rooms at Albuquerque, New Mexico.

Of this same type of weaver is Bileen Alpi Bizhaahd, discovered by Mr. J. B. Moore, of Crystal, New Mexico, and now in the regular employ of his successors, the J. A. Molohon Company. She has never been known to copy the design of another weaver, and though often delighted beyond measure at the charm and beauty of some design she has just made, she positively refuses to weave a second blanket from the same pattern. Hence, if it is to be duplicated, some other weaver must be found who is more complaisant. Such idiosyncrasies as this reveal that the "artistic temperament" is to be found among the aborigines as well as in the most "advanced" civilization.

There is a great deal of human nature displayed in the diversity of designs found in Navaho blankets, and also in their similarities. Human nature, as is tritely said, is very much the same whether found in civilized, uncivilized, black, white, bond, free, or in dogs. In the conventional, ordinary, commonplace designs one finds the timid, the conservative, the satisfied, the mentally contented, the orthodox. Why change these patterns? They have been good enough in the past; why try to alter or improve them?

But there are those who are not satisfied. Their minds are mentally alert for the new, the original. They seek new paths. They disregard the conventional bounds. Life is life, and life is to be known only in the living, and *every* avenue that opens is a new avenue of experience, knowledge, and possible improvement. So the iconoclastic designer makes "something different." She prefers living figures to geometric designs; she even dares to reproduce the *Yei* of the sacred sand-paintings, as I shall show in a chapter devoted to that feature of the art; and of late years there have developed the unbelieving, the irreligious, the scoffer, the atheist, who have dared to violate the taboos and picture everything their vagrant fancy dictates.

Occasionally a weaver thinks out a design and proceeds to incorporate it into a woven blanket. When completed it is so different from what she expected, or conveys to her mind some strange or peculiar impression, or arouses some superstitious fear, that she either destroys it or gets rid of it as speedily as possible. Of this character is the zigzag-design blanket shown in Fig. 143. This was given, many years ago, to Mr. Hamilton Noel, whose trading post is at *Tees-nas-paz,* or, as it is sometimes spelt, *Teas-nos-pos,* Arizona, which is Navaho for "the circle of cottonwoods." This blanket was woven by a man, and while it was still on the loom, after he had completed it, there came a day when the heavens were clouded and a severe lightning and thunder-storm arose. Suddenly the sun shone through the clouds and lit up the blanket in such a fashion that the zigzag design of the lightning seemed actually to live. This so scared the superstitious weaver that he brought it to Mr. Noel, with the request that he take and hide it, or much evil might come to them both. The trader gladly accepted the responsibility and always managed to secrete the dangerous blanket when its weaver came around, but when I desired to purchase it I found that no offer I was able to make could shake, in the slightest, Mr. Noel's determination not to part with it. The remarkable thing is that, even to the non-superstitious, there is a peculiar flash of the pattern, when it is seen under certain conditions of light and

Fig. 141.
Elle, of Ganado, Ariz., One of the Best of Living Weavers.

Fig. 142.
Tuli, the Child Weaver.

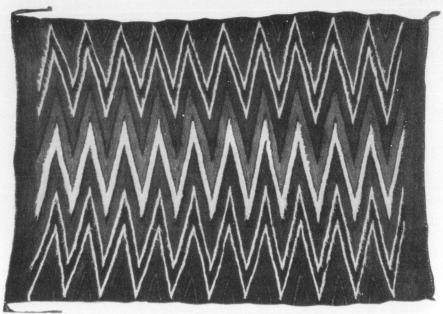

Fig. 144.
Lightning Design Blanket.
(Author's Collection.)

Fig. 143.
Lightning Design Blanket.
(Collection of Hamilton Noel.)

shade that give one an uncomfortable sensation. The reproduction fails
to give any suggestion of this, as the color is lacking. The colors are red,
green, and white. Apparently there are two zigzags of white running
through the center, from top to bottom, but in reality there is a break in
the white, and green is substituted. But at these substituted points the
white is introduced on the sides, and thus, mayhap, the peculiar effect may
be accounted for, in that the white, representing the more brilliant lightning, darts to right and left here, and is then caught lower down and
brought back into line with the point from which it started. Anyhow, the
effect is peculiar and most startling.

This zigzag design is by no means uncommon. Indeed, it is the
motif of many thousands of blankets, some simple as in Figs. 144 and
145, and in others, like Fig. 195, in which the zigzags are converted into
diamonds.

Figs. 144 and 145 are the blankets referred to on page 108 as
demonstrating the individuality of the weaver's method, in that the weft
threads are not taken directly across the face of the warp, but obliquely
to conform to the slope of the design. In Fig. 144 this is done in a
fairly successful fashion, interfering only a little with the general "square-
ness" of the blanket, but in Fig. 145 the difficulty of mastering this
"oblique stitch" is apparent, for it clearly got beyond the control of the
weaver, so that the blanket is much wider at one end than the other.

One of the most imaginative weavers of the tribe lives near Canyon
Gallegos, New Mexico. She is especially inventive in her designs. Were
this woman of a civilized race she would become another Rosa Bonheur,
for her love of animals is such that she constantly depicts them in her
blankets, and always with considerable artistic skill. Her work is eagerly
sought for, and no sooner is one of her blankets on the loom than,
regardless of what the pattern is to be, there are several purchasers ready
to buy it when completed.

With some weavers, even as with some authors of "best-sellers,"
this promptness of sale, or eagerness of purchasers, leads to a deterioration of the work, but with this weaver it seems to have had the opposite
and beneficially stimulating effect. The more her blankets are desired
the more desirable she determines to make them. In other words, she is
a true artist and finds great delight in her weaving. The result is her
latest blankets are her best. She never begins to weave until a design
has taken full possession of her and demands outward expression, and
then she sets up her loom and goes to work with an almost feverish eagerness, as anxious to see in objective form what her brain has conceived as
is a mother to see her new-born child.

One of her blankets is that pictured in Fig. 200 and described in

Chapter XVII, but, unfortunately, I am unable to show any of her "animal designs," for the blankets were sold to strangers, and no photographs were made of them.

That weavers *are* influenced in their choice of design by their environment I have illustrated a score or more of times, but never more forcefully than by the weaver from whom I purchased the fantastic blanket pictured in colors in Fig. 146.*

This weaver's summer *hogan* was not far from a siding on the main line of the Santa Fé Railway, some fifty miles west of Gallup, New Mexico, over the state line in Arizona. She was a skilful weaver, and I had bought several of her blankets at different times, all of them containing the usual type of design. On this occasion, however, she brought forth something of a different character. I was interested enough to seek to penetrate fully into the mystery of the change, and as I stayed at the *hogan* for several days, and she and her husband were most friendly and chatty, I succeeded in gathering the following, which, pieced together, is the story of how she came to depart so far from the usual.

One day after she had set up her loom, and while she was thinking over several designs that had suggested themselves, she was aroused from her thought by the arrival of a train going west. That immediately suggested to her that she attempt to reproduce the engine and train of cars in her blanket. The sun was glistening on the rails, and this effect she reproduced by alternations of white and blue. The wheels are diamond-shaped lozenges, while the cow-catcher, headlight and tender, the cab with its two windows, the smokestack belching smoke, and the steam-chest with its escaping white steam are all well represented. The train was of passenger coaches, and there was room on her loom for only two cars, and these of rather compressed dimensions. To denote that they were passenger cars she introduced two human figures in each. While this work was progressing certain birds appeared on the scene, together with two women, one walking east and one west. A "light" engine also came traveling east, and as the sun happened to be shining upon it as it passed it had a bright, glistening appearance, so she represented it by weaving it in white, while the windows of the cab are picked out in dark blue. A large and small rain-cloud also appeared on the horizon and these are duly represented.

Having thus begun with the railway, she determined to continue, and when she was ready for the next portion of the design a cattle-train came along, which she duly incorporated in the next horizontal panel. Her cattle are of a species known only to the "rarebit fiend." They are of a wilder type than even Gelett Burgess's "purple cow." After getting ready for the next panel and no train appearing, she pictured six flying

* In color section.

Fig. 145.
Lightning Design Blanket.
(Author's Collection.)

birds alighting on the track and five walking female figures. A rain-cloud is at each end of the group of walkers. This panel is followed by one showing two engines together, going west, with flying birds and rain-clouds above them.

The next panel shows a sleeping-car, and the weaver's curiosity having been aroused since her endeavor to picture these strange objects of the white man's travel, she had mustered up courage enough to go to Gallup and ask to be allowed to enter a sleeping-car after the berths were made up in order that she might understand how men and women could sleep on a railroad train. After this personal observation she was able to produce the double-deck effect of the upper and lower berths, though she laughed heartily when I pointed out that people lie down when they sleep, even though it be in a railroad berth. This she had not got clearly through her mind, for to sleep in such a confined space as that tiny berth seemed to her almost impossible, hence she had represented, to the best of her ability, these strange white people sitting up in the tiny cubby-holes where a malign fate compelled them to remain over night while they were hurled across the great, free, open land. Pointing to the two cars above I asked why she had placed these above the sleeping-car. Her reply was to the effect that it was not enough to have only one car, but that when she began to put on the other cars it was day-time and the people were not sleeping, hence she had to represent them as up and moving about.

The result of her personal observation is also manifested in the representation of the side doors and ventilators in the car — things she had not known before, having observed the cars only from a distance. The remainder of this panel is made up of fleecy clouds, flying birds, and rain clouds, while the last panel is her very effective representation of a poultry train going west.

In his office at Ganado, Arizona, John Lorenzo Hubbell has scores of blanket designs, painted in oil, hung upon the walls, and they present a most surprising and wonderful combination. These are designs that have been found to be pleasing to purchasers, and when a special order for a blanket of a certain design comes in, the weaver is shown the picture of the one desired. She studies it a while, takes the wool provided, or herself prepares it, and then, with such slight variations as she is sure to introduce, goes ahead and makes her blanket.

In blanketry, as well as in basketry, there are fantastic and degraded designs, which clearly denote mental vacuity on the part of the weaver, or a vain and foolish desire to copy something, or to do what the trader desires, regardless of its appearance. Foolish lettering, imitations of the American eagle, and subjects entirely foreign to the native weaver's natural tastes are found. The intelligent purchaser and the collector will alike frown upon these specimens of degradation of the art, and do all that can be done to discourage their perpetuation.

The following is the list of the principal designs, with the Navaho names, given by Berard:

Fig. 147 — *Dakha nahalin* (card-like), a square.

Fig. 148 — *Beeditli nahalin* (slingshot-like), a diamond, also called *so tso,* big star.

Fig. 149 — *Beeditlihi* (slingshot), an elongated diamond.

Fig. 150 — *Tsin alnaozid* (sticks crossing each other), Roman cross.

Fig. 151 — *So* (star), St. Andrew's cross.

Fig. 152 — *Tqago deza* (three points), a triangle.

Fig. 153 — *So deshzha* (pointed star), four lines crossed so as to form a figure with eight points, or a St. Andrew's cross drawn through a Roman cross. If made somewhat larger than ordinarily, it is also called *so tso deshzha,* big pointy star.

Fig. 154 — *Tsiyel nahalin* (like a queue), two triangles touching each other with their apices.

Fig. 155 — *Tqago deza be digo desa* (four points with three points), four triangles touching with apices, a Maltese cross.

Fig. 156 — *Nahokhos,* said of large, long objects in horizontal rotation, a swastica cross.

Fig. 157 — *Dakha nahalingo nahokhos binisaa* (a *nahokhos* within a card-like figure), a swastica surrounded by a square.

Fig. 158 — *Dakha nahalinigi bealqiaza* (card-like figures within each other), square inside of another square.

Fig. 159 — *Beeditli nahalinigi bealqiaza* (slingshot-like figures within each other), diamond within diamond.

Fig. 160 — *Noltlizh,* a zigzag line.

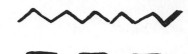

Fig. 161 — *Be'ndastlago noltlizh* (cornered zigzag), irregular zigzag.

Fig. 162 — *Danaazkhago noltlizh* (a row of empty places in zigzag order), a line resembling the crown of a battlement.

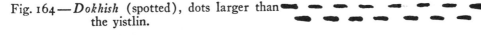

Fig. 163 — *Yistlin* (freckled), small dots.

Fig. 164 — *Dokhish* (spotted), dots larger than the yistlin.

Fig. 165 — *Dadestso,* spots somewhat longer than dokhish.

Fig. 166 — *Beeditli baba dolaghas* (slingshot with serrated edge), diamond with serrated edge.

Fig. 167 — *Dolaghas,* a serrated line; *besdolaghas* (ancient knife of chipped flint).

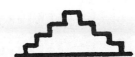

Fig. 168 — *Kos yishchin* (cloud image), a terraced figure on side of blanket.

Fig. 169 — *Hokha* (a large empty place or receptacle), a large terrace-edged diamond, usually in the center of a blanket.

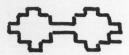

Fig. 170 — *Hokha bealkheaznil,* two *hokha* following each other.

Fig. 171 — *Honakha,* a *hokha* with a half *hokha* on either end.

Fig. 172 — *Noltlizh alniaznil,* a figure with zigzag edge in the center.

Fig. 173 — *Dolaghas bealkheaznil,* two figures with serrated edges following each other.

Fig. 174 — *Alkhe ndazha* (pointed ones following each other), a row of small figures with points, for instance V-shaped figures not too near together.

Fig. 175 — *Anikhe* (tracks), a double row of *alkhe ndazha.*

Fig. 176 — *Aqidelnago ndazha* (sticking in opposite direction), same as *anikhe* only that the figures of one row are reversed.

Fig. 177 — *Alkidot'ezh* (touching each other), a row of small figures, one touching the other, for instance a row of small flat-based triangles, set on edge, so that the apex of the one touches the preceding one at the center of the base.

Fig. 178 — *Alkheyit'ezh* (following and touching each other), a row of small
figures connected by short lines.

Fig. 179 — *Alkheyit'ezh dakha nahalingo,* a
row of small squares connected
by lines between them.

Fig. 180 — *Delzha,* battlement-like eleva-
tions, especially along the
border.

Fig. 181 — If another color is woven next to
delzha, and the intervening
spaces are left a distinct color,
they are called *inil,* enclosed,
encased.

Fig. 182 — *Alqihadot'ezh* (touching, following
within each other), said of a
succession of small figures,
usually along the border, of
such a form that the space between them is a reverted reproduction of same.

Fig. 183 — *So aqadenil* (two stars together), two large
diamonds in center of blanket.

Fig. 184 — *Hoshdudi,* the name of the whip-poor-will,
strewn with spots.

Fig. 185 — *Alni azi* (standing in the middle), said of
any central figure of extraordinary shape.

Fig. 186 — *Aqidinlnago da-
na'azkha* (spaces
opposite), a suc-
cession of small figures whose intervening
spaces show the same figure inverted or
opposite.

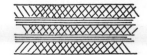

Fig. 187 — *Aqedzeba* means a gray stripe or border all
around. This is used with other colors:
dzegai, white; *jichi,* red; *dzetso,* yellow;
jijin, black; *jidaetlizh,* blue.

CHAPTER XV

Navaho and Pueblo Belts, Garters, and Hair Bands

ALL visitors to the Navaho reservation and to the homes of the various Pueblo Indians of Arizona and New Mexico, especially in early days (twenty or more years ago), were astonished and delighted at the beautifully designed and woven belts worn by the women around their waists, and the garters and head bands worn by the men.

Dr. Washington Matthews thus describes the methods followed in weaving these:

Their way of weaving long ribbon-like articles, such as sashes or belts, gárters, and hair-bands, which we will next consider, presents many interesting variations from the method pursued in making blankets. To form a sash the weaver proceeds as follows: She drives into the ground four sticks and on them she winds her warp as a continuous string (however, as the warp usually consists of threads of three

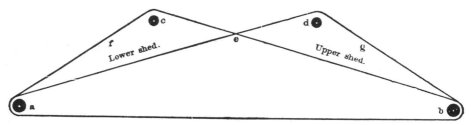

FIG. 188—Diagram showing formation of warp of sash

different colors, it is not always *one* continuous string), from below upwards in such a way as to secure two sheds, as shown in the diagram, Fig. 188.

Every turn of the warp passes over the sticks *a* and *b;* but it is alternate turns that pass over *c* and *d.* When the warp is laid she ties a string around the intersection of the sheds at *e,* so as to keep the sheds separate while she is mounting the warp on the beams. She then places the upper beam of the loom in the place of the stick *b* and the lower beam in the place of the stick *a.* Sometimes the upper and lower beams are secured to the two rails forming a frame such as the warp of a blanket is wound on, but more commonly the loom is arranged as follows: The upper beam is secured to a rafter, post or tree, while to the lower beam is attached a loop of rope that passes under the thighs of the weaver, and the warp is rendered tense by her weight. Next, the upper shed is supplied with a shed-rod and the lower shed with a set of healds. Then a stick is inserted at *f;* this is simply a round stick, about which one loop of each thread of the warp is thrown. (Although the warp may consist of only one thread, I must now speak of each turn as a separate thread.) Its use is to keep the different threads in place and prevent them from crossing and straggling; for it must be remembered that the warp in this case is not secured at two points between three stranded cords, as is the blanket warp.

When this is all ready the insertion of the weft begins. The reed-fork is rarely needed and the batten used is much shorter than that employed in making blankets. Fig. 189 represents a section of a belt. It will be seen that the center is ornamented with peculiar raised figures; these are made by inserting a slender stick into the warp, so as to hold up certain of the threads while the weft is passed twice or oftener underneath them. It is practically a variety of damask or two-ply weaving; the figures on the opposite side of the belt being different. There is a limited variety of these figures. I think I have seen about a dozen different kinds. The experienced weaver is so well acquainted with the "count" or arrangements of the raised threads appropriate to each pattern that she goes on inserting and withdrawing the slender stick referred to without a moment's hesitation, making the web at the rate of ten or twelve

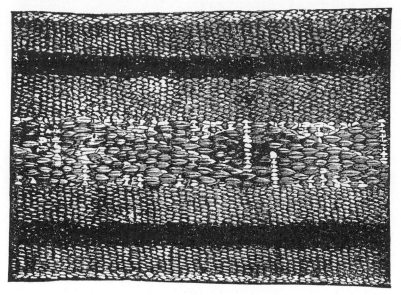

FIG. 189—Section of Navaho belt

inches an hour. When the web has grown to the point at which she cannot weave it further without bringing the unfilled warp nearer to her, she is not obliged to resort to the clumsy method used with blankets. She merely seizes the anterior layer of the warp and pulls it down towards her; for the warp is not attached to the beams, but is movable on them; in other words, while still on the loom the belt is endless. When all the warp has been filled except about one foot, the weaving is completed; for then the unfilled warp is cut in the center and becomes the terminal fringes of the now finished belt.

The only marked difference that I have observed between the mechanical appliances of the Navaho weaver and those of her Pueblo neighbor is to be seen in the belt loom. The Zuni woman lays out her warp, not as a continuous thread around two beams, but as several disunited threads. She attaches one end of these to a fixed object, usually a rafter in her dwelling, and the other to the belt she wears around her body. She has a set of wooden healds by which she actuates the alternate threads of the warp. Instead of using the slender stick of the Navahos to elevate the threads of the warp in forming her figures, she lifts these threads with her fingers.

This is an easy matter with her style of loom; but it would be a very difficult task with that of the Navahos. The wooden healds are shown in Fig. 190. The Zuni women weave all their long, narrow webs according to the same system; but Mr. Bandelier has informed me that the Indians of the Pueblo of Cochiti make the narrow garters and hair-bands after the manner of the Zunis, and the broad belts after the manner of the Navahos.

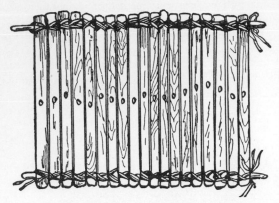

FIG. 190—Wooden heald of the Zunis

It will be interesting to compare the photographs of Navaho weavers and Fig. 191. In the latter a girl of ancient Mexico is weaving a web of some description. The former are from photographs taken from life; the other I have copied from Taylor's *Anthropology* (p. 248); but it appears earlier in the copy of *Codex Vaticana* in Lord Kingsborough's *Antiquities of Mexico*. The way in which the warp is held down and made tense, by a rope or band secured to the lower beam and sat upon by the weaver, is the same in both cases. And it seems that the artist who drew the original rude sketch sought to represent the girl, not as working "the cross-thread of the woof in and out on a stick," but as manipulating the reed-fork with one hand and grasping the heald-rod and shed-rod in the other.

Mr. A. M. Stephen, a careful observer, who lived in close contact with both Navaho and Hopis some forty years ago, thus wrote (in an unpublished manuscript) of Navaho belts, etc.:

Aside from the products of the vertical loom, smaller fabrics are woven by different methods, as in the making of the girdle. A woman prepares to make one of these by spinning the warp on her primitive spindle to the requisite fineness, not thicker than knitting cotton, and often as small as sewing thread. She then selects a level place and drives two stout pegs in the ground, from four to six inches apart, and two others parallel to these, at a distance of from eight to twelve feet, according to the width and length proposed for the girdle. Across the ends of each pair of pegs, which project not higher than a foot above the ground, a slender stick is fastened, and around these two sticks, the warp, of different colors,

FIG. 191—Girl weaving (from an Aztec picture)

is wound in the desired order and tightly stretched. A common arrangement in a girdle, say seven fingers wide, is to wind threads of dark blue so as to form a border on each side of one finger-width; next adjoining these, on the inside, another finger-width of light green, leaving three finger-widths between, which is then stretched with scarlet, and in the center, where the design is to be wrought, an additional finger-width of black thread is stretched over the scarlet. A black weft, wound upon a short twig, is then looped upon the outside warp-thread and carried across, above and below each alternate warp, then looped upon the outside thread on the opposite border. This is continued along the entire length of the girdle, and as the upper and under warp-threads are brought very compactly together, the weft is entirely concealed, and the process is really an inversion of ordinary weaving, the warp forming the surface instead of the weft.

A favorite design in the center of the girdle is a zigzag band extending its whole length, with a conventional figure of a bird, with outspread wings within each angle; this is produced on the upper or obverse side, by passing the weft under two or more threads of scarlet at once, leaving a single black thread below; the design is thus thrown in scarlet relief with black interstices, upon the obverse or outside of the girdle as worn, and a fringe of the warp, about six inches long is left at each end. The women alone wear girdles, and only the men wear garters to support their buckskin leggins. These garters are made by a method slightly modified from the above, but are, of course, much smaller, although woven with equal nicety, and are usually about two inches wide and four feet long.

Cinches or saddle girths are also made in decorated patterns, but instead of being woven between pegs, the warp is passed directly between the large iron rings or buckles at each end. After the warp has been thus arranged, one of the rings is fastened to the branch of a tree, or other convenient support, and the weaver attaches the other ring to her waist girdle, seating herself on the ground in such a position as to give the required tension to the warp, and the process she follows is more of close, neat braiding than weaving. These cinches are from four to six inches wide, and from two feet to thirty inches long.

Dr. R. W. Shufeldt, who thirty years ago spent many years on the reservation, thus describes and pictures the Navaho belt weaver at work. He says:

Among the Navahos one will see a great many blankets made before an opportunity will be presented for him to observe the labors of a belt-weaver. The reason for this is, that blankets are a universal necessity with them, while the belt is principally used as a supplementary adornment in dress. As my time for leaving the country drew near I almost despaired of getting a good photograph of the belt-weaver and the study of the loom she used. But a month before my departure an Indian came into my study one morning, beaming all over with the welcome information that one of the best weavers in the tribe had started the making of a belt in front of one of their huts. These Indians were then building close to the confines of the garrison.

The first day I studied her methods of procedure and the second day I succeeded in obtaining several excellent pictures of this weaver at work. My best result is here offered as an illustration, and it well shows the entire scene. The woman has rigged up her loom in front of her house; she is busily employed in her weaving and her child sits beside her. (Fig. 192.)

* * * * * * * * *

The weaver had constructed the subvertical, outside part of the frame of her loom of two trunks of small pine trees, averaging a little over three inches in diameter, and from which the bark had not been removed. Parallel to each other, and placed about a yard apart, these she had placed in a slanting position against the front of her

By courtesy of the National Museum, Smithsonian Institution.

FIG. 192—The Navaho belt weaver at work

house outside. The upper ends were strapped to the house, and the lower ends slightly planted in the earth, being held more secure there by a few stones. Next she had firmly tied on cross pieces, a double one a few inches from the top, and a single one at about a foot above the ground. Over these cross pieces the warp passes, and in such a manner as to produce a double shed only. Then a smooth short rod is made to take up the alternate threads of the warp above the intersection or in the upper shed. This is easily seen in the engraving. Below the intersection of the threads of the warp the weaver serves the lower shed with a set of healds, which are usually composed of yarn, have their own rod, and as in the case of the rod above the intersection, include alternate threads of the warp. When drawn towards the weaver the healds serve the purpose of opening the lower shed, and still another short rod is used to keep the threads in place, which is also well seen in the figure, where the woman has her hands resting upon the batten, a smooth, flat, and rather narrow piece of hard wood. This is the last and yet one of the most important adjuncts composing this primitive loom, and is used by the weaver in turning it horizontally to open the shed to admit the passage of the weft, and afterwards to pound the latter down firmly into its place as the weaving proceeds.

These belt-looms as in use among the Navahos are not always exactly alike in their construction; for we find in some of them that the side posts of the frame are omitted, and the upper cross piece is fastened to a tree, and the lower one served with a loop of rope through which the weaver passes her limbs and then sits down upon, thus holding the warp of her belt firm and tense by her own weight as she sits cross-legged afterwards at her work. Other modifications of this simple loom are also to be seen in the contrivances in use among the Zunians and other Pueblo tribes, and there are a number of departures from the main details of the weaving (also to be noted), as we have described them above.

CHAPTER XVI

The Outline Blanket

BY AN "outline blanket" is meant one the designs of which are set forth in lines of another color, as illustrated in the color plate of Fig. 195. This outlining of the design produces a most charming and striking effect, inasmuch as it sets out the design with greater clearness. Just as a frame separates a painting from its surroundings and determines its *individualness,* so does an outline, if the colors are harmonious, show forth the beauty and striking character of the design.

There are those who deem the outline blanket a recent, or modern, innovation in Navaho weaving. Such is not the case. Many of the older and better blankets are in outline, and it is interesting to discover that long before the Navahos made blankets they were in the habit of using the outline in their sacred dry- or sand-paintings. A full account of these is given in Chapter XII. It should be observed, however, that while the use of the outline is very common in the sand-paintings it is by no means universal. I have examined and carefully studied many of these paintings, both in the medicine *hogans* and in the pictures drawn by the Navaho shamans, and in some they appear on every figure, in others they are absent, while in some paintings the outlines are placed around some figures, and omitted from others.

From these facts, therefore, it is easy to infer from whence the keen-witted and observant Navaho weaver gained the idea of her outline blanket. Her artistic perception showed her the great improvement and enhancement of beauty the added outlines would afford, and she sought and found the most suitable and harmonious combinations of color for the purpose. Only the real artist, however, would do this. The merely commercial weaver, or the inartistic, could see no reason why she should go to the added labor of outlining her design. Hence it is a general rule that can be relied upon almost to a certainty that an outline blanket is well woven. A weaver whose artistic perceptions demand of her the increased labor of adding the outline would naturally be offended with poor weaving.

One who did much to further the development of the art was Mrs. Peabody, an eastern lady who took so great an interest in the Navahos that she went and lived on the reservation for a while. At this time, some twenty-five years ago, she found the outline work almost abandoned. But

136

Fig. 194.

A Fine Germantown Blanket with Good
Outlines.

(Vroman Collection.)

Fig. 193.

A Fine Germantown Blanket with Delicate
Outlines.

(Author's Collection.)

her keen eye happening to find a few choice specimens of this type she began, with foresight and inspiration, to urge upon the better weavers, with whom she had influence, that they reintroduce the outline. Encouraged by her intelligent appreciation and the more material fact that they were able to obtain a larger price for outlined blankets, a keen rivalry sprang up between the best weavers of the district in which she worked, and today it is from this portion of the reservation that the major part of the best "outlines" come.

Naturally the traders of other sections desired to reap the advantage of these blankets of higher value and they began to urge upon their weavers of the better class the introduction of the outline. To some extent they succeeded; hence, now and again, an excellent and choice outline blanket will come from a region where one scarce expected it.

Fig. 193, described on page 157, is of a fine Germantown blanket in which there is considerable outline work of delicate and artistic skill. Even in the illustration, which gives none of the striking color effects, and where, indeed, the effect of the design on the sides is almost lost, the rare delicacy of the white pencillings which outline the zigzags of color is clearly evidenced.

Fig. 194 is of an exquisitely designed Germantown blanket in the Vroman collection, in which the outline is used in the inside of the oblique, or St. Andrew's Cross, as well as on two sides of each of the four-sided figures which terminate each leg of the cross. This emphasizing of the color of the design within is a powerful device, with wonderful capabilities in the hands of a skilful and artistic weaver.

Fig. 195 shows the white outline zigzag used to set off a heavier line of color.*

Fig. 196 is of a blanket in the Fred Harvey collection of modern weave, in which a delicate outline of red around the inner side of the border and the outer edge of the two diamond designs of the center give it a distinction and artistic attractiveness that materially enhance its value. The body of the blanket is in silver gray, which is naturally varied in shade.

A good modern specimen of the outline type of blanket is illustrated in Fig. 197. This was taken up from the floor of my living-room, where it has been in constant daily use for between seventeen and eighteen years. In color it is as rich and striking as the day I purchased it on the Little Colorado River, some fifty miles or so from the Santa Fé Railway at Canyon Diablo. The design is almost entirely of zigzags, arranged in diamond patterns with four other figures, two at each end. The basis of the blanket is red and orange. The two center diamonds contain centers in orange, outlined in lemon yellow. Each of these two large diamonds is

_____
* In color section.

bordered with black, and the black border, on each side, is outlined in white. Half diamonds treated in the same fashion throughout appear on each side of the blanket. On each side of the center diamonds are lemon yellow centers, outlined in purple, followed with a red border, outlined in rich green. The two half diamonds at each end are in red, bordered with violet, outlined on the outer side with a lighter and a darker shade of the same color, and on the inner side with black. The four figures (two at each end) are in black and green, outlined in yellow.

Fig. 198 is a fairly representative outline blanket, of single saddle size, made of Germantown yarn, in my own collection. Here the center diamond is twice outlined in serrated lines, and the four corner diamonds are also outlined, thus bringing out the colors in striking relief.

There is great scope afforded for artistic and creative ability even in so simple a matter as these outlines, and this not merely in the fineness or coarseness of the weave. The outline may show all the difference between the one slight touch of color change, that gives artistic attractiveness, and the heavy *overtouch* which is an impertinence and intrusion. It is not good for a careless weaver to attempt the outline.

Fig. 196.
A Fine Modern Blanket of the Best Type.
(Fred Harvey Collection.)   [Page 137]

Fig. 198.

Single Saddle Blanket with Outlines.

Fig. 197.

Good Representative Specimen of Outline Blanket.

(Author's Collection.)

CHAPTER XVII

Kachina or Yei Blankets

IN THE Hopi and Zuni pantheons there are certain divinities of greater or lesser power and importance, called *Kachinas*. These are often represented upon the baskets of the Hopi, as in Fig. 199, and these are called *Kachina* baskets. Corresponding somewhat to these Pueblo divinities are the Navaho *Yei,* representations of which are common in the sand-paintings. To reproduce these, however, in any unauthorized or secular fashion has always been deemed impossible by the reverent and devout Navaho. Even to see a photograph of a sand-painting, if it contained a representation of the *Yei,* gave a shock to most Navahos, and while the medicine-men chanters never resented Dr. Matthews's making pictures of the paintings, and, indeed, as he says, often came to ask to look at them when instructing younger members as their assistants, this may be regarded as the familiarity of the professional rather than the normal attitude of the ordinary lay member of the tribe.

Possibly strict truth demands that a little explanation be made of the feeling of the Navahos about reproducing pictorial representations of the *Yei.* While in many there is no doubt that reverence and devout feeling enter into this disinclination to reproduce the sacred *Yei,* to others, especially of the men, fear and superstition have a large place. One may have both fear and superstitition and yet be reverent and devout, but, too often, alas, not only with Navahos but also with whites, there is such a thing as being possessed by the spirit of the former and not of the latter. It is when fear and superstition reign supreme, unsanctified, unmodified by reverence and devotion, that fanaticism, bigotry, and cruelty control.

With these thoughts in view it can well be understood with what shocked surprise, thrilled horror, and fierce condemnation the Navahos learned that a blanket, clearly of Navaho origin, was on exhibition at a certain trader's store into which was woven as the design the figure of one of the yei. It is almost impossible for a white man to comprehend the vast sensation this caused. Councils were held over the reservation to discuss the matter, and the trader was finally commanded to remove the blanket containing the offending emblems from the wall of his office. He refused, and for a time his life was deemed in jeopardy. But he was a fearless and obstinate man, and resisted all the pressure brought to bear upon him, though among themselves the Navahos still argued and discussed the sacrilege, and a shooting-scrape in which one man lost his life was the outcome.

For a long time it was not known who the weaver of this blanket was, but it eventually became known. She is one of the inventive geniuses in design, whose taste invariably goes to figures. Horses, sheep, cattle, men, women, etc., she loves to picture as she weaves, and her skill in manipulating the yarn is as great as her designing ability. She it was who, having lost the superstitious fear that oppresses most Navahos, men or women, as to the evil power of the *Yei,* determined to make the blanket, incorporating their sacred figures as her design. The blanket was seen by a collector and sold to him for several hundred dollars. For some time the weaver refused to make another, but finally produced one of others of the gods, and later still another. There are only some six or seven of these *Yei* blankets known to exist. Two of them are now in the possession of Mr. Richard T. F. Simpson, Indian trader at Canyon Gallegos, near Farmington, New Mexico, one of which is reproduced in Fig. 200,* and another is owned by Mr. William MacGinnies, of Boulder, Colorado.

Fig. 201 is a half-tone reproduction of one of the earlier of this woman's *Yei* blankets. This is clearly an attempt to produce in weaving one of the figures from one of the sand-paintings used in *The Night Chant.* The figure is that of a *Yebaad,* or female divinity, for the Navahos provide all the male gods of their pantheon with wives. This may account for the fact that Navaho women are equally influential in the affairs of the tribe as the men. Or it may be the other way, viz., that because Navaho women are powerful and influential in tribal matters they therefore occupy an important place in the Navaho pantheon.

In *The Night Chant* the female divinities are supposed to exercise great healing influence, and they generally appear in the dances on the two last nights. In these dances the character is generally assumed by a youth, largely naked, the exposed portion of the body being painted white. He wears an ornate scarf or skirt around the hips with a belt, the ends of which are fringed or tasselled, and from which depend pieces of twigs of juniper or other ornamentation.

These are crudely represented in the figure, while the skirt or loin cloth is represented by the widening out of the design above the knees. The peculiar dangling objects at the two bottom corners of the skirts are bunches of tassels or other ornaments of which the Navahos are inordinately fond. The head dress or mask of the *Yebaad* is of the female type, which differs fundamentally from that of the *Yei,* or male gods. While the latter, like a bag inverted, covers the entire head and neck, and completely conceals the hair of the wearer, the former conceals only

* In color section.

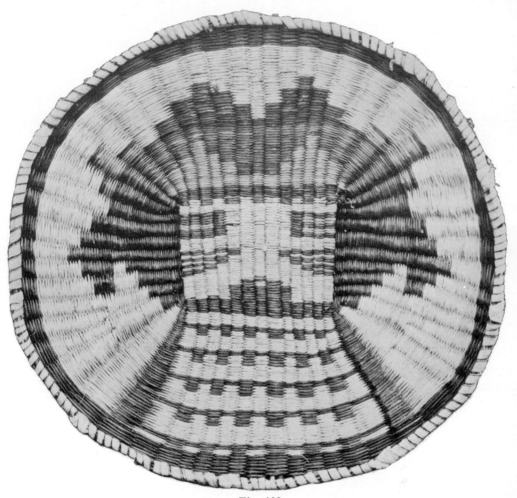

Fig. 199.
Hopi Basket, Showing Figure of Kachina.

the face and throat and allows the hair to flow out freely over the shoulders. The *Yebaad* actor never wears the hair bound up in a queue. While the male mask is soft and pliable, the female mask is stiff and hard, being made of untanned skin. It is nearly square in shape; the top is slightly rounded and in some cases the base is a little broader than the top. There is a flap or wing, called the ear, on each side about two inches broad, as long as the margin of the mask proper, and indented or crenated on the outer margin. The margins are all alike in each set of masks, but not in any two sets. The hole for the mouth is square. The holes for the eyes are triangular — the apices pointing outwards. The mask is painted blue, the ears white, a square field around the mouth-hole, and a triangular field around each eye-hole are black.

The *Yebaad* holds a bunch of spruce twigs in each hand and long arm pendants hang down from elbows to wrist. The lower legs are uncovered, to denote that the figure is standing or dancing, the skirt always covering the legs of a sitting figure.

Fig. 202*is from a painting made of another noted *Yei* blanket, owned by Mr. W. MacGinnies. Its size is fifty-eight by eighty-seven inches, and it is made throughout of wool, both the warp and weft. The background is a beautiful silver gray, somewhat similar, and as closely approximating as the dyer could attain, to the gray sand used in the sacred paintings. The chief and outside figure, which makes the border for three-fourths of the way around the blanket, is that of the rainbow deity.

In the paintings it consists of two long stripes, each about two inches wide, one of blue, one of red, bordered and separated by narrow lines of white. At the southeastern end of the bow is a representation of the body below the waist, such as the other gods have, consisting of pouch, skirts, legs, and feet. At the northeastern end we have head, neck, and arms. The head of the rainbow is rectangular, while the heads of the other forms in the picture are round.

There are those who have seen this blanket who affirm that it is a reproduction of one of the pictures of a sand-painting used by either Dr. Matthews or Colonel Stevenson to describe certain ceremonies of *The Night Chant,* in one of the reports of the Bureau of American Ethnology. Such is not the case. There are some points of similarity, but in some most important points this blanket is strikingly dissimilar.

Mr. MacGinnies informs me that certain Navahos gave him the following explanation of the design:

The outside figure, the one extending three-quarters around the rug, is the god of double sex, being the Navaho way of expressing their conception of the deity, who never dies, constantly reproducing himself, so to speak, the red part representing the male and the blue the female. This was the being who, according to their traditions, gave them the corn, and you will notice an ear of corn pass between the hands of this figure and of the god next to it on the blanket.

* In color section.

The other figures are shown as giving the lightning and the rain; the corn stalk with its symbolic number, three ears of corn; the bluebird, representing the messenger, resting upon the tassel at the tip of the stalk; the rainbow colors, which are also the colors of the Summer People under the feet of the figures. The long strings of half diamonds depending from the hands of the two inner figures have been explained to me as being the calendar sticks, they being divided into certain numbers of different colors to represent different epochs or pages in the history of the people, the true crosses at the end of the strings being either symbolic of the deity or being phallic symbols.

I am inclined to the belief that Mr. MacGinnies has been misinformed. As I have elsewhere explained, the Navahos believe there are five colors in the rainbow, and some assert that each color is a different individual. Hence, according to this theory, there are five rainbow goddesses. It will be noticed that there are five distinct lines in the outside figure, the white and yellow separating the red and the black. This gives the five colors, or the five goddesses, as the case may be. The bird represented is the bluebird (*Sialia arctica*), which is called by the Navahos *Tholy*. He is of the color of the south, and the upper regions. He is the herald of the morning. His call of "Tholy, Tholy" is the first that is heard when the gray dawn approaches. Therefore, is he sacred, and his feathers form a component part of nearly all the plume-sticks used in the worship of the Navaho. Two bluebirds, it is said, stand guard at the door of the house where the gods dwell; hence they are represented in the east of the picture.

There is little or no doubt in my own mind that this blanket is a more or less accurate reproduction of some sand-painting used in a ceremony to which the women have free access, and that the white race, as yet, has no photograph or drawing of. As I have before explained, we have but few of the sand-paintings pictured, and no one as far as I know, save Mrs. John Wetherill, is now engaged in study upon this important and instructive branch of Navaho ceremonial and religious art.

The rarity of these *Yei* blankets makes them highly desirable, and happy is that collector who has one in his possession.

Another blanket that contains some of the sacred symbols of the sand-paintings is shown in Fig. 203,[*] designed and woven by Dug-gaueth-lun Bi-dazhie. It is 64x92 inches in size, and the swastikas, with their flying terminals, are regarded with great reverence and superstition by the devout Navahos. This woman and her near relatives who are weavers have overcome their superstitious dread about the making of such blankets, for they have repeated this and similar designs in a dozen or more blankets during the past ten years. They are ready to make them to order in any colors, sizes varying from 45x75 inches up to 6x9 feet. These blankets are classed as extra standard.

* In color section.

Fig. 201.
Yei Blanket.

[Page 140]

CHAPTER XVIII

The Classification of Modern Blankets

THE chief points to be considered in determining the value of a modern blanket are—

1. Size and Quality of Warp.
2. Size and Quality of Woof or Weft.
3. Quality and Harmony of Color.
4. Firmness and Regularity of Weave.
5. Originality and Attractiveness of Design.

Let us look at each of these points with a view to aiding the intending purchaser to know intelligently what he is doing.

Size and Quality of Warp. — Except in very light weight blankets an all-wool warp should be insisted upon. As I have shown in the chapter on the deterioration of the art, cotton-warps were introduced to cheapen the price by saving the time of the weaver. Unfortunately, it did not have the desired effect. The weaver expected as much for her cotton-warped blanket — which warp she had bought for a small sum — as she did for the blanket made on honestly-woven, strong, and durable wool warp which would have taken her several days to spin. A cotton warp is less yielding than wool; its tensile strength is very much less, hence when there is any pressure placed upon the fabric a cotton warp will often give way and the blanket is then on the way to speedy dissolution.

The size of the warp is a matter for serious consideration, and the tightness with which it is spun. It is, as it were, the skeleton upon which the flesh of the woof or weft is hung. It must be large enough and tightly woven enough to bear the weft to stand all the ordinary and expected strains that may be made upon it. Many an otherwise good blanket is almost valueless because the warp strands are not thick and strong enough, by tight spinning, to bear the strain of shaking or using in the fairly rough manner such household articles are commonly subjected to.

Size of Woof. — It must be evident to every purchaser that a coarse, loosely-spun yarn cannot make as durable, beautiful, or desirable a blanket as one made from a fine tightly-spun yarn. Many blankets of harmonious color and striking design are undesirable because the weft is not composed of a fine and tightly-woven yarn. Then, too, no fine blanket can be made from a coarse yarn. The finer the yarn the greater

143

demand upon the weaver to "batten" it down well in weaving. Hence a fine yarn blanket is *prima-facie* a better-woven and, therefore, more dur-- able one than one with a coarse yarn.

In the working out of design, too, a fine woof or weft yarn is essen- tial. The fine lines that often delight the eye, and the introduction of slight touches of color here and there that make all the difference between the mediocre or commonplace and the striking and distinctive are impos- sible with a coarse woof yarn.

Quality of Woof Yarn. — But not only must the woof yarn be tightly spun; it must be of good quality wool, silky in texture, of long staple, and of great tensile strength. Where it is possible — and if there is a fringe made of the same yarn as the woof it answers as if prepared for the purpose — the yarn should be carefully examined. The finer the wool, the softer and silkier to the feel, the longer the staple, and the stronger it proves itself, the better the blanket. But even with all these qualities in its favor the wool may be dirty, and therefore unable to receive or retain the color in which it is dyed. Hence its cleanliness and freedom from extraneous substances, as small burrs, pieces of vegetable fibre, small sticks, etc., should be considered and carefully examined into. Where one has the opportunity of comparing the grade of blankets I have designated as "common" with the "extra standard," or "native wool fancy" grades, he will readily note the differences, and understand why he should pay more for the better class of blankets than the former, even though the former *look* quite as well, or even better, to his eye, than the latter.

Color. — Color is a most important factor in a blanket. In the first days of aniline dyes when the Navahos were suddenly awakened to the fact that the whole rainbow gamut of colors was open to them at ten cents a package, they indulged in a riot of colors that was a debauch and delirium combined. There are still some remnants left of this wild frenzy of unrestrained color in the Navahos' minds, though the conser- vative traders have ceased to supply certain of the colors whose use is likely to be disadvantageous. So long as the Indians were left to their own unperverted tastes their color harmonies were pleasing, and though somewhat limited, perfect and satisfying. But when they were given unrestrained freedom, with the idea that the white man desired the frenzy of color, their normal tastes became perverted, and it is one of the unfor- tunate facts of life that ten years of exercise of a perverted taste takes four times ten years to eradicate.

Hence determine whether the colors are pleasing in themselves, har- monious in relation to each other, and then whether they will harmonize with the color-scheme into which you wish to introduce the blanket.

It should also be remembered that Time is a kindly ministrant to loud or unrestrained colors. Even as he tones down the exuberant boisterousness of youth, so does he subdue, soften, and render mellow and harmonious the riot of colors some otherwise excellent blankets contain. This has been proven in many cases, where twenty-five years have worked wonders on highly colored blankets and toned them down to soft and pleasing blends.

Weave. — Now comes the question of weave. Is the blanket well woven? Square? Even in stitch? In some places the weaver "bungles" her work. (See Fig. 207.) In other words, she does not take her woof straight across where there is nothing to hinder, and then she "fills up" the space awkwardly and clumsily to the manifest injury of the looks of the blanket. Regularity should be insisted upon, and then, for a good blanket, be sure to see that each row of woof is well "battened" down — in other words, that it is tight and solid.

And yet, somehow, there is another side to what I have termed above "bungling." In this blanket from which the illustrative photograph is made (Fig. 207), as well as others in my possession, this very irregularity of the weave produces a pleasing effect on the mind. It arouses thought. What made the weaver do it? Why did she not go directly across the fabric with this yarn when she desired it to be of the same color and stitch?

Then a picture comes to me of a somewhat tired weaver, squatted before her blanket, the sun just happening at that time of the day to be in such a position that if she moved a trifle to right or left her tired shoulders would come directly under its powerful rays. Too weary to make the effort to move or to place a screen between herself and the sun, and made a trifle careless by her weariness, her tired hands reach as far as the shade goes, and then sends the ball of yarn back, thus making the "bungle" or irregularity that nothing but the destruction of the blanket can efface. How human and how real. How close it brings one to the blanket. It is a "bungle," but it makes the blanket mean more than it did before. It gives it the *human touch,* that flash of life and reality that sets it distinct and apart from machine work. It makes it the work of a personal, living, sentient human being. And these recognitions of humanity in such work are good. They are, in reality, most precious in the things we are able to purchase.

In this connection my attention has been called to the assertion made that when these "bungles" appear in Oriental rugs they are done purposely, in order to confuse the evil spirits who might otherwise work injury to the weavers or users of the rug; and the question is asked, May not the Navaho weavers be controlled by the same idea?

I do not think so. While superstitious, the Navaho weavers' dread is not aroused in this direction, and in all my talks with them, while this kind of question has often been asked, there has never been any response given that suggested such fear. Furthermore, if it were a general superstition all the blankets would show similar erratic weaving. The fact that very few blankets in a thousand are so woven is conclusive proof that they are not influenced by such a fear.

Design. — The marvel of the infinite variety in Navaho blanket designs never grows less. The more one sees and knows the more the marvel grows. From the simple and plain alternate bands pictured in Fig. 204, of the common type, to the complex, highly ornate, and brilliantly colored designs created by a modern genius is a gigantic step in artistic development, and one for which the aboriginal weaver is entitled to our highest consideration and appreciation.

Naturally in choosing a fine blanket the quality of the design is a matter the importance of which cannot be too highly estimated. Personal taste, necessarily, largely enters into the choice of a design. What will please one may be displeasing to another. The place the blanket is to fill should be a helping factor in coming to a decision. As a rule, however, too great complexity is not desirable, the plainer and simpler the design, in reason, the more pleasing it becomes with time. There are some designs, however, such, for instance, as that shown in Fig. 205, that are too simple, too plain, too large, for general use. A plain series of stripes or bands would be much preferable to this "Greek key" on so large a scale.

On the other hand the one large panel of Fig. 206 is so broken up by the black and white bands that it does not seem too large, and although the blanket is 60x96 inches in size, and the single panel practically fills up the whole space, there has never been a moment when it has seemed inappropriate or unpleasing.

In considering this subject of design the reader should not overlook the fact that the Navahos have proven themselves possessed of inventive genius in this department of art. There are no "stock" designs as far as they are concerned. Repetition of design comes from the desire of the white race for duplication — "I want a blanket exactly like that one" — never from the unperverted, natural instincts of the weaver. And while I feel that my publishers have been generous in the number of illustrations they have included in this book, to me the number is inadequate and altogether limited as far as conveying to the reader anything like an idea of the vast and marvelous variety a study of the Navaho's textiles affords. Multiply the designs reproduced herein by *ten thousand* and still new and striking designs will continually be found. Hence the exacting connoisseur should not hesitate to discard a thousand designs, if necessary, to secure what he desires, for he may rest assured that if he is patient and persistent, the one design of his longing will ultimately come into his hands.

Fig. 205.
Key Design, Too Large for Blanket.

Fig. 204.
Simplest and First Deviation from a Flat or
One-Color Blanket,

Fig. 206.
Blanket with Large but Pleasing Design.
(Author's Collection.)

While I have thus attempted to analyze the elemental factors that go to the making of a good Navaho blanket, no one knows better than I how inadequate my attempt is.   For after all, when the fire of genius burns it will manifest itself even though the instrumentality be poor warp, and unclean, ill-spun, poorly dyed weft.   Genius rises triumphant over all adverse conditions and compels admiration and respect in spite of them. But, when genius triumphs and is enabled to use perfect and fitting manifestations for its soarings, then — when the result is a Navaho blanket — one has a poem of weaving, shot through and through with an exquisite melody, accompanied by glorious harmonies of color that make the design. These are the priceless treasures one occasionally sees in the collections of connoisseurs, more rarely has offered to him for sale, and now and again triumphantly finds when rambling in solitary and wild places on the reservation, far, far away from the haunts of civilized and artistically sophisticated mankind.

In what is presented above there is that which will enable a tyro to determine the relative value of a Navaho blanket, but to those engaged in the purchase and sale of them as a business, there is still another individualistic analysis of blankets for purposes of broad classification which others may find helpful and suggestive.

It must be recognized, however, at the outset, that it is impossible to classify and describe a Navaho blanket as the products of the white man's loom are classified.   The colors are dissimilar, the weave is different, the designs are individualistic, and, therefore, play up and down a marvelous gamut, the warp and woof threads are spun tighter or looser according to the whim of the weaver, the finished product is closely or more loosely woven according to the time taken or haste shown in the work.   Hence, practically every Indian blanket must be examined for itself and then placed in a broad classification to which it belongs, only, however, by a consideration of its general characteristics.

This broad classification scheme is as follows, with examples and descriptions which will broadly typify each class:

I. Common

Generally these are woven of coarse yarn, an eighth of an inch more or less in diameter, made of wool that has been indifferently cleaned and dyed.   They are usually made for saddle-blankets, and are in reds, blacks, dirty whites, and grays, with other colors occasionally appearing.   No first-class dealer ever cares to handle this type of blanket, unless it be that some one orders a quantity for a special purpose or that he pick out a few of a little better quality than the average. There is no reliability to be placed upon the warp, anything being used that is most readily at hand. It may be strong and even of wool, but, equally, it may be rotten and cotton. Generally they are of a simple striped pattern, though sometimes I have bought them of a coarse diagonal weave, and twenty years or so ago one could occasionally pick up a well-woven blanket in this class.

The average size of a saddle-blanket may be said to be in the neighborhood of 36x48 inches; some being a trifle larger and some smaller. A "common" blanket larger than this size is seldom to be desired, though often found in the cheaper "curio" stores, where trashy blankets are disposed of to the unwary. Beware of these places. There are plenty of reliable dealers to be found, and the mail order business, referred to in the chapter devoted to reliable dealers, places any would-be purchaser in the United States in immediate contact with those whose knowledge and experience are safeguards and assurances against deception.

Blankets of the "common" variety can generally be bought, in quantity, by the pound. All else are now sold, as a rule, by the piece, though there are still a few traders who sell certain grades to their retailers by the pound. The public, however, can seldom buy in any other way than the piece.

It should not be overlooked that, comparatively speaking, there are a great many of this poorer quality of blankets made which find their way into circulation through the hands of irresponsible traders. And by this I do not mean dishonest traders — they buy these blankets at a low price and sell them correspondingly. But they often come into the hands of dealers — wholesale and retail — who care nothing for quality or price so long as they can collect their toll from everything that passes through their hands. Hence, while compared with the number of the superior grades of blankets that the reliable Indian traders and wholesalers succeed in obtaining the number of these poor blankets is small, in the aggregate they amount to a large enough quantity to lead the wise purchaser to be cautious. Unless one is assured that *he knows* it is far better to trust to the judgment of an expert, or purchase only from those who deal in no other than first-class and unquestionably desirable blankets, than to run the risk of having one of these common grades thrust into one's possession.

Now and again where one has large experience and knowledge he may "pick up" either from a trader on the reservation, or a weaver, one or more of these common type of a little better quality and finer weave, and such are often good enough to use for places where a first-class and expensive blanket is not desired. Occasionally I have made purchases of this kind and have always found a ready market for them amongst those

Fig. 207.
Navaho Weaver, Showing "Bungling" in Weave on
Left-Hand Side.

[Page 145]

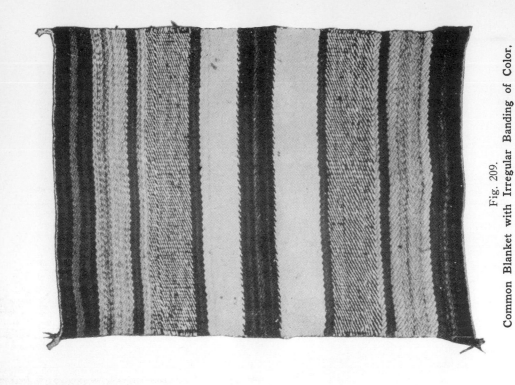

Fig. 209.
Common Blanket with Irregular Banding of Color.

Fig. 208.
Common Blanket of Simple Design.

Fig. 210.
A Closely Woven Blanket, Practically Waterpoof.
(Matthews Collection.)

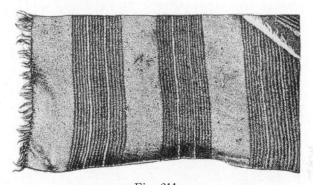

Fig. 211.
Good for Rough Use.
(Matthews Collection.)

Fig. 213.
Standard Blanket in Gray, Red, and White.
(Author's Collection.)

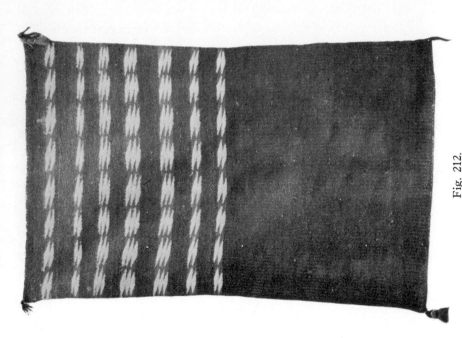

Fig. 212.
Double Saddle Blanket.
Plain half is placed next to the horse.
(Author's Collection.)

of my friends and others who desired a cheaper blanket, and yet who did not wish to waste their money on a worthless one.

Of this class of blanket the one in the loom and covering the knees of the weaver in Fig. 207 may be regarded as a type, though it does not always follow that blankets without design or color (as is the one in the loom), are always trashily *common*.

Fig. 208 is also of what might be termed a little better quality of common blanket. Here bands of color are introduced, in which geometrical figures are worked in simple but effective fashion. Fig. 209 also is another specimen of this class. While of a cheap variety, it is not unpleasing, the banded and colored effect being variable enough to destroy monotony.

Fig. 210 is of a *common* blanket in the Matthews collection, closely woven, twilled and practically waterproof, while Fig. 211, not being so closely woven, is better fitted for rough use as a camping-out blanket.

This fact should ever be borne in mind, viz., that a heavy, closely woven blanket is not suited either for a bed-blanket or for camping-out purposes, unless one places it underneath him. The stiffness makes the blanket so that it does not fit snugly to the body, and the result is that if one attempts to use one of this type for either of these purposes he is sure to be disappointed.

On the other hand, the loosely woven blankets, especially if the yarn is not too coarse, are highly suitable for both these purposes, though the ordinary types are much too heavy for bed use except in a very cold climate.

Now and again what may almost be regarded as another type of common blanket finds its way to the market, or can be purchased on the reservation. I have had many of them during the past twenty-five years. This type is illustrated in Fig. 212. At first the stranger to it wonders why it is woven half with a design and half without. Here is the reason. It is a saddle-blanket, which, before being placed on the horse's back, must be *doubled*. The plain portion is then next to the horse — because it is hidden — while the "designed" half is outside and exposed. While at first when these are placed upon the floor, or on a porch, as rugs, they have a peculiar and sometimes unpleasantly strange effect, I know of many cases where their owners have become quite fond of them and have learned to enjoy their singularity.

II. Standard

In the earlier days of the awakening industry there was a grade regularly known by the name of "Extra Common." It was made of finer yarn, cleaner wool, better dyes, and greater variety of designs than the "common." The sizes varied from saddle-blankets to the largest products of the loom. Today, however, these are mainly graded as "Standard," and comprise the general run of ordinary Navaho blankets. In this grade will be found every color of the rainbow (though the less harmonious pieces are rapidly disappearing), the coarser of the outline blankets, and the coarser of the native grays, blacks, whites, and browns. These are literally turned out by the hundreds, though, as knowledge increases, and purchasers are willing to pay a trifle more per blanket, the demand for the better quality blankets will cause the supply of this grade to diminish. At the same time it must be remembered that all Navaho weavers are not alike. There are the shiftless and the indifferent among them just as there are among the whites, and so long as a weaver knows that she can take even an indifferently woven blanket to the trader and get enough for it to buy flour, baking-powder, coffee, and sugar to last for a month or two, she will not go to the trouble of improving the quality of her work.

Fig. 213 is of a size rather smaller than what might be regarded as an ordinary standard size. It is 46x75½ inches, with body color of gray, and the triangular designs in red, white, and black, the red being inside. The border at each end is gray, white, and black.

Fig. 214 is 48x79 inches in size, with a dark gray body. The border, however, is red, two and a half inches wide on the sides, and three and a half inches at each end. The designs throughout are in black and white, save in the center, and the four diamonds nearest to the center, where there is an inner touch of red. Fig. 215 is of about the same size, with a gray body, the designs being in gray, white, and a little red.

These are typical specimens, although as elsewhere explained, the sizes vary from saddle-blanket size to twelve or more feet square, and the designs are as many and varied as there are blankets.

A rather unique and pleasing blanket of the standard class is one made expressly for me as a gift by the widow of the last great warrior chief of the Navahos, Manuelito. The dear old lady and I became great friends. I made many excellent photographs of her, one of which is reproduced in Fig. 139, and some months after my leave-taking and return home, I received the blanket shown in Fig. 216, with a message of appreciation and affection. The blanket is closely woven, though of heavy yarn. The body is white; the Greek border in gray, outlined in black, while the center figure is of maroon, outlined or bordered with green, orange, blue, and lemon yellow. While these colors — to read about them — may not seem to harmonize, the blanket itself is pleasing to most eyes, and, anyhow, color harmony is largely a matter of individualistic taste.

Of this *standard* type is Fig. 217.* This is about 38x76 inches in

* In color section.

Fig. 215.
Standard Blanket in Black, White, and Gray.
(Collection of C. C. Manning Co.)

Fig. 214.
Standard Blanket of Fine Quality.
(Collection of C. N. Cotton.)

Fig. 216.
Made by Manuelito's Widow for the Author.

[Page 150]

Fig. 220.
Standard Quality Blanket, Good Design and Color.
(Author's Collection.)

Fig. 221.
Standard Blanket, Saddle Size.
(Matthews Collection.)

Fig. 222.
Standard Blanket.
(Matthews Collection.)

size, with a red body, with the central diamond, and the centers of the two end figures in gray. Gray and black also appear in the borders.

Occasionally a blanket similar to Fig. 218[*] will be found in this class, 5x7½ feet or thereabouts in size. There is no certainty, however, that blankets of *standard* quality will be found like this, as most of the weavers now seek, when they make a blanket as large and well designed as this, to have it so good that it is immediately recognized as of the *extra standard* quality.

Fig. 219[*] is an excellent *standard* blanket, with gray body, and red interior design picked out in white. Its size is about 5x7 feet, and the design is peculiarly striking and forceful. It was made by Hastin Deet-si Be Ahd, who is very proud of it, and who occasionally makes up a similar blanket in native wools, undyed.

Fig. 220 is a *standard* quality blanket, in my own collection, which I bought some years ago. It is saddle size, viz., 30x45 inches, body in red, the design down the center in black and brown, although in the illustration the brown is scarcely distinguishable. The zigzag outlines on the side set off portions of diamonds in violet, brown, and black, while the two striking white designs on each side are joined to a light blue design of equal size, which the photograph fails to reveal.

Two *standard* blankets of saddle size, both of which, however, were being worn by children when he secured them, are in the Matthews collection. These are Figs. 221 and 222, and the designs of both are effective and pleasing, especially as they are of a better quality than ordinarily found in saddle-blankets. In commenting on the border in Fig. 222, Dr. Matthews says such regular border of uniform device all the way around is a very rare thing.

This may have been so in the Doctor's day, but, as many illustrations in this book show, the weavers have made it now quite a familiar sight.

III. Native Wools, Undyed

The undyed native wools are those that come naturally from the sheep. They are whites, blacks, browns, and grays, the last being either a natural growth (of which there is comparatively a small shearing), or made by a judicious admixture of black and white while spinning the yarn. The demand for this class of blanket, when the design is good, has been a steadily growing one, as the public taste has been cultivated during the past ten to fifteen years. I well remember when I used to buy a fine quality of this type at a less price than that now charged for "standards." Indeed, there was comparatively small call for them. Those bought in the earlier days were urged upon the taste of the critical for use in bed-

* In color section.

rooms, or other places where quiet shades were desirable, and a ready market was soon found for all that could be procured. Slowly, then more rapidly, they grew in favor, until now many weavers spend their whole time in making them.

This type as a rule, is made from wool that has no acquaintance whatever with dye. The sheep of the Navaho grow wool that is black, white, gray, and brown. There are some black and brown native wools, however, that are not pronounced enough to be pleasing, and in such cases the wool is cleaned, carded, spun, and dyed—that is, the black is put into black dye to make its blackness uniform, and the same is done with the brown.

In many cases the gray of a gray blanket is made by carefully carding together black and white wool. When this is properly done a pleasing gray is the result, but the most desirable gray is that which comes from a special breed of sheep and is silver gray of itself. This is a glossy wool, of a bright and attractive gray, and blankets made from it, with due introduction of design or outline in black, white, or brown, are eagerly sought after. They, however, are generally extra well woven, so come into the class called "extras."

Figs. 223-227 and 39 are all of native wool, undyed, but the five latter are so well woven and of such excellent and pleasing design that they would immediately be graded as "Extras" of this type.

Fig. 227 is one of the modern blankets of this type made by the best weavers on the reservation of today, and is one of the many found in the Fred Harvey collection. The body of the blanket is gray with alternate rows of diamonds extending across the blanket. The first row has one center diamond, with a half-diamond on each side, the outer line of the figure being in black. The second row comprises two complete diamonds, the outer line being in white. They thus alternate from bottom to top.

Blankets of this kind are especially adapted to be used as rugs in dining-rooms, bedrooms, sitting-rooms, or porches, and are capable of enduring the roughest kind of wear.

A peculiarly attractive blanket that contains a great deal of native wool, undyed, is shown in Fig. 228.* The body color is of natural brown, carefully cleaned, deodorized, and spun. It was designed and woven by Chas-cin-ni-bit-See, and is 60x90 inches in size. Like the native silver gray, this pure brown is rather rare, and blankets made from it are to be prized, especially if the designs are artistic and pleasing. In this case the red and blue of the design are of dyed yarn, but where black and gray are introduced with the brown the color effect is even more pleasing than with the red and blue.

* In color section.

Fig. 224.
Extra Quality Native Wool Blanket.
(Wetherill & Coleville Collection.)

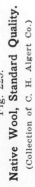

Fig. 223.
Native Wool, Standard Quality.
(Collection of C. H. Algert Co.)

Fig. 226.
Extra Quality Native Wool.
(Vroman Collection.)

Fig. 225.
Extra Quality Native Wool Blanket.
(Vroman Collection.)

Fig. 227.
Extra Quality Native Wool.
(Fred Harvey Collection.)

A little native brown is introduced into Fig. 227. This is 58x113 inches in size, and each of the diamonds has one of its panels in brown. This is a blanket secured on the reservation in the winter of 1912-13, and is one of the finest specimens of modern weave I have ever seen. While not so fine as the oldtime bayetas, it is equally well woven and is a splendid specimen of the weaver's art, though the design is neither so striking nor individualistic as many others herein pictured.

IV. Extras: Outline, Standard, or Native Wools, Undyed

Naturally, certain weavers excel no matter what form of work they produce from their looms. When such specimens of excellence are brought to the traders they grade them as of "extra" quality and charge an extra price for them. The determining points of "extras" are wool-warp, fineness of woof-warp, good color, excellence of design, harmony of color and design, and general superiority and fineness of weave.

This is the class of blanket of which Fred Harvey makes a specialty. He keeps no cheaper grades. His weavers are constantly urged on to the production of "extras." This, and even better qualities, are the only types he recommends or guarantees, and on blankets of this character he is ready to give the most comprehensive guarantees.

J. A. Molohon & Co. have also gained a reputation for this class of blankets, though they announce that they keep the ordinary standard grades at a lower price.

Fig. 229 shows one of especially fine effect, designed and made by Hastin Dug-agh-eth-lun Be-Ahd. It is about 52x84 inches in size, and is in gray, white, and black. Blankets of this type are made by the same weaver in sizes ranging from 45x76 inches up to 6x9 feet. Occasionally she will introduce a trifle of color into the border, or interior figures, but, as a rule, she prefers to stick to the native undyed wools.

Of equal quality and even more striking in design is Fig. 230,* designed and woven by Bi-leen Al-pi-Bi-zha-Ahd. This woman has never been known either to copy the design of another weaver or to repeat one of her own. Every blanket must be an original. She is of an essentially artistic temperament, and has the creative instinct developed to a high degree. In this blanket the native brown is introduced with pleasing effect. This is 75x115 inches in size. A blanket of this size and type is worth, according to quality and fineness of weave, from $60 to $150.

It is a source of great pleasure to know a weaver of this woman's natural aptitude. If she can be found alone and induced to speak freely she converses interestingly and fluently of the influences that determine the designs of her blankets and the reasons she will never duplicate them.

* In color section.

In effect she says that if she duplicates, the voices of "Those Above" will no longer inspire her to make new designs. In other words, she must trust the gods to supply her artistic needs and ever be in the receptive condition to take in what they send.

Occasionally blankets of these sizes and similar designs are brought in to the traders of the *standard* class, then the prices are correspondingly lower.

Very popular both in design and color is Fig. 231,[*] which originated from the busy brain and fingers of Bi-leen Alpi Bi-zha Ahd. The soft gray of the body and border, with the white panel picked out in a small design of red, white, and black, makes an effective and pleasing combination. The size of the original is 56x86 inches, but it is made to order in *extra* grades from 45x76 inches up to 6x9 feet, and is often kept in stock in some of those sizes. While originally made in the *standard* quality, it is seldom found in that grade, though occasionally one is brought in of similar though not exact duplicate pattern in that quality.

The same weaver also designed Fig. 232.[*] This is 5x7½ feet in size, in which grays, blacks (or deep blues), browns, and reds are skilfully commingled in a daring design. She has also woven the same design in red, white, and black. These are made to order in the *extra* class, in any colors required and in any of the standard sizes.

Fig. 218 is of an *extra* quality blanket. This was designed by Meh-li-to Be Day-zhie and is 5x7½ feet in size. The major portion of the body is red, with white, black, and blue, or gray in the design. This is one of the stock designs of the Manning Company, and can be made up in any color, such as gray, white, and black, when it would be classed as a *native wool, undyed,* of the *extra* quality. The sizes, too, vary, and are often found "in stock," as, for instance, 45x76 inches up to 65x96 inches.

Fig. 219 shows a striking and original blanket, which, while classed as *standard,* is often made up in *extra* grades, of sizes from 48x72 inches up to 6x8 feet or more. This was designed by Hastin Deet-si Be-Ahd, and has been so popular that she has been kept weaving on similar blankets ever since to meet the demand.

Similarly Fig. 233,[*] while occasionally found in the *standard* class, is regularly made up in a variety of sizes from about 48x72 inches up to 6x8 feet in *extra* qualities, either in native wools, undyed, or in standard colors.

Fig. 234[*] is an *extra* grade, designed and woven by Yeh-del-spah Bi-mah, size 64x85 inches. The body color is gray, with a panel of red all around, in which the designs are worked out in white and black, while the inner panel is in white, red, and black.

* In color section.

Fig. 229.
"Extra" Blanket in Gray, White, and Black.
(Courtesy of J. A. Molohon & Co.)

Equally original is Fig. 235,*designed and made by Bit-se Bi-Ghay Bit-Se, size 64x84 inches, with a body mainly of red. The black and white, or deep blue and white, make striking and effective contrasts.

Figs. 234 and 235 can both be made to order, in any color and size, from 45x76 inches up to 6x9 feet.

To those who enjoy the full flood of "sunshine red" Fig. 236*will especially appeal. It was designed and made by Toh-dichin-e Bi-Ahd, and is 64x98 inches in size. The red picked out in light gray, with the inner panel in white, with design in black, or deep blue, with slight dashes of red, make striking contrasts, and one must know definitely where such a colored blanket will "fit" or it will strike a discordant note. But on a light wood floor, with no other deep color note to conflict with it, such a blanket would light up and warm a room with a glow such as covers the earth at sunset. The weaver who made this is ready to make others similar to this, in the same or different colors and of sizes varying from 45x76 inches up to 6x9 feet.

V. Native Wool, Fancy

There is, however, another fine and distinctive grade, known as Native wool, Fancy blankets. It used to be well known in the trade and included all the very fine native wool blankets as differentiated from those made of Germantown yarn.

The same tests are put to this type as to the "extra" qualities, only carried to a still finer point. Such blankets are exceedingly desirable and when found fully justify the words of Father Berard, elsewhere quoted, to the effect that the Navahos of today are making just as fine blankets as they have ever done.

Some of the finest of these blankets are made by men, more to show what they can do, perhaps, than for sale purposes. Several of those I have secured have been of this class, and, tell it not in Gath! others were woven by maidens for the young men of their choice, to use as saddle-blankets, and were disposed of when the flames of affection had burned low, or some other flame had taken the place of the "light that had failed," or gone out. Practically all of these are single size saddle-blankets, viz., 15x24, 21x24, and 17x22 inches, thus demonstrating how individualistic is the taste in size, as well as design and color, of the weavers even in those blankets that are to be used for a common purpose.

Fig. 237 is of the choicest specimen of this type in my own collection. It is 21x25 inches in size, and is used as a table-cover. The panels of small lozenges or diamonds are daintily done. The main color is red, while different colors are used in the fourfold portions of which the diamonds are composed.

* In color section.

Fig. 238 is of almost as fine yarn, spinning, and design.   It is 15x24 inches in size, of closely spun red, with unusual figures combined with those that are more common.   The fringe and tassels at the ends are extra elaborate.   Well do I remember the place and occasion on which I purchased this.   I had been to little visited portions of the reservation, around the dreaded Navaho Mountain, where renegades of several races and tribes are said to congregate, and where some wonderful cliff dwellings are found, and was now crossing, on horseback, alone, to Shiprock, on the northeastern border of the reservation.   My mount was not of the best, and could not be urged beyond a limited speed, the roads were somewhat uncertain, and late afternoon found me at the Cornfields, where several families had built their *hogans,* in the midst of a fairly large area of cultivated land.   I had no blankets or bedding of any kind, but the hospitality of a rude *hogan* was preferable to nothing.   The nights were exceedingly cold and frosty, so I intimated that I should be glad to remain. There were families of two generations, with grandpa and grandma, to occupy the *hogan,* and only enough blankets to go around.   But I was supplied with a sheepskin to lie on, and with my overcoat wrapped around me and a small saddle-blanket I endeavored to be content.   We were stretched out with feet towards the fire, but I kept up a fairly constant roll all night, warming first one side and then the other, as the temperature declined.   The roof of the *hogan* was partially open, though a blanket was hung over the doorway.   During the night the head of the family did a most gracious thing.   He arose and took down this doorway blanket, and, assuming that I was asleep, carefully and gently spread it over me, tucking it around me so that I might secure its full benefit.   That blanket secured me several hours' extra sleep, for in its warmth I was able to defy the cold.   Early the next morning his son brought me the blanket pictured (Fig. 238), and, as they would take no money for my "lodging," I was glad to purchase and pay extra well for this dainty little piece of weaving.

Fig. 239 is of a less fine and striking quality of weave, yet one which would properly come within this class.   It was made by a Navaho maiden for her lover, who for some reason or other jilted her, and then was willing to sell me the blanket.

Fig. 240 is a native wool, fancy blanket in the Matthews collection. When secured by Dr. Matthews it was being worn by a woman.   Its size is 5 feet 4 inches by 3 feet 7 inches, and its colors are yellow, green, dark blue, gray, and red, all but the latter color being in native yarn.

Fig. 241 is one of the best representatives of the earlier type of native wool dyed blankets made by the Navahos prior to the deterioration of the art.   It is in the American Museum of Natural History.   The body of the blanket is red, and the wool used is of several different dyes, which is

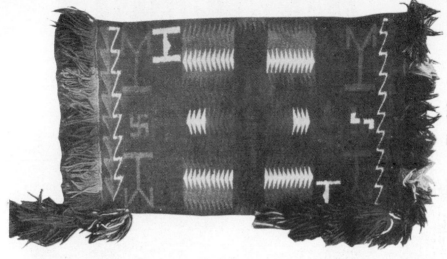

Fig. 238.
Fancy Blanket, Native Wool.

Fig. 237.
Native Wool Fancy Blanket.

Fig. 240.
Native Wool Fancy Blanket.
(Matthews Collection.)

Fig. 239.
Fancy Saddle Blanket, Native Wool.

evident from the variations of tone to which time has softened the original color. The general effect is a delicious soft old rose. The three inner diamonds of each design are all in black, followed by a fourth in white, which produces a bold and striking, yet pleasing effect. The zigzags, top and bottom, are in white and black.

Fig. 196 is a typical specimen of a first-class native wool fancy blanket, modern in weave throughout, but of old design. The body of the blanket is gray, the center diamonds are of red outlined in brown, white, and black. The stepped figures surrounding the center diamonds are in black and white, while the conventional stepped diamonds of the center are outlined in black, brown, and white. The border is of white, surrounded with black. Blankets as good as this are often woven by Fred Harvey's best weavers.

VI.   Germantowns

These, as the name implies, are Navaho blankets made throughout of Germantown yarn. In the chapter on the development of the art I have already referred to the introduction of Germantown yarn, and how, for a time, it led to the deterioration of blanketry. "Haste to get returns" became the cry of both Navaho weaver and trader, regardless of quality and durability. The weaver was glad to get rid of the trouble of cleaning, carding, washing, dyeing, and spinning the yarn, when she could secure it from the trader all ready to be woven. And so cotton-warp, Germantown-woof blankets for a time had a great run. Then, as suddenly as the trade had grown, there came a slump, and trader and weaver meaningly asked: "Why?" The answer was not far to seek in the angry cry of purchasers, dinged into the ears of blanket sellers, and by them echoed to the traders: "We thought we were buying good blankets. We find we have almost thrown our money away." This speedily led to a change, and today only the smallest and lightest "Germantowns" are made with a cotton warp, while all the larger ones handled by reputable dealers have wool warps, and are woven both with care and skill.

Fig. 193 is of a very fine blanket of this type which I purchased over twelve years ago. It has been in constant and rough use ever since. While it has a cotton warp, it is an extra strong one, and is so carefully woven that it is in good condition. The body of the blanket is in red, the lozenge figure in the center in white, blue, white, and maroon, with the very delicate outline in white. The upper and lower diamonds, with the serrated edges, or really outlines, are in red, with a blue border inside and a maroon border outside the dainty serrated line, which is in white. From top to bottom on each side are two rows of *alkidot'ezh*, or triangles placed one above another, touching. The outer rows are in green, while the inner rows are in orange brown. These latter scarcely show in the reproduction.

Fig. 132 is of a Germantown yarn blanket which used to be in Dr. Matthews's private collection. He described it as follows: "This blanket measures 6 feet 9 inches by 5 feet 6 inches, and weighs nearly six pounds. It is made entirely of Germantown yarn in seven strongly contrasting colors, and is the work of a *man* who is generally conceded to be the best weaver in the tribe. A month was spent in its manufacture. Its figures are mostly in serrated stripes, which are the most difficult to execute with regularity. I have heard that the man who wove this often draws his designs on sand before he begins to work them on the loom."

This is the only case in which I have ever heard of a weaver making a design in the sand, or otherwise. In my many years of familiarity with the Navahos, and varied wanderings over the whole of their reservation, my constant inquiry has failed to find me one weaver who has ever followed this practice, or known of anyone doing so.

Figs. 242 and 243 are of two single saddle-blankets made with Germantown yarn. Fig. 242 is fairly well woven and with a good color scheme. The design is familiar and frequently found, and lends itself to as varied a color harmony as there are bands. This comprises white, deep blue, cherry-red, salmon-pink, and deep green, and they are combined with a keen eye to color effect. The size is 17½x23 inches, with fringes at both ends fully two inches long.

Fig. 243 has a red body color, is 20x24 inches in size, and is completely surrounded with a so-called Greek-key border, which Dr. Matthews claimed was exceedingly rare in the eighties of the past century. The key is in green, with an orange insert; the geometrical figures on each side are in black, yellow, and green; while those of the center row are in black, yellow, green, and gray. The blanket has a four-inch fringe at each end, with double tassels at one corner of each end.

Fig. 241.
An Old Native Wool Dyed Blanket.
(Courtesy of American Museum of Natural History.)

[Page 156]

Fig. 243.
Germantown Yarn Saddle Blanket.
(Author's Collection.)

Fig. 242.
Germantown Yarn Saddle Blanket.
(Author's Collection.)

CHAPTER XIX

Imitation Navaho Blankets

THERE is an impression abroad, quite widespread, that there are many so-called Navaho blankets which are machine-made. To those who are familiar with the subject this impression is absurd. He would be credulous, indeed, who, knowing a real Navaho blanket, could ever imagine one made on a machine. The thing is impossible. A so-called machine-made Navaho blanket can be discerned by the knowing a hundred feet away. And writers who ought to know better — or else they should not be allowed to publish what they write in high-class papers and magazines — often assert the most foolish things. For instance, in *The Saturday Evening Post* for June 25, 1911, a contributor thus writes under the title, "Faking the Antiques." About some of the things of which the article speaks I am not competent to offer an opinion, but in regard to Navaho blankets I *know* whereof I speak, with the knowledge gained by thirty-two years of personal and intimate experience and study. He says:

In the curio dealer of the western part of the United States the fellah who sells fake scarabs has no mean rival. Ninety per cent of the Indian moccasins, blankets, and baskets sold in western souvenir shops are the machine-made output of a thriving factory that employs not only "squaws," who are nimble-fingered girls, but a dozen salesmen, who travel from Seattle to Key West, from Los Angeles to Bangor. Real Indian craftsmanship finds it so hard to compete that beading and blanket weaving of the old kind will soon be a lost art. In the very heart of the Indian country — at Flagstaff, Cheyenne, Albuquerque, and Bismarck — the curio stores are packed with Indian wares that no Indian ever touched. Even if you distrust the shops and decide to buy only from an Indian, you may be bitten. A crafty buck struts along the street in Albuquerque with a gorgeous blanket carelessly flung over his shoulders.

"How much?" you ask, fingering the thing with greedy digits.

"Thirty dollars," he answers, with an appraising glance at your scarfpin, your shoes, and other indices of your prosperity.

You pay. It is more than you expected; but, at least, the blanket is genuine. Six months later you learn that your blanket was made in a factory and that your Indian warrior probably divided his gains with a white employer.

In the main this charge is not in accordance with facts. It may be true that ninety per cent of the "Indian moccasins that are sold in western souvenir shops are the machine-made output of a thriving factory that employs 'squaws' who are nimble-fingered girls," but there is not the slightest particle of truth in the statement that ninety per cent of the Indian blankets and baskets so sold are the product of anything but Indian fingers. I am personally familiar with every Indian trader on the Navaho Reservation; I know all the wholesale dealers in Indian blankets that are secured from the Navahos, and I personally know ninety per cent of the Indian curio dealers of the Southwest and all those of Los Angeles, Flagstaff, and Albuquerque. Of Cheyenne and Bismarck I am unable to speak. I venture the assertion that it is not possible to find in all the stores in all the centers I have named one basket, professedly made by an Indian, which is made by a white person, and the same can be said of the blankets. But it must be remembered that some blankets are sold as Indian blankets which are made by Mexicans, and it requires knowledge to differentiate between an Indian blanket and a Mexican blanket, though both are hand-made on primitive looms.

As far as the purchase of the blanket from the back of an Indian is concerned, for which the author claims to have paid thirty dollars, the deception in that case was self-deception or ignorance rather than any intent to deceive on the part of the Indian. Indians seldom, if ever, wear blankets of their own manufacture. They make no pretense of wearing them. Their blankets are too thick, rough, and stiff for use as personal wraps. They are fit only for rugs, portieres, or buggy robes.

I have just returned from a prolonged trip to the Navaho Reservation, and it was a daily occurrence when I was in the stores of the Indian traders to see Navaho weavers bring their blankets and sell them for amounts varying from ten to sixty dollars, part of the proceeds of which they immediately invested in the purchase of a machine-made blanket. This latter style of blanket, while it possesses Indian designs and is made in striking colors, is no more intended to be an imitation of the Indian blanket than a chromo is *intended* to be a *deceptive imitation* of a painting by Raphael or Corot, and he is a self-conceited ignoramus who could possibly be deceived by such a blanket.

The fact of the matter is that when the Navaho found she could sell her blanket for enough to purchase a dozen American blankets she promptly did so, for the reason before stated, viz., that most of her own blankets are too stiff to give warmth and comfort when wrapped around her. A good three-dollar comforter is worth half a dozen fifty-dollar blankets as far as comfort when lying down and sleeping is concerned. The closely-woven Navaho will shed the rain and keep out the wind, and the thick, fuzzy type is good as a mattress, but none familiar with Navaho blankets ever buys them for bed-covers or wraps. As soon as this fact dawned clearly upon Messrs. Hubbell and Cotton, and the C. H. Algert Company they immediately began to negotiate with the blanket weavers of the East and Northwest for the manufacture of blankets, especially designed for the Navaho trade, containing those designs and colors which they knew would be pleasing to their Indian customers. They themselves provided the designs — these men, be it especially noted and remembered, whose greatest income is from the sale of *genuine Navaho blankets,* and whose business would suffer materially if the notion ever became broadcast that the real Navaho could be successfully imitated. They now purchase these blankets by the *carload,* and there is not a trader on or off the whole reservation who does not carry a quantity of them in stock; but the idea has never entered their minds that anyone could purchase them for genuine Navaho blankets. No man has a right to slander and vilify an honorable body of business men, nor is he justified in awakening the suspicions of the purchasing public in regard to a staple article of goods about which only those who have had no opportunity to be informed can be imposed upon. Such is my confidence in the reliable blanket dealers of the Southwest that I will undertake to buy back at the full price, with interest, every blanket purchased from a dealer of repute in his own community who knows Indian goods, and who has knowingly and wilfully deceived an ignorant purchaser into buying a machine-made blanket.

On this subject even so careful an authority as General U. S. Hollister, in his *The Navaho and His Blanket,* gives out misleading ideas. He says (the italics are mine) :

It is frequently said that many of the so-called Navaho blankets are now made in eastern factories, but this is not true *to any great extent.* Some garish things *in attempts at Navaho designs* are so made, but the likeness is too poor to be called even an imitation; and no dealer with the slightest sense of honor would offer one of the horrid things as a Navaho blanket. Tourists have only themselves to blame if they are sometimes thus deceived.

The error and unconscious mischief of this statement is its implication that *to some extent* so-called Navaho blankets are made. They are not made to *any* extent. There is *not one* that for a moment can deceive anyone reasonably familiar with the hand-woven Navaho product. That tourists sometimes have themselves to blame for their own deception is true, as General Hollister thus remarks, though, as a rule, the only blankets used by the Navahos today are those especially woven for them.

The Navahos often prefer to wear blankets made in the East, for two reasons: one is that they are lighter; and the other, that they can sell a good blanket of their own make for a sum sufficient to purchase a " Mackinaw." Not long ago a lady visitor saw one of these Mackinaw blankets on the back of a Navaho buck at Gallup, New Mexico. She immediately began negotiations, and finally got the blanket for about three times what it cost " poor Lo," and went away rejoicing, believing she had a genuine Navaho blanket. Why? Because she had bought it from a Navaho Indian! Incidents of this kind having been repeated frequently have, no doubt, given rise to the story and belief that a large proportion of what are said to be Navaho blankets are not made by the Navahos, but are the products of eastern looms. Nothing, however, can be further from the truth. A visit to the establishments of all the Indian traders in or about the Navaho reservation, or to those in any of the cities of the East or West in which Navaho blankets are offered for sale, will fail to find a single blanket represented as of Navaho origin that was not made by the Navahos themselves or in similar style on primitive looms by imitative Mexicans.

There is another reason, however, which ought forever to satisfy the intelligent reader that Navaho blankets can never be imitated. As is shown in nearly all of the colored plates in this book, the colors of a certain line of weave are *not alike* all the way across the blanket. There may be two, or three, six, a dozen, even twenty colors on one line or row of cross weave. And the colors are alike on both sides. This is possible only in hand work, where a weaver may take her color as far as she chooses, and then substitute another. The following letter quoted by General Hollister explains the limitations of machine-weaving and satisfactorily demonstrates that it can never successfully imitate the hand-weaving of any people:

PENDLETON WOOLEN MILLS

Fleece Wool Blankets, Indian Robes and Shawls

PENDLETON, OREGON, June 23, 1902.

Dear Sir—We have your letter of the 17th and also the sample of the Navaho. We note what you say about blanket people saying this has never been successfully imitated. It is for a good reason. It is impossible with any machine yet made to get this effect. On our looms there are but two shuttle boxes on a side. Running a different shuttle in each box only allows for four colors at a time. In this robe a certain color appears and then is cut out. On a machine when a color once starts across the beam, it must be carried clear to the other side, either on one side or the other. If you lose it from the upper side, it must appear somewhere on the bottom. It is necessary for it to go clear across to be able to return. In weaving by hand, one can simply take the shuttle out any place desired and lay it aside until wanted again, covering the end between the filling threads and warp.

We can get this diamond pattern, however, if you think it would do, but cannot get the effect nor the weave as it appears in this robe. The Racine people are making a shawl something after this pattern, but can use only a limited number of colors, for the reasons explained above.

We could do this. We could get something like this pattern and then work with two colors for a certain width, and then change to two others, giving a striped effect. For instance, we could work with black and yellow, the diamond pattern appearing in yellow and the background in black, and then change to green and red, for a certain width, and so on. This, however, would not produce the effect you are after.

On this kind of a proposition we can quickly tell you we cannot do anything except go ahead and try to get up something that is impossible. If you think a robe something like we have described would sell, let us know and we can get out some, but they will be far, far from the Navaho effect.

Yours very truly,
PENDLETON WOOLEN MILLS.

Further, to confirm my assertions, I again quote General Hollister, and assure the reader that this is the universal testimony of all who know:

I have traveled extensively throughout our Southwestern country, and have examined the stocks of nearly every Indian trader and dealer in Navaho fabrics; and in no instance has a spurious blanket or rug been offered me as of Navaho make. I have not always agreed with the dealers' statements regarding the age, composition, or coloring of their blankets, but I am, however, pretty well satisfied that in the main they are sincere in their representations, and place their goods before their customers with the best knowledge they possess. Some of them have been so long in the business that they are authorities upon the subject.

CHAPTER XX

Pueblo Indian Weavers

WE have already seen that the art of weaving was known to the Pueblo Indians long prior to the coming of the Spaniards into New Mexico (and Arizona) in 1540. They were also growers and weavers of cotton. In the American Museum of Natural History, in New York, is a fine specimen of cotton weaving taken from a prehistoric cliff-dwelling. It is from a cotton blanket that was originally about three by five feet in size. It is in colors and the designs are similar to those found on the pottery of an earlier or contemporaneous period.

In spite of the oft-made assertion that "the Pueblos appear to have soon discarded the spinning of cotton for the easier spinning of wool," there is plenty of evidence that they have never discontinued cotton-weaving, and they still (1914) make many of their garments of this material. Every wedding dress of a Hopi maiden is of cotton, and I have half a dozen or more ceremonial costumes of cotton, embroidered with wool of different colors in striking designs. Fig. 34 is of a rare old Hopi woman's blanket, with a white cotton body and a border of deep blue with stripes of white cotton and red bayeta. Blankets of this type are very rare and seldom found, even in the best collections. The cotton weave is of twilled design and is a beautiful specimen of artistic work, while the border is in two panels, the wider of which is crossed with double diamonds. On the inner edge of this panel are a row of triangular figures placed one upon another. The white of the cotton has taken on a rich creamy hue, which gives the blanket as a whole a very pleasing effect.

In practically all of the various pueblos of the Rio Grande, of New Mexico and Arizona, one or more weavers can be found who make blankets that cannot be distinguished from those of the Navaho. At the Hopi House, near El Tovar, at the Grand Canyon, Fred Harvey generally has a Hopi weaving *Navaho* blankets. Mrs. Matilda Coxe Stevenson, whose colossal work on the Zunis occupies the whole six hundred pages, with scores of additional plates, of the *Twenty-third Annual Report of the Bureau of American Ethnology,* states that:

in 1881 a young boy about twelve years of age became jealous over the writer's admiration for the blankets of the Navaho and determined to see what he could do. Going to work with no design before him, he produced a saddle-blanket of exceptional beauty.

The elaborate figures were woven in various colors on a red ground.   In 1902 a Zuni priest presented the writer with a blanket of his own weaving, which, though not fine, was elaborate in design and color.   It was made in order to show the writer that the Zunis possess the art of weaving blankets in the Navaho style even though they do not practice it.   They prefer to purchase blankets of the more elaborate kind from the Navahos and give their time to other things.

During the past twenty years since active and open hostilities between the Navahos and Pueblos have terminated there has been a commingling which has somewhat disturbed the old and rigid lines of racial or tribal divergence.   This has manifested itself in weaving as in many other ways. For instance, time was when one familiar with the different tribes could immediately point out a Navaho-woven blanket from that of a Hopi, Zuni, or Acoma, etc.   But that day has gone by.   A Navaho woman weaver may be found making a dress in the Hopi weave, or a Hopi man weaving a Navaho blanket.   In my collection I have a squaw-dress which was woven by a Zuni man, but it has none of the characteristics of the twilled or diamond weaving so often found in Pueblo squaw-dress weaving. Indeed, it is a simple Navaho weave throughout.   It is woven broad side on.   The two plain striped portions are in black and dark gray.   The center design is in red, with the crosses in orange, with a smaller cross inside each in black.   The upper and lower stripes are in red, with the "square-eyed" design in red, purple, and orange.

Fig. 244 is of a Hopi weaver at Sichomovi, on the first mesa.   It will be observed that, in the main, this loom is exactly the same as that of the Navaho weavers, though the weaver is a man.   Here, too, is another evidence of individuality in weaving methods.   This man, having woven the diagonal portion of the squaw-dress at one end, turned the loom over so that he could complete the diagonal weaving of the other end before he began the plain or simple weave of the center of the dress.

That this method, however, is not uncommon is shown by Fig. 245, which depicts a Hopi man weaver at the most western of the Hopi pueblos, Oraibi.

One of the most interesting of sights is to see a Hopi weaving a white cotton garment, full blanket size, from cotton of his own growing, cleaning, carding, and spinning.   This is generally done in the sanctity of the kiva, or secret underground ceremonial chamber, because the dress, when completed, is to be worn by his bride at the wedding ceremony. Such a blanket has no color to it whatever, but is adorned with carefully made and most elaborate cords and tassels at each corner.   A reed case is also made for carrying it.

For dance and other ceremonial purposes, however, cotton dresses of this type are beautifully embroidered in black, green, and red, similar to the kilt shown in Fig. 246.   The Hopis are great adepts in this kind of work.

Fig. 247 shows a member of the Antelope clan at Oraibi weaving a ceremonial sash or kilt, which he is to wear at the forthcoming Snake Dance, in the manner shown in Fig. 248.   This dance is fully described in my *Indians of the Painted Desert Region* and is one of the most remarkable and astounding religious rites of the pagan world.   The sash is shown in Fig. 246, with one of the Pueblo and Navaho belts worn around the waists of the women.

Fig. 244.
A Hopi Weaver at Sichomovi.

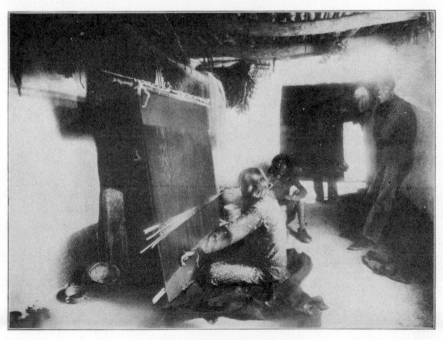

Fig. 245.
A Hopi Weaver at Oraibi.

Fig. 246.
Hopi Ceremonial Sash, and Woman's
Sash or Belt.

Fig. 247.
Hopi Weaving Ceremonial
Sash.

Fig. 248.
Hopi Priests. Method of Wearing Cere-
monial Sash or Kilt in the
Snake Dance.

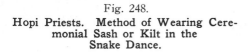

CHAPTER XXI

The Chimayó Blanket

WHILE the aborigine of North America was familiar with the art of weaving prior to the coming of the Spaniards, it was much modified and improved after his advent. The Navaho brought a rude loom and rude methods of work with him. Here he found the Pueblo Indian and from him learned much. Then, when the Spaniard came, both Pueblo and Navaho had sheep added to their possessions, the wool from which practically changed the future of the art of weaving as far as they were concerned.

The Spaniards and Mexicans also brought with them their weaving arts. Many of their numbers were able to weave blankets and the finer serapes. Hence, side by side, three different types of blanket-weaving were carried on. These were, first, that of the Pueblos; second, that of the Navahos, and, third, that of the Mexicans. Almost every Mexican settlement had its weavers in the early days of their occupation of what is now United States territory, but here and there the art declined and finally disappeared, while in other settlements but one or two families preserved their looms and continued to use them. One settlement, Chimayó, however, kept up its weaving, and has so persistently continued in its practice that Chimayó blankets have become known all over the civilized world, and its older and better types are highly prized by collectors. The Mexican settlements known as Chimayó are about thirty miles north of Santa Fé and ten or twelve miles from Española, a station on the narrow-gauge line of the Denver & Rio Grande Railway, which runs from Santa Fé to Denver, changing at Alamosa, Colorado, from the narrow to the broad gauge.

It was a sharp, clear, snappy afternoon in December, 1912, when I walked from Española to Santa Cruz, two miles away, getting a "lift" in a friendly buggy as I crossed the bridge over the Rio de la Santa Cruz.

Chimayó is not a town in the sense that Americans understand the term. It is the name given to ten or eleven little settlements, stretching out for six miles or more along the Santa Cruz River. The name implies "the meeting of the streams." Just above the uppermost settlement the Rio Cundiyo and the Rio Chiquito unite and form the Santa Cruz. The dwellers in the Chimayó settlements call it the Rio Chimayó until it reaches the town of Santa Cruz, when they are then willing to call it the Rio de la Santa Cruz — a change rather confusing to the ordinary American not accustomed to the idiosyncrasies of the Mexican mind. The settlements that form Chimayó are known as follows, coming up the river from west to east — all are on the north side of the stream except *La Puebla* to the west and *Potrero* to the east — *Cuarteles,* so called because a body of Mexican soldiers was once quartered there; *La Puebla; Plaza Abajo,* the lower plaza; *Los Ranchos; La Cuchilla,* so-called because it is located on a small hill with a knife-like ridge; *Plaza del Cerro,* the plaza of the hill (this is commonly known as *Chimayó* on account of its possessing the post-office bearing that name); *Rincon,* the corner settlement; *Potrero,* "the opening" — into the canyon above; *Los Ojuelos,* the little springs; *El Llano,* the plain; and *Rio Chiquito,* the Little River.

The locations of the Chimayó settlements were occupied by Indians long prior to the advent of the Spaniards and Mexicans. All the way up the banks of the stream there were small Indian rancherias or pueblos, and these people all called themselves Chimayó. It was in 1714 that a few Spanish families came and settled along the river, and little by little the Indians disappeared, or were absorbed by marriage, until now there is not a single Indian family left. This also accounts for the Mexican names given to the different settlements.

After spending the night in the parsonage of Santa Cruz, I hired a buggy to take me to Chimayó the next morning. The road for the major part of the distance is up the course of the Rio Santa Cruz, which at this time of the year spreads out into two, three, or more rapidly flowing creeks. The road was rocky in most places, sandy, and rough. We crossed the stream many times, the separate channels being lined with thick ice. In spring, when the ice thaws out, the road is muddy in places, as well as sandy and rocky; in summer, when the rains and cloudbursts come one cannot venture to guess where and what the road is, for they tell me there is no other way of going back and forth, and the stream spreads out until all roads are obliterated, and, at times, the river becomes a raging torrent, pouring down its flood with great rapidity to the Rio Grande. In the fall it is rocky, muddy, sandy, and rough; and winter, spring, summer, and winter it is uniformly hard, uphill, and disagreeable, except to those who choose to take their daily exercise by being jolted, jarred, jounced, and jiggered from one side of the buggy or wagon to another, up and down, back and forth, and sometimes all directions in one grand bounce, which jerks the head half off the shoulders, and semi-dislocates the spine.

But immediately on reaching *Plaza del Cerro* all memory of the discomforts suffered disappear. A drive of two hours and a half has

Fig. 249.
An Old Chimayó or Mexican Blanket.
Called by the Navahos nak hai bicliidi.   [Page 169]

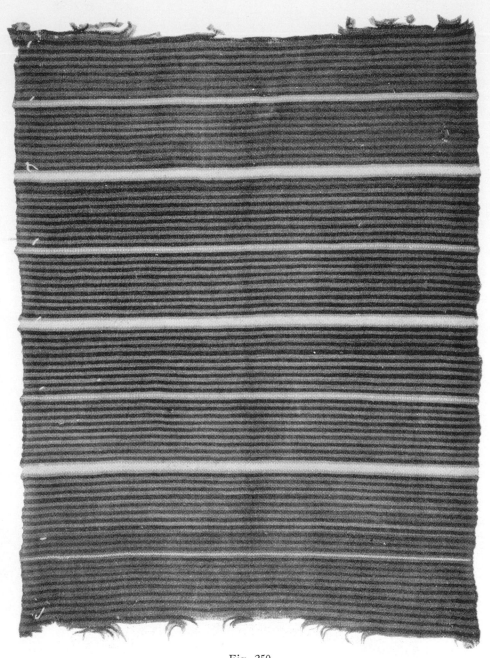

Fig. 250.
Rare Old Chimayó Blanket in Black, Blue, and White.
(Fred Harvey Collection.) [Page 169]

Fig. 251.
Handsome Chimayó Blanket.
(Made expressly for Rev. G. Haelterman,
Santa Cruz, N. M.)

brought us to the settlement, snugly nestled along the foothills, beyond which snowy-clad peaks of the Rocky Mountains tower into the New Mexico sky. It is a straggling place, with streets that remind one of Sam Walter Foss's poem of the Boston "Calf Path," in their irresponsible and altogether unsuspected twinings and twistings. Here a large plaza is surrounded by well-built, thrifty-looking Mexican houses. Though built of adobe, and with flat roofs, most of them are whitewashed and attractive, and a few glimpses through open doors as we pass suggest what our later observation confirms, that here is no lazy, indifferent, drinking, gambling Mexican settlement, but the home of self-respecting, hard-working, thriving, law-abiding men and women, who could well set an example to many far more pretentious towns and villages in our eastern states.

On every hand are evidences of prosperity. Fruit orchards are found in all directions. Apples, peaches, plums, and cherries grow abundantly and of finest flavor, and a ready market is found for them in Santa Fé, Albuquerque, and other points on the Santa Fé Railway. The plaza itself is cut up into gardens belonging to those who dwell around it, and in spring and summer it supplies their tables with a varied and abundant supply of vegetables, while it charms the eye of residents and visitors alike with the riot of color of its fragrant flowers.

During the fruit and vegetable season the people are fruit growers and agriculturists, but in winter, when the ground is frozen, they uncover their looms, and in three-fifths of the houses the bump of the batten and the jerk of the treadle may be heard as the busy weaver plies her shuttle to and fro.

Here everything is different from the methods followed by the Navaho. The loom, though rude and roughly built, is not unlike those which George Eliot described in *Adam Bede,* or which even now may be found in many of the older and quieter village communities of New England, New York, and Pennsylvania.

The spinning wheel is different, however, in appearance from the old wheels which we find now and again in ancient houses, or exalted to places of honor in local museums, although, of course, the principle of working is practically the same.

Being made by Mexicans, the older types of Chimayó blankets were made in two parts, as are the serapes, sewed together down the middle. Of late years, however, as there has grown up a demand for Chimayó work, the double, center-sewn blanket practically has been abandoned, and it is now made in one piece, complete.

Figs. 249, 250 are representative Chimayós of the oldest and best types. The warp is of home-grown, home-cleaned, home-carded, homespun, natural white wool. Two threads are spun together to give the blankets strength and body. The weaving is simple, as is also the design, while the colors are but white, black, and blue, the two former being the native colors of the wool, and the blue made by dyeing with indigo. In some of the stripes that separate the black it will be observed that blue and white alternate. This alternation is caused by the weaver holding a shuttle of blue in one hand, and one of white in the other, and throwing them simultaneously in opposite directions.

Fig. 249 is of much the simpler form, though the colors in both blankets are the same, and only straight lines are used. Fig. 250, however, is much better woven and a far more desirable blanket. It is of full size and weighs about seven pounds. The general effect of its simplicity in color and design, enhanced by a peculiar charm bestowed by age, gives it a dignity altogether foreign to the later and more pretentious work.

Now and again a Chimayó weaver, embued with the love of colors apparently inherent in all Mexicans, wove a blanket with a wider gamut, and I was fortunate in securing a rare and beautiful specimen of this type especially woven for my friend, the Rev. G. Haelterman, the Catholic priest of Santa Cruz, in whose parish all the Chimayó settlements are, and to whose people he has continuously ministered for a score or more years. This blanket, Fig. 251, is 42x75 inches in size, though, as it is woven in two parts and sewn down the center, it is really two strips 21x75 inches long. The basic color is white with the lines of the serrated diamonds in a light red, dark brown, dark blue, rich maroon-chocolate, with touches of lemon-yellow. The blanket has been washed many times and some of the colors have slightly "run" into those of other lines, and this seems to have enhanced the color values instead of detracting from them.

The blue dye of the old Chimayó blanket is indigo. This was brought from Mexico in lumps about the size of a walnut. A number of these lumps were placed in a small sack made of cheese-cloth or its equivalent, which was then thrown into a small earthenware bowl of urine. As soon as the indigo showed signs of disintegrating a larger bowl was put out of doors, on a fire, and the urine and indigo stirred now and again while it came to a boil. When all the coloring matter was thoroughly dissolved and the liquid boiled, the wool was immersed several times until the color was thoroughly absorbed. The yarn was then allowed to drain for a short time, after which it was hung out to dry.

The yellow was gained from the same flower used by the Navahos.

The red used was exactly as described in the chapter on the bayeta blanket. For the New Mexican trade it was generally purchased in "Brazil sticks."

When attention was directed by experts to the fine weaving of the

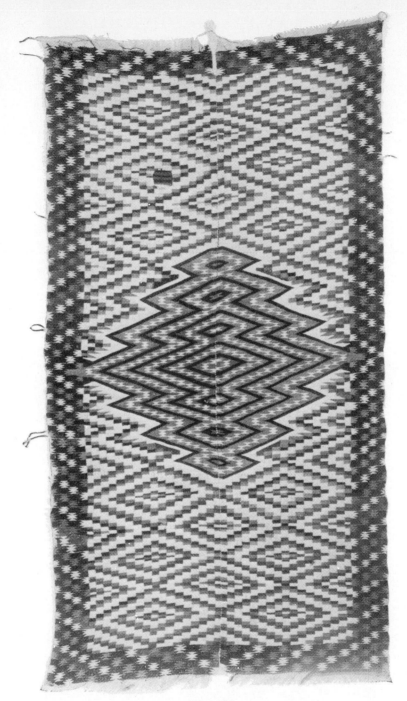

Fig. 252.
Old Chimayó, Black, White, and Blue.
(Fred Harvey Collection.)

The usual type of old Chimayó is plain blue and white stripes,
though diversified in the arrangement of the stripes. The type here
illustrated is rare, and the design is really derived from the Saltillo
blanket of Old Mexico. The Chimayos are part Indian and part Mexican, and their style of weaving and designs can be traced to both.

Fig. 253.
Rare Old Chimayó of Simple Design.
(Author's Collection.)

Navahos, and the traders sent collectors all through New Mexico to gather every old bayeta, native-wool and native-dyed blankets, they brought in quite a number of these Chimayó blankets. The collectors did not gain their history; they were simply informed they were not Navahos, but were made in New Mexico by Mexicans. The name was spelled, therefore, in Mexican or Spanish fashion, Chemallo, and it was not until a comparatively recent date that those outside of New Mexico began to learn the real story of the Chimayó settlements, as I have herein recounted it.

The output of old Chimayós, while apparently large, was very small in the aggregate when such a population as that of the United States is considered. All told there never were more than a hundred weavers (so I am informed), and if each wove three blankets a winter — a large average — that would be but three hundred a year. The ordinary life of an old Chimayó, receiving the rough usage the Mexicans give their blankets, was possibly not more than ten years; hence many of them have passed out of existence. Mexico also absorbed quite a number, for in spite of the fact that the Mexicans weave their own *serapes* and blankets, the Chimayó weaves were much sought after. The result is there are, I suppose, not more than a score of good old Chimayós now offered for sale in the country. The only dealers that I know who have a few fine and desirable specimens are Fred Harvey, of Albuquerque, New Mexico, and the Burns Indian Trading Company, of Los Angeles.

Fig. 252 is a fine, representative example in the Fred Harvey collection. The colors are black, blue, and white, the only dye used being that of indigo for producing the blue. The black varies in color just as the black is found to vary on the backs of the sheep, and in one or two cases a little gray has been introduced instead of black, which gives a unique and pleasing variety.

This blanket throughout is of native wool — not too closely woven — and the warp is of wool. The center design is of conventionalized diamonds, while the remaining part of the design is made up of diamonds, or lozenges of various sizes made of rectangular blocks or diamonds. The border, which is uniform in design throughout, is mainly black with a slight mixture of gray (before referred to) with blue and white figures interwoven throughout.

Those who are familiar with the Mexican *serape* inform me that this design is very often found in the *Saltillo* serape. Chimayós of this type are very desirable for portieres or couch-covers, where they do not get rough usage.

Fig. 253 is of an old Chimayó in my own collection. It is 48x65 inches in size, and is all wool, warp and woof, and as light a specimen as

I have ever seen. It is soft and pliable and perfectly suited either for a bed-blanket or wrap. Its colors are white, indigo-blue, and black, but the latter has softened until it is a rich brownish-black that gives a wonderfully beautiful effect to the blanket as a whole.

At Chimayó, however, as among the Navahos, modern methods have entirely revolutionized the industry. A modern Chimayó blanket is still a distinctive creation, but it is no more like the old type than a common Standard Navaho is like a bayeta. It must be remembered, however, that the Chimayó weavers have never made as tightly-spun a yarn, or as closely-woven a blanket as did, and do, the Navahos. Their blankets are softer, more adapted for bed coverings, or for actually wrapping around the person.

In nearly all modern Chimayós cotton warps are used instead of wool. These are easier to get, being purchasable at the nearest store; and, though not quite so easy to work, as they do not lend themselves to the strain of the shuttle as do the wool warps, they preserve the shape better. They are also cheaper, thus making the actual cost of the blanket less to the weaver. And, as in thousands of cases, the buyer knows no difference between wool and cotton warps, and is willing to pay as much for the latter as for the former, the short-sighted weaver argues that it is to her advantage to use cotton.

Little by little, however, the same check will be put upon cotton-warped Chimayó blankets as has been upon the Navaho, and the art will improve as the result.

But not only do the modern Chimayó weavers use cotton warp. They have grown weary in well-doing, and no longer cut, clean, dye, card, and spin the wool themselves. It is so much easier to buy Germantown yarn all ready for the loom; hence most modern Chimayós are made of Germantown yarns woven on cotton warps. Most of them have solid body colors with small designs interspersed throughout.

When I asked a keen-brained Mexican father of a family why native spinning and dyeing were abandoned, and cotton warps were used in place of the more satisfactory home-made wool-warps, he exclaimed: "Our girls do not want to work so hard as their mothers did. They would rather go to school and make a speech [recite] than card, spin, and dye wool. They no longer *sabe* how to make *atole*. If they pretend to make it they don't cook it enough, and it gives one indigestion to try to eat it."

I replied that it was "Too bad!" and he added, with a melancholy air: "They should not forget the old things unless they learn something better."

I could not help thinking how appropriate this was to all industries.

It is a bad business to forget the old good ways, especially when there are substituted for them new and worse ways.

For small pillow, cushion, and table covers cotton warps may answer every purpose, as the sizes demand so little weight, and the wear is so small that the cotton is equal to every strain. Some of the designs of these covers are exceedingly attractive, and they are worked out with artistic skill. Taste in color necessarily is a personal matter. What pleases one will not please another, and the Chimayó weavers are no exception to this universal rule. There are a few weavers, however, whose tastes seem more critical than those of others, and their work meets with the approval of those best qualified to judge.

In order to meet the great demand for modern Chimayó blankets of this and the better class Mr. Burns, of the Burns Indian Trading Company, of Los Angeles, personally visited Chimayó, bought several looms, and engaged the best weavers he could find to come to Los Angeles and there weave regularly for his growing trade. The looms were set up, and for the past two or more years have been steadily at work. While small covers with cotton warps are made, and a cheap grade of the larger blankets, the choicest weaves all have wool warps. Many of these are in almost solid colors, of reds, browns, blacks, grays, etc., with small designs in the center or at the ends in some relieving color or colors.

CHAPTER XXII

Cleaning the Navaho Blanket

TO THE housewife it sometimes becomes a serious matter how to direct the cleaning of blankets that she knows are valuable and highly prized without injuring them.

The Navahos themselves have two methods of cleaning them. One is to take the soiled blanket out into the sand of the cornfield, and then shovel damp sand upon it and allow it to remain buried for a day or so (see Fig. 254). It is then well scrubbed with the sand, thoroughly beaten and shaken and allowed to fully dry and air in the sun.

Where a more thorough cleansing is required the saponaceous roots of the *amole* are taken, macerated into shredded fibre, beaten up and down in a bowl of water until a rich lather is produced. With this suds and a rude brush made of shredded cedar bark the blanket is soaked and scrubbed on both sides, after which it is rinsed with as much water as these desert-dwellers can spare. If the colors are not well-mordanted this process naturally makes them "run" and commingle, and this often spoils a blanket, but where the colors are fast, or the wool of the blanket is the native white, black, gray, or brown, no injury can result, and there is no soap known to modern civilization that equals this natural soap used for so long by these Bedouins of the Painted Desert.

The Mexicans use the same *amole* root for the purpose of cleaning their brilliantly-colored serapes and the Chimayó blankets of their own weave.

Of course, since the modern vacuum cleaner has come into use it will solve the problem for all but extreme cases, and, perhaps, in such cases, the unaware would better consult an expert before running any risks.

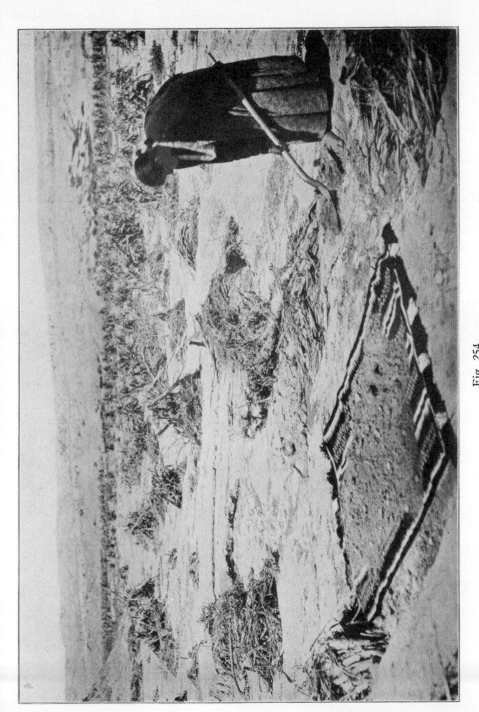

Fig. 254.

Navaho Woman Cleaning Blanket.

[Page 174]

APPENDIX

I

The Navaho Indian

OF ALL the North American Indian tribes none is more interesting than the Navaho. Occupying a reservation in the northeastern corner of Arizona and the northwestern corner of New Mexico — the largest Indian reservation in the United States, with an area of 12,360,723 acres, or about 19,313 square miles, larger than the states of New Hampshire, Vermont and Rhode Island combined — the Navaho tribe is rapidly on the increase.

While the Navaho are supposed to remain on their reservation, they pay little attention to suppositional requirements. They occupy, in addition to their reservation, about 2,304,000 acres, or 3,600 square miles, of Government and railway land, together with a large portion of the Hopi Indian Reservation. It is said that fully 2,000 Navahos are now living on the lands of the Hopi. I suppose it is owing to the rapid increase in the number of these people, their industrious trading, farming, and sheep-herding occupations, and their peaceable character that they are accorded these freedoms. The Hopis do not seem to need all their land, and little or no objection is made to the presence of the Navahos, and the white people are so eager and anxious for the trade of a thrifty, prosperous, and wealth acquiring race that they welcome, rather than object to, their presence and bartering proximity.

Yet it must not be thought that the Navaho is a weak, subservient, dependent Indian. Even in his trading he is bold, independent, self-reliant, and self-assertive. The most skilful traders on the reservation assure me that they are as alert as the most wide-awake white men, and that the wits of the latter are often taxed to the utmost to keep pace with them. The major portion are honest and reasonably truthful, but they are ready and quick to seize every advantage, and are unscrupulous in dealing with a too-confident, boastful, or ignorant white.

It can scarcely be said of them that they are — what Inspector James McLaughlin, in his admirable *My Friend the Indian,* terms the Utes — "unwhipped." From time immemorial they are said to have warred upon the Pueblo Indians, and, after the Spaniards settled in New Mexico, upon these invaders also. It was not so much enmity or hostility as "benevolent assimilation" that was the motive of these wars. The industrious and home-loving Pueblos and Mexicans accumulated possessions that the Navahos envied and coveted. The next step was to seize, and, as they were numerous, crafty, and reasonably brave, they generally managed, either by stealth, craft, or force, to obtain what they wanted. Many a story is told of fights with the Navahos by the Mexicans prior to the seizure of New Mexico by Kearny, August 15, 1846. Some of these form thrilling chapters in the books of Charles F. Lummis — stories told to him by his Spanish friends, the Bacas, Chaves', Hubbells, and others of early New Mexican days.

Major Emory, who accompanied Colonel Kearny, thus writes of Las Vegas, N. M., and the attacks made upon it by the Navahos:

The village, at a short distance, looked like an extensive brick-kiln. Approaching, its outline presented a square with some arrangements for defense. Into this square the inhabitants are sometimes compelled to retreat, with all their stock, to avoid the attacks of the Utaws (Utes) and Navahos, who pounce upon them and carry off their women, children, and cattle. Only a few days since, they made a descent on the town and carried off 120 sheep and other stock. As Captain Cooke passed through the town ten days since, a murder had just been committed on these helpless people.

And September 30, 1846, looking out over the mountainous country northwest of Santa Fé, he wrote:

I saw here the hiding places of the Navahos, who, when few in number, wait for the night to descend upon the valley and carry off the fruit, sheep, women, and children of the Mexicans. When in numbers, they come in daytime and levy their dues. Their retreats and caverns are at a distance to the west, in high and inaccessible mountains, where troops of the United States will find great difficulty in overtaking and subduing them, but where the Mexicans have never thought of penetrating. The Navahos may be termed the lords of New Mexico. Few in number, disdaining the cultivation of the soil, and even the rearing of cattle, they draw all their supplies from the valley of the Del Norte.

This was the common reputation of the Navahos when the Americans first began to come in contact with them. The Mexicans and the Indian tribes dreaded them as a hostile, thieving, quarrelsome, yet brave and daring, people. They were in constant fear, and tried again and again to make treaties with them, which were no sooner made than they were broken.

The United States Government, through its officials in the field, started in on the same plan. Rumors were current that the Navahos had a great and impregnable fortress in the heart of their country; they were reputed warlike and treacherous, and the better and wiser plan seemed to be to conciliate, rather than provoke them to declared hostility.

When Colonel Kearny left Santa Fé for California he placed the responsibility of the government of New Mexico upon the shoulders of

Colonel Alex. W. Doniphan, of the First Missouri Volunteers. But he had not been gone long before he sent Doniphan a special order to organize and conduct a campaign against the Navahos, who had been raiding the valley in the neighborhod of Polvodera. Doniphan immediately left, placing Colonel Price in command at Santa Fé, and finally, at Ojo del Oso (Bear Spring), after a campaign of six weeks, a treaty of peace was concluded.

A remarkable speech was made at this treaty which has been preserved. In his negotiations Doniphan outlined the policy of the United States in New Mexico, and he was then replied to by Sarcilla Largo, a young, bright, and aggressive Navaho, as follows:

Americans! You have a strange case of war against the Navahos. We have waged war against the New Mexicans for many years. We have plundered their villages, killed many of their people, and have taken many prisoners. Our cause was just. You have lately commenced a war against the same people. You are powerful. You have great guns and many brave soldiers. You have therefore conquered them, the very thing that we have been attempting to do for many years. You now turn upon us for attempting to do what you have done yourselves. We cannot see why you have cause to quarrel with us for fighting the New Mexicans on the west, while you do the same thing on the east. Look how matters stand! This is our war. We have more right to complain of you for interfering in our war than you have to quarrel with us for continuing a war we had begun long before you got here. If you will act justly you will allow us to settle our own differences.

It was left for "Kit" Carson, who served in New Mexico in 1862-6, under General James H. Carleton, completely to break the warlike and treaty-breaking spirit of the Navaho. James F. Meline, in his *Two Thousand Miles on Horseback*, thus tells part of the story:

Soon after General Carleton assumed command in New Mexico, an eminently respectable deputation of eighteen Navaho chiefs, with keen perspective of indefinite presents, called upon him to know if he would make a treaty. The general is from the state of New Hampshire and characteristically answered their question with another question: "What do you want of a treaty?" "That we may hereafter have peace." "Well, then," was the unexpected reply, "go home, stay there, attend to your own affairs, commit no more robberies or murders upon this people, and you have peace at once, without the trouble of a treaty." Treaties, the general informed them, appeared to confuse matters and involved the double labor to the Navahos of making and breaking them. They, the Navahos, well knew they never kept them, and he, the general, was not a child to be beguiled by them. "Now," he continued, "go; and if you rob or murder any of this people, so surely as the sun rises, you shall have a war that you may not soon forget." Navaho, discomfited, said he had never been treated that way before. Refused a treaty! Was such a thing ever heard of? They were good Indians though. They would return to their country and try to persuade their young men to behave. The result was that in a few weeks the robbery and murder of Mexicans began again. Then came a Navaho message that a large number of them were peaceably disposed. This was in the spring of 1863. General Carleton sent them word that, as they all lived together, he could not distinguish friends from foes; that those who claimed to be friendly should come out from among the others and go to the Bosque Redondo, a large and beautiful tract of land forty miles square, with six thousand acres of arable land, on the Pecos river, where they should be cared for and allowed to want for nothing. Indian reply was not polite, but it was perfectly intelligible. Not a Navaho would come. Another message from the General that they had better consider the matter more maturely. They might have until the 20th of July with the door of peace left wide open. Once closed, it should never be opened again. But the Navahos said they had heard "Big Talk" before that meant nothing; had listened years to the cry of "Wolf" that came not. And they scouted the soldier's warning. True to his promise, the war opened on the very day set by General Carleton, July 20, 1863. A regiment of New Mexicans, with more than a century of accumulated wrong and oppression to avenge, were at once placed under the command of a man who understood his Indian well—Kit Carson. These troops knew neither summer rest nor winter quarters, but pursued the Indian foe relentlessly, month after month, night and day, over mesas and deserts and rivers, under broiling suns and the rough winter snows, killing and capturing them in their chosen retreats, until finally, broken and dispirited under a chastisement the like of which they had never dreamed of, small bands began to come in voluntarily; then larger ones, and finally groups of fifties and hundreds, nearly comprising the strength of the tribe. The prisoners as fast as received were dispatched to the Bosque Redondo and those who remained in arms sent out white flags in vain.

One feature of Carson's method of warfare Mr. Meline does not comment upon, yet it reveals more than anything else Carson's keen insight into Indian character. Instead of arguing pow-wowing or threatening, Carson *acted*.

From General Carleton's report, as quoted by Twitchell, we find that in five counties alone, in the year 1863, the Navahos stole 224 horses, 4,178 cattle, 55,040 sheep, and 5,901 goats, besides killing sixteen citizens. Carson's method was to retaliate in kind, but in such swift and merciless fashion as to stun and bewilder the Navahos, unused, as they were, to quick and forceful action on the part of the Mexican soldiers. Carson fought as did De Wet and the other generals of the Boer war. They had no evolutions, no marching battalions advancing upon the foe in lined-up battle-array. Stealthily, in the night, by forced marches in unsuspected places and at undreamed-of times, Carson's men moved and acted, hit suddenly, hit hard, killing all the horses, cattle, sheep, and goats they saw, remorselessly, relentlessly, and swiftly. Carson made war *hell* to the Navahos, and such swift and persistent hell that they began to realize— as nothing had ever made them realize before—that now they were fighting with men who knew no defeat, and who also knew how to conquer. *There is no other way of dealing with an Indian when he has once gone on the warpath.*

Thus deprived of food and of wool with which to make blankets, the ending of the year 1864 practically saw the major portion of the Navahos surrendered and over 7,000 of them living at the Bosque Redondo. In the transporting of the prisoners to Bosque Redondo such great hardships and terrible exposures were experienced that many of them died, and the few who were allowed to retain their flocks and herds lost most of them in crossing the snow-covered mountains.

During the time they were kept here the fates seemed against them. Year after year their crops failed. Even at the best they were not expert farmers, and the corn-worm ravaged the few crops they did persuade to grow. The grazing was insufficient to nourish their flocks and herds, and they died in large numbers. Even the natural increase that took place was a disadvantage rather than a benefit, for the mother-sheep, weakened by insufficient food, not only could not nourish their lambs, but they were unable to recover their own strength, and perished. To add to their miseries their hereditary foes, the Comanches and other Indians of the plains, defying the forces of the United States that were supposed to protect them, stealthily fell upon them and punished them severely. Weakened by want of food, stricken by disease, broken in spirit, they were in sorry plight.

Then came Congress to their rescue, under the administration of President Grant. A Peace Commission was appointed, and if any of my readers have felt that my many strictures, written here and elsewhere, upon the criminal wickedness of the white men who were the provoking causes of Indian wars — even those of the Apache and Sioux, as well as the Navaho — have been too severe, I would urge upon them a careful perusal of its report. The Commission claimed (and proved its claims) that in fifty years the United States Government had spent *five hundred million dollars,* besides the loss of twenty thousand lives, and, it unhesitatingly affirmed, had been *uniformly unjust* toward the Indian.

June 1, 1867, General Sherman and Colonel Tappan signed a treaty with the Navahos — the terms of which I beg my readers to note carefully — by which they should be returned to their own country in New Mexico and Arizona,

Schools should be established and schoolhouses built for every thirty children between the ages of six and sixteen years among them, their education made compulsory, the heads of families given one hundred and sixty acres of land for individual ownership, seeds and agricultural implements, flocks of sheep and cattle, and one hundred dollars the first year, twenty-five dollars the second and third years, with clothing and other articles needed to encourage and aid them in beginning and living a civilized and industrious life.

I have given these promises in the words of Colonel Twitchell. How were they carried out? The flocks were given to them, and some money, clothing, and food. But in the main they have been left to themselves to develop and prosper in their own way. The Government has done little for them, save the comparatively recent establishment of more schools. Today there are seven government schools on the reservation, in addition to those of the various religious bodies. None of the latter, however, receive any aid from the United States Indian Department.

It should be noted with gratification, at this time, that there is a decided tendency to improvement in our treatment of the Navaho. And it may be that for many of the past years there has been an earnest desire to help them on the part of the high officials at Washington, which — broadly and generally speaking — was frustrated by the incompetency and inefficiency of the agents and superintendents in the field. I am led to this conclusion by recent personal investigations which have demonstrated that where an agent or superintendent really has the welfare of the Indian at heart, and his knowledge and ability are commensurate with his sympathies, he is left to carry out his plans, not only unhampered by the department in Washington, but, in the main, with their cordial cooperation, sanction, and financial help. At the San Juan Agency, locally known as Shiprock, Superintendent W. T. Shelton took hold of matters with the clearest understanding of any man I have yet met in the Indian service in over thirty years of experience. He perceived, what all other workers with Indians have always learned, that to educate a boy or girl born in a *hogan,* away from all of the life he, or she, would naturally lead if left alone, and then return such an individual to the original conditions and environment, was to waste time, energy, and money, just as if he were to prepare a beautiful garment, carefully laundering, embroidering, and decorating it, merely to throw it, when completed, upon a dirt pile to be trampled under foot by wild and unclean animals. The simile may seem unduly strong, but it is not any exaggeration upon the actual conditions that Mr. Shelton knew to exist. Hence, he determined to care for the life of the Navaho boys and girls of his school (and other schools) after their scholastic education was completed. With the vigor of the superior man who knows what he wants and how to obtain it he has gone ahead, backed up generously in the main by the department, and has set aside 5,000 acres of land to be used as home plots for the Indians when they need them. This acreage is near enough to the San Juan Agency to allow daily contact with the life of the school and church, and to give the superintendent and teachers opportunity for watchful care and guardianship over their whilom scholars.

As soon as the young people graduate each one is given one of these house plots of five acres and aided in building a house, planting out the ground, and carefully cultivating the crop. Fine sheep, horses, pigs, and oxen have been bought for breeding purposes, and each scholar is given

an opportunity to purchase these at the lowest possible price. If a couple
desire to marry, their two plots are given together, if possible, and thus
they are encouraged to settle down to a life of useful and civilized
industry. The land is irrigated by a well-constructed system.

Being on the reservation, their parents and friends are able to visit
them and are encouraged to do so. In this way it is hoped the good
influence will spread and the whole tribe ultimately be permeated with the
better ways of the industrious white man.

This plan of Superintendent Shelton cannot be too highly commended,
and it is one which, if persistently followed, will do more to civilize the
Navaho, or any other Indian, than a thousand years of the methods
hitherto followed.

There seems to be some conflict as to the number of Navahos now
found on the reservation. Their number as given in 1869, when they
returned from their banishment at Bosque Redondo, was nearly 9,000.
In 1890, though the census is acknowledged to have been faulty, the
figures returned were 17,204. That of ten years later gave more than
20,000, and in 1906 the Indian Department reported a rough estimate
of 28,500. On the other hand, Father Berard, of St. Michaels, in his *An
Ethnologic Dictionary,* published in 1910, confuses the census of 1890
with that of 1900, assuming that that of 1900 gave the return of 17,204.
Hence, he infers that 20,000 is as near as one can now estimate. Still
others assert that, as many of the Navahos never submitted to "Kit"
Carson, and have always lived in more or less inaccessible places, and yet
have partaken, directly or indirectly, of the benefits that peace has brought
to the tribe, they have increased to such an extent that it would be safe to
say there were 35,000 of them.

The report of the Indian Department for 1912 gave the following
figures of the Navahos who came under the observation, more or less, of
agents and school superintendents at the agencies named. The gross
totals are merely estimated and make no pretence to numerical accuracy.

Children of School Age—		Gross Total of Children and Adults
Moki (Keam's Canyon)	462	2,000
Navaho	2,500	9,990
Leupp	425	1,342
Western Navaho	1,409	6,131
Albuquerque	62	208
Pueblo Bonita	1,221	2,685
San Juan	2,500	8,000
Grand total of children	8,579	Grand total.. 30,356

While I have no desire to be an alarmist, it seems to me that the Indian Department will some day have a new Indian problem on its hands. As I have elsewhere shown, the Navaho is not confined strictly to his own reservation. He has reached over and seized all the available water-holes, springs, pasture, and corn-land on the Hopi Reservation that are not in the actual occupancy of the Hopis. He has done the same on the Zuni Reservation, and has not a few locations on the public domain. Being prosperous and well fed, he is naturally virile, and the women of the tribe being uniformly healthy and vigorous, families are sure of increase. The ratio of births enlarges as the years go by, and it will not be long before there will be 50,000 Navahos on territory that is none too large as it is. What then? If the Hopi and Zuni demand the clearing of their own reserves, how will the Government meet their demands? If uninterrupted occupation confers certain rights, what will be said to the Navahos when they assert such a claim to springs and land on the public domain? And it must be remembered that the Navahos of this generation know little or nothing of the Bosque Redondo experience, and, in their prosperity, have come to regard themselves as their original name, Di-né, implies — *the people*. They will prove to be no easy-going, peace-loving tribe who will meekly submit to what they regard as injustice. They will assert what they conceive to be their rights and bravely stand by them, and it behooves our Indian Department and the wide-awake statesmen of the land to begin to consider what course of action can righteously and properly be taken when these contingencies arise.

About the name Navaho, its derivation, significance, and spelling, there has been considerable controversy. Here are the salient facts. The name first appears in literature in Benavides' *Memorial to the King of Spain,* written in 1630. He there says, after describing the Gila Apaches, that more than fifty leagues north of these—

One encounters the province of the Apaches of Nauajo. Although they are the same Apache nation as the foregoing, they are subject and subordinate to another Chief Captain, and have a distinct mode of living. For those of back yonder did not use to plant, but sustained themselves by the chase; and today we have broken land for them and taught them to plant. But these of Nauajo are very great farmers, for that is what Nauajo signifies — great planted fields.

Upon this matter Father Berard sagely concludes:

From the expression, "the Apaches of Nauajo," it is evident that the word Navaho was not given to the people, but was the name of the province or territory in which they lived; or, in other words, the Indians themselves were called Apaches, and their country was called Navaho, until, later, the name Apache was dropped and the name of the territory applied to the inhabitants.

Dr. Edgar L. Hewett says:

The Tewa Indians assert that the name "Navahu" refers to a large area of cultivated lands. This suggests an identity with Navaho, which Fray Alonzo Benavides applied to that branch of the Apache nation then living to the west of the Rio Grande, beyond the very section above mentioned. . . . It would seem, at any rate, that the Tewa origin of the tribal designation, *Navaho,* is assured.

As to the spelling: Father Berard adopts *Navaho* in his *An Ethnologic Dictionary,* as did Dr. Washington Matthews in his *Navaho Legends, The Night Chant,* and all his later writings on these people. These two men are by long odds the chief authorities upon the subject, and the "Bureau of American Ethnology," which is the official guide to all matters Indian in the United States, has formally adopted it; also the "Board of Geographic Names" and most leading writers. Why, then, others should object to Americanizing a name which had its origin in this country is to me a perversity and a mystery. Is there any pleasure to be derived from spelling a word so that hundreds of thousands of reasonably cultured Americans will mispronounce it? I am glad to follow the true American style.

Father Berard says:

In the English pronunciation of the word Navaho the first a is short and sounded as a in "hat"; the second a is indistinct; the h is strongly aspirated; the final o has its natural sound, and the accent is on the first syllable. Thus, in reading the word, the vowels and the v and h have about the same sound as in the sentence, "have a hoe." The Mexicans place the main accent on the last syllable, pronounce the h slightly guttural and sound the a as in "ma" and "pa." The Navahos themselves, when using this name, pronounce it thus: Na-we-hó.

Their own name for themselves, however, is not Navaho. They are the Di-né (Tinneh)—*the people,* relatives of the Tinnehs of Alaska, and the Apaches, of the great Athabascan stock.

II

The Religious Life of the Navaho

TO a proper comprehension of the place the blanket and its decoration have in the life of the Navaho it is essential that we know some of the more important features of his religious life, and to understand, even though in an incomplete manner, his mental processes.

That this is not an easy task is manifested by the fact that early and late writers have affirmed that the Navaho is irreligious, ignorant, and without tradition. As early as in the *Smithsonian Report* for 1855 Dr. Letherman, who resided for three years at Fort Defiance, in the heart of the Navaho country, wrote as follows:

Of their religion little or nothing is known, as, indeed, all inquiries tend to show that they have none; and even have not, we are informed, any word to express the idea of a Supreme Being. We have not been able to learn that any observances of a religious character exist among them; and the general impression of those who have had means of knowing them is, that, in this respect, they are steeped in the deepest degradation. . . . Their singing is but a succession of grunts, and is anything but agreeable. . . . Their lack of traditions is a source of surprise. They have no knowledge of their origin, or of the history of the tribe.

As late as 1903 General U. S. Hollister wrote:

Most authorities agree that the Navaho is not a particularly religious Indian, for the reason, I suppose, that he does not make much ado about it. He has no public Snake Dances or other ceremonies that are likely to attract attention of a casual visitor; nor does he set up totem poles or idols in his public places. His only conspicuous appliance of worship is the altar in the medicine lodge, which is hidden from the sight of white men, excepting those who are in great favor.

These altars are fantastically ornamented with feathers, stalks, and tassels of corn, grain, grasses, and the like, and on the floor in front of the altar are strewed strange symbols in colored sand — "sand paintings," as they are called by white folks; and over these the incantations are made, prayers are said, and songs sung, to invoke happiness, and success in their every undertaking.

In contradiction of these statements let me present what Dr. Washington Matthews and Father Berard have to say upon this subject, both of them men who have given years to a thorough and persistent study of the Navaho. Dr. Matthews thus comments upon Dr. Letherman's statement, which he notes is confirmed by Major Kendrick, who for many years commanded the military post of Fort Defiance:

The evidence of these gentlemen, one would think, might be taken as conclusive. Yet, fifteen years ago, when the author first found himself among the Navahos, he was not influenced in the least by the authority of this letter. Previous experience with the Indians had taught him of how little value such negative evidence might be, and he began at once to investigate the religion, traditions, and poetic literature, of which, he was assured, the Navahos were devoid.

He had not been many weeks in New Mexico when he discovered that the dances to which Dr. Letherman refers were religious ceremonials, and later he found that *these ceremonials might vie in allegory, symbolism, and intricacy of ritual with the ceremonies of any people, ancient or modern.* He found, ere long, that these heathen, pronounced godless and legendless, possessed lengthy myths and traditions — so numerous that one can never hope to collect them all, *a pantheon as well stocked with gods and heroes as that of the ancient Greeks,* and prayers which, for length and vain repetition, might put a Pharisee to the blush.

But what did the study of appalling "succession of grunts" reveal? It revealed that, besides improvised songs, in which the Navahos are adepts, they have knowledge of thousands of significant songs — or poems, as they might be called — which have been composed with care and handed down, for centuries perhaps, from teacher to pupil, from father to son, as a precious heritage, throughout the wide Navaho nation. They have songs of traveling, appropriate to every stage of the journey, from the time the wanderer leaves his home until he returns. They have farming songs which refer to every stage of their simple agriculture, from the first view of the planting ground in the spring to the "harvest home." They have building songs, which celebrate every act in the structure of the hut, from " thinking about it " to moving into it and lighting the first fire. They have songs for hunting, for war, for gambling — in short, for every important occasion in life, from birth to death, not to speak of prenatal and *post-mortem* songs. And these songs are composed according to established (often rigid) rules, and abound in poetic figures of speech.

Perhaps the most interesting of their metrical compositions are those connected with their sacred rites — their religious songs. These rites are very numerous, many of them of nine days' duration, and with each is associated a number of appropriate songs. Sometimes, pertaining to a single rite, there are two hundred songs or more which may not be sung at other rites.

In confirmation of the above statements, some of which I have italicized, Dr. Matthews was able to publish before his death, in various monographs, books, and scientific reports, a large number of these songs. For instance, in *The Night Chant,* which is a marvelously interesting nine-day healing ceremony of dances, songs, chants, and ritual, there are constant references to the power of beauty to transform the sick into the healthy. In the *Legend of the Dawn Boy* the priest, shaman, or medicine man who represents the Dawn Boy sings a song in which are the following lines:

> In the house of long life, there I wander.
> In the house of happiness, there I wander.
> Beauty before me, with it I wander.
> Beauty behind me, with it I wander.
> Beauty below me, with it I wander.

that comparatively little has as yet been achieved by way of offering a comprehensive study of Navaho mythology, which, in reality, forms the basis and ritual for the chants, since the origin and motive for each chant is based upon its own peculiar legend. . . . [Then he expresses regret that] many chants are becoming extinct, and the singers conversant with legends, songs, and prayers are fast disappearing, without a possibility of filling such vacancies. It is also well established that much *singing and exorcising* is continuously practised by a class of inferior and ignorant apprentices, whom the Navaho designate as *aza oniligi* — those who offer a mouthful, implying that they make a few prayer-sticks accompanied by a song or two. . . . Hence, the extinction of the existing and more difficult chants is conceded as inevitable by the remnant of conservative and studious members of the chant lodges, for want of proper pupils. Efforts are consequently being made to obtain a complete account of the various legends, with a view of supplementing those already existing.

He then enumerates the list of chants in two classes: first, those that do not directly deal with the *yei,* or gods; and, second, those as originated with and from the gods. Let us look at the wonderful scope of this first list. There are chants dealing with the " Moving Upward," or the beginning of things in the lower worlds, and their emergence upwards. The *Moving Upward Chant* is still largely in demand, as it is supposed to have great power in dispelling witches and their evil craft. The *War Dance,* which is for the dispelling of foreign enemies; the *Rite of the God Men,* which was extensively in demand on raids and in war (though, as now, raids and war are prohibited by the United States government, this is seldom sung nowadays). Then there is the *Rite for Dispelling Monsters* — or the blackening and driving out of witches and native enemies, in contradistinction to the driving out of foreign enemies. A ceremony or chant continuously called for is that of *Renewal,* or *Benediction.* This is an essential feature of every Navaho chant. Hence, in the *Night Chant,* which requires nine days for its observance, one night is set apart for this chant of blessing.

Outside of its connection with the longer chants, it appears as a one-night ceremony of blessing upon the *hogan,* the members of the family, their chattels and real estate, their crops and occupation, such as weaving and singing, their propensities to greed, at the nubile ceremony, or the birth of a child, the dedication of a new set of ceremonial masks, for the purification of the ceremonial paraphernalia — in fact, for almost any phase of domestic life.

Then there is the *Chant for Dispelling the Darts of the Male Powers of Evil,* such as the lightning, rattlesnakes, and the like. When the first moccasin was made an *Awl Chant* was composed and handed down, but of late years it has dropped into disuse. There is also an extinct *Hail Chant,* and one almost extinct called the *Corral Rite.* It was used for corralling antelope and deer, and in the chase at large; but, as the rifle and modern weapons have almost entirely done away with the old methods of hunting, the old chants are no longer sung. Those that are still in vogue are the *Big Star Chant;* the *Wind Chant,* to propitiate the winds that so often are harmful and injurious; the *Coyote Chant,* and a similar one for the removal of mania and prostitution; the *Water Chant,* the *Female Lightning Chant,* and the *Chant for the Trapping of Eagles.* The *Feather Chant* is sometimes in demand, but the fact that many requisites, such as baskets, buckskins, feathers, and numerous prayer-sticks, all the latter of which have to be made expressly for the particular ceremony in which they are to be used, militates against its popularity.

The other chants are in some way connected with the Holy Ones. These are the *Mountain Chant of the Maiden Becoming a Bear;* the *Chant of Beauty,* by which the bear and copperhead inveigle two beautiful maidens into marriage with them; the *Night Chant,* of which Dr. Matthews says:

It is really a healing ceremony. It is celebrated primarily for the cure of a rich invalid, who pays the heavy expenses; but the occasion is devoted to other purposes also, to prayers for the benefit of the people at large, and, among other things, to the initiation of youths and maidens, and sometimes people of maturer years, into the secret of the Yébitsai.

After explaining the ceremony, the Doctor then continues:

The secret of the Yébitsai is this: The *Yéi* are the bugaboos of Navaho children. These Indians rarely inflict corporal punishment on the young, but, instead, threaten them with the vengeance of these masked characters if they are unruly. Up to the time of their initiation they are taught to believe, and, in most cases, probably do believe, that the *Yéi* are genuine abnormal creatures whose function it is to chastise bad children. When the children are old enough to understand the value of obedience without resort to threats, they are allowed to undergo this initiation and learn that the dreaded *Yéi* is only some intimate friend or relation in disguise. After this initiation they are privileged to enter the medicine lodge during the performance of a rite.

One evening I attended a Yébitsai dance, a few miles from Ganado, Ariz., on the Navaho Reservation, and, making application to the Chief Chanter of the Dance, my companion, Mr. A. W. Dubois, and myself were permitted (as I had been before) to undergo the rite of initiation. We disrobed in the medicine *hogan* and went through the whole rite. Afterward we took part in the concluding ceremonies of the nine days of the *Night Chant,* of which this Yébitsai initiation forms a part of but one night's rites.

Then there are the *Chant of the Clan Dance;* the *Feather-Shaft Chant,* sometimes called the *Knife Chant,* or the *Life Chant,* as often upon the directness of feather-shaft of the shot arrow or the piercing power of the knife one's life depends; the *Bead* or *Eagle Chant of the Great Ship-*

rock, which is connected with the legendary advent of the Navahos into this country; the *One Day Song,* so called because it recounts the legend of a man slain by a bear and revived in one day; the *Red Ant Chant* — the Navahos dread these tiny but active creatures; the *Big God Chant;* the *Chiricahua-Apache Wind Chant;* the *Lightning Chant;* the *Female Lightning Chant,* and the *Mountain Chant to the Small Birds.*

Who shall say that here is not material for study? And all are interesting. I have sat for nine nights in succession and listened to songs that must have consumed, say, five or six hours of each night in *continuous performance,* and there are few repetitions, yet each one must be sung correctly and entirely from memory or the whole nine days' ceremonies are vitiated and must be gone over again. Many of the songs are beautiful, as one can conceive on re-reading those of the blessing of the *hogan,* which are elsewhere quoted.

As can well be understood from all that has gone before, the Navaho is a firm believer in spells, charms, portents, signs, wizardry, and witchcraft. His religion, naturally, is a crude religion largely composed of Nature Worship, and his primitive mind has sought to explain all the many diverse, strange, and especially harmful and hostile forces he finds around him, in accordance with the workings of his simple and untutored intellect. From the legends of the people we gain much information as to their beliefs. Some of these legends are quaint, interesting, beautiful, and instructive. These four adjectives may seem to be carelessly chosen, but they are not. They truthfully designate these stories. Naturally, when one gets a real peep into the mind of the Indian, his methods of thought are found to be quaint. And in these legends this quaintness is enhanced by the fact that the stories are old and have all that peculiar flavor that belongs to stories that have been handed down for many hundreds of years. And how can the stories that account for the origin of the Navaho which are different from our origin stories, be other than interesting to those who like to know how the human mind works with different people, influenced by their own peculiar environment. That some parts of their stories are horrible and dreadful may be expected, for they deal with the primitive instincts of man, where cruelty, even to murder, is no uncommon thing, and blood is made to flow freely. But just as the fierce thunder and lightning storm is often followed by the most exquisite and tender sky-effects, so are these harsh and bloody stories preceded and followed by revelations of exquisite tenderness, gentleness, kindness, and love. The instructiveness of these legends is in the opportunity they afford for the student to see the working of the primitive mind. The human mind is subject to laws of development exactly as is the body, and it has grown up from its childhood just as each man has grown up from babyhood. In studying these Indian stories we are getting back to the period of the child-mind of the race, and such revelations are found to be in the highest degree instructive.

To tell the whole story of the origin of the Navahos would fill a good-sized book. The first part of the legend recounts the emergence of the people from the four lower worlds into the fifth world. The second part tells of their experience in the fifth world. The third part tells of the war gods. The fourth, of the growth of the Navaho nation.

It is in the third part that we learn the story of Yeitso, who was slain by the two heroes of the tribe who cut off his head and placed it to the east of Mount San Mateo, where it is known as Cabezon and where the lava flow is regarded as the flow of his blood.

Soon after these two heroes were born, while their mothers were baking corn cakes, Yeitso, the tallest and fiercest of the alien gods of the Navahos, appeared walking rapidly towards the *hogan*. Knowing that he was a fierce cannibal and would slay and eat their children, one of the mothers hastily grabbed them up, earnestly cautioning them to be perfectly silent and hid them away in the bushes, under some bundles and sticks. Yeitso came and sat down at the door just as the women were taking the cakes out of the ashes. He wanted one of the cakes, but the women refused it. "Never mind," said Yeitso; "I would rather eat boys. Where are your boys? I have been told you have some here and have come to get them." Putting Yeitso off as well as they could, they finally made him believe that there were no boys around.

It was not very long after he had gone before one of the women, having to go to the top of a near-by hill, saw a number of these alien gods hastening towards their *hogan* from all directions. Hurrying down in great distress, she told her sister. This sister had magical power, and, picking up four colored hoops, she threw the white one to the east; the blue one to the south; the yellow one to the west and the black one to the north. These magic hoops produced a great gale which blew so fiercely in all directions from the *hogan* that even the great power of the alien gods was not sufficient to allow them to approach it.

The two boys that Yeitso was hunting were little fellows of super-human origin, and, having no fathers as other boys had, were curious to find their fathers, and, in spite of the prohibitions of their mothers, would keep journeying first in one direction and then in another, determined to find their fathers, and the stories of their adventures are strange and wonderful.

One of these stories was about their visit to the underworld, where they found the "Spider-woman." She it was who gave them their magic charms and taught them many magic formulae. One of these explains why the Navahos gather and use so much pollen in their ceremonies. Pollen, while plentiful in the aggregate, is very light, airy, floating stuff, and exceedingly difficult to gather. Yet the Navaho medicine men are indefatigable in procuring certain kinds of pollen at certain times of the year when the moon is in certain exact locations.

When these boys met their giant enemies, all they had to do was to sprinkle towards them some of a certain kind of pollen and then repeat this formula: "Put your feet down with pollen. Put your hands down with pollen. Put your head down with pollen. Then your feet are pollen; your hands are pollen; your body is pollen; your mind is pollen; your voice is pollen. The trail is beautiful. Be still."

Here is one of the incidents that occurred as the two boys left the house of the Spider-woman. They came to the place known as "Tse'-yeinti'li" (the rocks that crush). There was here a narrow chasm between two high cliffs. When a traveler approached, the rocks would open wide apart, apparently to give him easy passage and invite him to enter; but as soon as he was within the cleft they would close like hands clapping and crush him to death. These rocks were really people; they thought like men; they were *anaye* (that is, cannibalistic gods). When the boys got to the rocks they lifted their feet as if about to enter the chasm, and the rocks opened to let them in. Then the boys put down their feet, but withdrew them quickly. The rocks closed with a snap to crush them; but the boys remained safe on the outside. Thus four times did they deceive the rocks. When they had closed for the fourth time the rocks said: "Who are ye; whence come ye two together, and whither go ye?" "We are children of the Sun," answered the boys. "We come from *Dsilnaotil*, and we go to seek the house of our father." Then they repeated the words that the Spider-woman had taught them, and the rocks said: "Pass on to the house of your father." When next they ventured to step into the chasm the rocks did not close, and they passed safely on.

The boys kept on their way and soon came to a great plain covered with reeds that had great leaves on them as sharp as knives. When the boys came to the edge of the field of reeds *(Lokaadikisi)*, the latter opened, showing a clear passage through to the other side. The boys pretended to enter but retreated, and as they did so, the walls of reeds rushed together to kill them. Thus four times did they deceive the reeds. Then the reeds spoke to them as the rocks had done; they answered and repeated the sacred words. "Pass on to the house of your father," said the reeds, and the boys passed on in safety.

The next danger they encountered was in the country covered with cane cactuses. These cactuses rushed at and tore to pieces whoever attempted to pass through them. When the boys came to the cactuses the latter opened their ranks to let the travelers pass on, as the reeds had done before. But the boys deceived them as they had deceived the reeds, and subdued them as they had subdued the reeds, and passed on in safety.

After they had passed the country of the cactus they came, in time, to *Saitad,* the Land of the Rising Sands. Here was a great desert of sands that rose and whirled and boiled like water in a pot, and overwhelmed the traveler who ventured among them. As the boys approached, the sands became still more agitated and the boys did not dare venture among them. "Who are ye?" said the sands, "and whence come ye?" "We are children of the Sun, we came from *Dsilnaotil,* and we go to seek the house of our father." These words were four times said. Then the elder of the boys repeated his sacred formula; the sands subsided, saying: "Pass on to the house of your father," and the boys continued on their journey over the desert of sands.

The boys finally reached the house of the Sun God, their father. It was built of turquoise, but square like a pueblo house and stood on the shore of a "great water." Here they were in much danger and would undoubtedly have perished had it not been that they were magically protected. For in a short time the giant who bore the Sun on his shoulder came in. He took the Sun off his back and hung it on a peg on the west wall of the room, where it shook and clanged for some time, going, "tla, tla, tla, tla," till at last it hung still. It took some time for the bearer of the Sun God to realize that he was the father of these boys, but when he did, he greeted them with great affection and asked them their mission. They explained that the land in which they dwelt was cursed and devastated by the presence of a number of alien gods who devoured their people. Said they: "They have eaten nearly all of our kine; there are few left; already they have sought our lives and we have run away to escape them. Give us, we beg, the weapons with which we may slay our enemies. Help us to destroy them." This petition pleased the bearer of the Sun God and he gave them clothing and a number of weapons which would enable them to accomplish what they desired. He took from the pegs where they hung around the room and gave to each a hat, a shirt, leggins, moccasins, all made of iron, a chain-lightning arrow, a sheet-lightning arrow, a sunbeam arrow, a rainbow arrow, and a great stone-knife or knife-club. "These are what we want," said the boys. They put on the clothes of iron, and streaks of lightning shot from every joint.

After more trials of their shrewdness and powers of perception, during which time the Sun God carried them through the heavens, he finally, after making them point out the place where they lived, spread out a streak of lightning on which he shot down the children to the summit of Mount San Mateo. Here four holy people told them all about Yeitso.

They said that he showed himself every day three times on the mountains before he came down, and when he showed himself for the fourth time he descended from the mountain to drink; that, when he stooped down to drink, one hand rested on the mountain and the other on the high hills on the opposite side of the valley, while his feet stretched as far away as a man could walk between sunrise and noon. This was the opportunity the boys wanted. While waiting, however, they decided to try one of the lightning arrows which their father had given them. When they shot it, it made a great cleft in the side of Mount San Mateo, where it remains to this day, and one of the brothers said to the other: "We cannot suffer in combat while we have such weapons as these."

Soon they heard the sounds of thunderous footsteps, and they beheld the head of Yeitso peering over a high hill in the east; it was withdrawn in a moment. Soon after, the monster raised his head and chest over a hill in the south, and remained a little longer in sight than when he was in the east. Later he displayed his body to the waist over a hill in the west; and lastly he showed himself down to the knees over a mountain in the north. Then he descended, came to the edge of the lake, and laid down a basket which he was accustomed to carry. He stooped down to drink, and so frightful was his appearance that it made the boys afraid, but by and by their courage came back and they taunted the giant when he made a threat that he was going to eat them. The Wind (which in Navaho mythology is a personification), in his kindness towards the boys, gave them warning as to the treacherous acts contemplated by Yeitso, and made it possible for them to dodge the lightning bolts that he rapidly hurled at them one after another. Escaping the giant's arrows, the brothers had time to put their own lightning arrows into place, pull the bow-string taut, and fire. Four times did the elder brother shoot, and when the fourth arrow struck the giant, it brought him to the ground, flat upon his face, his arms and legs outstretched. As he lay there, the younger brother stepped up and scalped him, and then they cut off his head and threw it away, where it may be seen to this day.

The blood from the body flowed in a great stream down the valley, and the boys stood watching it with no thought of danger until their friend, Wind, told them that it was flowing in the direction of the home of another alien god and that if it reached that far Yeitso would come to life again. Then the elder brother took his great stone-knife, which had magic power, and drew a line with it across the valley. When the blood reached this line it piled itself high until it began to flow in another direction. Here again was danger, for Wind whispered that it was flowing towards the home of another alien god known as "Bear That Pursues," and that if it reached this far Yeitso would come to life again. Again the elder brother drew a line with his knife on the ground and again the blood piled up and stopped flowing, and that is the reason the blood of Yeitso fills all the valley today, the high cliffs of black rock that you see being the place where the blood piled up after the elder brother had drawn the line with his magic knife.

This is but a taste of hundreds, possibly thousands, of pages that might be given of Navaho lore.

III

Navaho Land

NAVAHO LAND is not a land of cultivated areas, of smiling fields in fertile valleys, where the homes of happy and prosperous people, surrounded by merry and boisterous children, look out at you through the leafage of fruit-laden trees. No! no! Picturesque, certainly, it is in places; wild, rugged, and fantastic in others; but, as a rule, it is not alluring to those who look for pretty, cultivated, refined landscapes. A taste of Navaho land scenery may be had in riding on the main line of the Santa Fé Railway going to California on the border-line between New Mexico and Arizona. There are giant cliffs of different colored sandstones, some of the rocks having fallen in vast boulder-like masses. Between these cliffs extend great stretches of valley lands in which sagebrush and wild grasses grow in abundance.

In riding out to St. Michaels, Ganado, and Chin Lee from Gallup station, one gains a reasonable conception of this tumbled and upheaved land. First the road is fairly level, then there is a sudden and steep uphill. On the summit of this the road begins a long, slow, and very easy descent. Indeed, it is so easy that it seems almost level, and appears a fairly smooth valley. Then there is another brief and steep uphill beyond which another slightly sloping valley extends to yet another uphill, and so on, for thirty miles or more. Then we reach a higher "divide," or crest, covered with pinions — nut pines — small pines (the large ones have been cut out for lumber) and junipers, and great sandstone walls, vast, gigantic, towering, appear before us. In many regions these would be deemed titanic features, and would make a landscape famous, but here they are so common that one takes a good look and passes on. The stranger may try climbing to the top of a cliff to get a good outlook, but he soon grows tired of this if he travels further and deeper into the reservation.

The whole country is elevated, the lowest portions being about 4,000 feet above sea level, and the hilly parts from 6,000 to 7,000 feet, while the mountains tower to 9,000 and 10,000 feet. In their legends the Navahos regard certain high mountains as the boundary marks of their country. Each of these mountains is sacred, and has an important name. To the west is the San Francisco Range (seen from Flagstaff, on the line of the Santa Fé). This is *Dokoslid,* but when its sacred character is referred to it is *Dichilidzil,* the haliotis mountain, because yellow is the sacred color of the West. *Sisnajin*—the woman's standing black belt, or Pelado Peak, is the sacred mountain of the East, and its ceremonial name is *Yolgaidzil*—the white bead mountain. Mount Taylor—or as the Mexicans call it, Mount San Mateo—is the sacred mountain of the South. Ordinarily it is *Tsadzil,* the giant tongue (so called because one of its vast lava flows seems like a vast out-thrust tongue), but ceremonially it is *Yodotlizhidzil,* the blue turquoise mountain. *Debentsa,* the mountain of the sheep—or the San Juan mountain of the whites—is the sacred mountain of the North, and it is then *Bashzhinidzil,* or the cannel-coal mountain, black being the color of the North.

According to their origin-legends, these sacred mountains were brought from the lower worlds and placed in their present positions by the First Man. In their sacred sand-paintings these mountains figure largely and can always be told by their location and the colors by which they are represented.

Now and again great sweeps of country are presented which are practically bare, barren, desolate desert, with almost unclad hills rising from the plains and destroying the otherwise distressing monotony. Yet there are many mountains actually in the reservation, as, for instance, the Luckachuchai Mountains, so named from the Navaho word which signifies "the white reed patches." These are at the northwestern end. In the central part is the Tunicha Range (large water), and the southeastern end, the Chuska, or Chusca Range (white spruce). There are also a few isolated mountains, or groups, as the Carrizos (mountains surrounded by mountains), and the Black Mountains in the West. Not far from the junction of the San Juan River with the Colorado, is Navaho Mountain, which, on a clear day, can be seen from *El Tovar* hotel porch at the Grand Canyon.

On these hilly slopes the pinion grows naturally in abundance, and its nut is one of the crops of the Navaho which he is slowly beginning to use to his financial advantage. The day before this present writing I stood and saw a wagon-load of pinion nuts unloaded at a Navaho trading-store on the reservation. There was over a ton of the nuts and the Indian received about seven cents per pound for them. A week or two earlier I had seen three carloads of these nuts shipped on the railway. The pinion nut of these regions is of the same family as the *pinola* of Italy, but is much richer and sweeter. Experts tell us it abounds in proteids, and is one of the most nourishing of muscle foods. It certainly is the most delicious and tasty of all nuts. Unfortunately, the crop in the Navaho country is uncertain, there being a good yield but once every five to seven years. Of course it receives no cultivation or care whatever, and the traders never seem to have considered the advisability of trying cultivation, even though it went no further than dry farming. There is too little water in the Navaho country to allow for irrigation, even were it desirable with the pinion, a matter upon which I know nothing.

Yet if this could be made a reliable crop with a little extra labor, what a profitable yield these nature-planted trees would afford. Another thing, as yet the Navaho traders have learned no way of easy shelling these nuts, and to most people this is so slow and tedious a task that they will forego the pleasure of eating the nut rather than be bothered with it. Unshelled, the nuts are worth, probably, from nine to twelve cents per pound. Shelled, they would be worthy fully twenty-five cents to thirty cents per pound. The shells are exceedingly light, not weighing more, I should assume, than one-fifth to one-fourth of the nut itself.

This is the only natural crop, as far as I know, upon which any of the Navahos rely. They raise some corn, but use all they grow, hence commercially, corn-raising scarcely counts with them.

The high elevation, the want of water, and the general climatic conditions are not favorable to agriculture or pomoculture, for while it is hot in summer the nights are generally cool, and the time for maturing crops short. Hence, the Navahos have had to turn to other sources of wealth, and their land affording fairly good pasturage, it seemed as if a kind fate had turned their attention to sheep-grazing, wool-raising, and blanket-weaving; for, by making a specialty of these industries, they have sprung in a few years into a prosperity that makes them, from their standpoint, a rich and independent nation.

While much of Navaho land seems to be desert, there are, however, great stretches of a splendid growth of white pine on the Chuska Range, and there are forests of the red cedar *(Juniperus virginianus),* and western juniper *(J. occidentalis)* on the lower levels. Patches of scrub-oak are to be found anywhere on the mountains, and in the canyons cotton-woods, box-elders, aspen, alder, walnut, and peach thrive abundantly.

Through some of the mountainous plateaus, deep-gorged, tortuously winding canyons have been cut by corrosion or erosion, and through these the mountain rains, and the water of the melted snows are drained out into the valleys. The result is the Navaho reservation is not less noted for its canyons than its deserts and mountains.

One of the most world-famed of these is the Canyon de Chelly, a foolish (apparently Frenchified) spelling of the Navaho name for canyon, *tségi.* This is known because of the wonderful cliff-dwellings that have been discovered here, some of which rank as the most perfect specimens of aboriginal stone-work in the boundaries of the United States. Close by are the Canyon del Muerto, so-called from the many mummified human bodies found in the cliff-ruins, and Monument Canyon, the entrance to which is made dignified and impressive by a giant mass of rock that stands detached from the main wall as a lone sentinel guarding the gateway.

In 1912 I made a visit to these canyons while completing my book — *The Prehistoric Cliff Dwellings of the American Southwest* — and to the pages of that book I refer the reader for further impressions of these three wonderfully historic and scenic places. There are many other cliff-dwellings found within the boundaries of the reservation, and scores of ruins of houses, both singly and in groups, and even pueblos. All along the Little Colorado River many of these are to be found, and the Chaco Canyon country is almost as famous as Canyon de Chelly for its cliff and house ruins, which were first described over thirty years ago in *Scribner's Magazine*. Of some of these ruins Dr. Edgar L. Hewett, of the American Institute of Archaeology at Santa Fé, N. M., thus writes:

Another group of ancient towns, less picturesque in situation but of equal interest, is that of the Chaco Canyon in Northwestern New Mexico. These great houses, standing in the open, some five stories high, were built of sandstone blocks, in some cases so arranged in courses of varying thickness as to produce decorative effects. They had no natural security of situation on high mesas or in deep canyons, but stood in the open valley and on the sandy plain, entirely unprotected save by their own massive walls. Best known of all in this group is Pueblo Bonito, a huge structure five stories high, semi-circular in form, its walls still standing to a height of over forty feet. Not far away are the ruins of Chettro Kettle, Hungo Pavie, Wijiji, and Peñasco Blanco. This famous group of ruins stands in the midst of a desolate plain, the Navaho Desert, now almost devoid of water and incapable of supporting any population except of wandering Navahos.

Close to the San Francisco and San Mateo Mountains are vast areas of lava — flows that altogether surpass in extent and wildness the classic lava-flows of the South of France, and of which the legends are told referred to in a former chapter.

When one gives time to the study of the Navaho language he finds himself well repaid by the poetic descriptions that are used, for instance, in the names of places. One is called "Where the Cranes Stand," another "The Hawk's Nest." Here are others, "Where Water Flows in the Darkness under the Rock," "Where Water Flows out of a Canyon," "The Buttes that Stand like Twin Stars," "The Baby Rock," "The Small Canyon Meadow," "Where They Fall into the Pit of Water." This latter name is given to a pool in the Black Mountain region much frequented by game. Owing to the rocks of the pool sloping inward towards the center and not affording sufficient foothold, the thirsty animals are entrapped somewhat after the fashion of the early game-pit-traps of the natives. Here are a few more names: "The Sumach Spring in the Black Mountains," "Rough Rock Spring," "Antelope Spring," "The Water Flows through the Rock," "Tangled Waters," "Fringed Waters," "Slim

Water," "Crystal Water Flows Out," "Braided Willows," "Winged Rock," "Red Round Rock," "The Conical Sand Dune," "Beaver's Eye Spring."

In the reading of but one Navaho legend will be found the following rich list of poetic names: "One-eyed Water," "Rock Sticking Up," "Beautiful Under the Cottonwoods," "White Standing Rock," "Erect Cat-tail Rushes," "Clay Hill," "Scattered Springs," "Narrow Water," "Beautiful in the Mountains," "Circle of Red Stones," "Wind Circles Around a Rock," "Narrow Sand Hills," "Valley Surrounded on All Sides by Hills," "Rock That Bends Back," "Big Oaks," "Last Mountain," "Mountain Comes Down Steep," "Four Doorways Under a Mountain," "Where Yellow Streak Runs Down," "Where They Came Together," "House of Rock Crystal," "Broad Cherry Trees," "Leaf Mountain," "White Water Running Across," "Brown Earth Water," "Much Grease Wood," "Where Two White Rocks Lie," "Radiating White Streaks," "Lone Juniper Standing Between Cliffs," "Woods on One Side," "Standing Rock Above," "Sheep Promontory," "Sheep Lying Down," "Rock Cracked in Two," "Hill Surrounded with Young Spruce Trees," "White Ground," "Dipping Rocks," "Cold Water," "Black Mountains," and "Hard Earth."

With such a splendid catalogue of place-names, who shall say the Navahos have no eye for beauty and no poetic facility in describing it.

As already shown, inclination and interest have led the Navahos to take the fullest possible opportunity of availing themselves of the grazing features of their reserve. Not hundreds or thousands, but hundreds of thousands of sheep are found in bands wherever grazing and water are assured. One will pass half a hundred bands of several hundred each in a day's journey. These are always in the charge of the women, or girls and boys of adult years.

As a sheep-herder the Navaho woman has no superior in the world. She shows patience, skill, and real tenderness in her dealings with her flock. Indeed, on two or three occasions I have known of Navaho women suckling at their own breasts new-born lambs whose mothers had died. It is no uncommon thing to see them ahead of their flocks, the sheep following contentedly, just as is described by David the Psalmist.

The herds are generally taken out in the morning, guided all day, kept moving to better pasture, and to water, and then returned to the corral at night. Owing to the increasing number of the flocks and the constant treading down of the grass, the pasture is growing scarcer each year, and this is going to add ere long to the problem the Indian Department will have to solve regarding the Navahos.

As yet the Navahos have not seen the wisdom of preparing for the winter. They cut no hay, hence when the pasture is gone, the herds must do the best they can on the sage-brush and what withered grass they can find; or, when it becomes worse still, the herders cut pinion and cedar branches for them to gather therefrom what scant nutriment they can find.

Often, if one approaches these bands of sheep unseen, he will hear the loud and musical, though peculiar and characteristic, voices of the herders raised in song. They are great singers, and singing plays a remarkably important part in their ceremonial and religious life.

Experts tell us that many improvements are to be desired in the Navaho sheep-herds, yet they are beginning to see that better stock means better prices. Hence, some of the wiser Navahos are killing off their old rams and selecting new stock with judicious care. They are also separating their herds of sheep and goats. Hitherto this has not been done, to the immense detriment of the herds. A real Navaho goat, two years old, will give a pelt weighing about two to two and a half pounds. It is worth about forty cents per pound. This makes the pelt worth from seventy-five cents to one dollar. The meat is good, and, properly cooked, is both tender and tasty, though slightly "stronger" than ordinary mutton. The animal itself, too, is hardier than the sheep, can stand drought better, and is less liable to disease. The goat-skin is largely used for book-binding purposes, much of the so-called morocco and French morocco being nothing but our Navaho friends' goat-pelt under an aristocratic name. On the other hand, sheep pelts are worth but from eight to ten cents per pound, and a two-year-old sheep will give a pelt weighing three to four pounds. Yet, sheep for the white market are more profitable, as on the hoof they bring nearly twice as much as goats of the same weight.

The traders and the government officials are now trying to show the Navahos that it is to their best interest to keep sheep and goats apart, to kill or sell off as soon as they can all cheap cross-breeds, to kill their poor stock rams and buy those of pure breeds, and breed them only with sheep of assured wool-giving qualities, when wool is desired, and with good mutton producers, when they are to be sold on the hoof to the white packers.

IV

Reliable Dealers in Navaho Blankets

IT IS scarcely to be expected that every purchaser of a Navaho blanket will be interested enough to go as deeply into its history and manufacture as has the author. Nor can he expect to absorb in a brief perusal of a few pages sufficient knowledge to make him an expert in judging the value of any blanket that may be offered to him if he place himself in the position of a possible purchaser. But I can do such possible purchaser, who values my judgment and word, a great and lasting service by placing him in direct touch with dealers who are thoroughly familiar with all phases of the business, and whose reliability many years of experience have proven to be unquestioned.

When I suggested the introduction of this chapter to my publishers, they felt considerable hesitancy as to its propriety. They argued it was not customary, and it might seem to savor of invidiousness. My replies are that new conditions require new methods of meeting them. High class newspapers and magazines have long ago adopted a system of genuine helpfulness towards their readers in guaranteeing the reliability and honesty of their advertisers. In this case there is no advertising, but my readers are entitled to the results of my experience and knowledge as far as I can give them. The fact that there are *unreliable* dealers in Navaho blankets, who cheat and deceive their customers, and that, on the other hand, there are those whose integrity and knowledge are unquestioned, is my justification for calling specific attention to the latter.

As for the possibility of involving the publisher in any trouble I hereby personally agree to refund to any purchaser any sum he may lose through misrepresentation or dishonest treatment at the hands of any of the dealers herein named.

Foremost among those to whom the collector must turn for the rarest, choicest, and finest specimens of the Navaho, Pueblo, and Chimayó weavers' art now on the market is Fred Harvey, whose principal blanket exhibit is at Albuquerque, N. M., in one portion of the picturesque Santa Fé depot offices, and hotel, named after Alvarado, one of the Captains of Artillery who accompanied Coronado on his journey of exploration and conquest of New Mexico in 1540.

For a number of years Fred Harvey has had collectors gathering up every old blanket of superior worth, whether of Navaho, Mexican,

Chimayó, Hopi, Zuni, Acoma, Laguna, or Alaskan origin. Money has been no object, but every good blanket must be secured. All the leading collections not already in museums have also been gathered in, first one, then another, until the Harvey collection is notable. Several of his choicest specimens are illustrated herein.

Those who travel on the transcontinental line of the "Santa Fé," as the Atchison, Topeka & Santa Fé Railway is popularly known, will need no assurance as to the integrity of Fred Harvey. Ever since the railway has been in operation he has had charge of the eating house and dining-car system, and his excellent service has made his name world-famed and synonymous with the best of foods, cooked and served in the best of style. The same business principles that have made the Fred Harvey hotels, eating houses, lunch counters, and dining-car service famed among travelers have already built up the largest business in Indian blankets, baskets, pottery, and curios in the world, and prospective purchasers may fully rely upon everything that they may secure either at Albuquerque or any of his branch establishments being genuine, and as represented.

Elsewhere I have referred to the work of C. N. Cotton and John Lorenzo Hubbell in furthering the development of the blanket-weaving art among the Navahos. These men are still in the blanket business, the former as a dealer, purchasing from the traders, while the latter still carries on the business directly with the Indians themselves. In 1884 Mr. Cotton, who had been the station agent of the Santa Fé Railway at Wingate, N. M., bought an interest in Mr. Hubbell's Indian trading post at Ganado, Arizona, which is some sixty miles northwest from Gallup, N. M. In those days the trade for blankets was small and insignificant. In 1884 all the new firm secured was two small bales of common blankets weighing not more than from 300 to 400 pounds, the designs being of the plain straight-line type. Saddle blankets were not purchased at all.

In 1894 Mr. Cotton gave up the direct trading with the Navaho, removed to Gallup, N. M., and ever since has dealt only with the traders, supplying them with all the goods they need to sell to the Indian and taking in return everything the traders secure from them. The special feature of his blanket trade, therefore, has been to secure a market. Each year the demand for good blankets has increased. The firm name is "The C. N. Cotton Company," Gallup, N. M., and it disposes of its blankets only at wholesale. The first illustrated and descriptive catalogue of the Navaho blanket ever issued, I had the pleasure of writing for Mr. Cotton nearly twenty years ago. He and Mr. Hubbell can truthfully be called the fathers of the business among the white race, and while Mr. Cotton is no longer in partnership with Mr. Hubbell they have a close business relationship, and many of the latter's finest blankets are purchased by

Mr. Cotton. So it is with traders all over the reservation. Their best blankets are shipped to Mr. Cotton as fast as the Indians bring them in.

Few men have ever held so honored and rare a position in the esteem of the Navahos and in relation to the blanket industry as does John Lorenzo Hubbell, of Ganado, Arizona. Indeed, it would be as impossible to write truthfully and comprehensively of the history of the Navaho blanket and leave out Mr. Hubbell's relation to it, as it would be to give the history of the phonograph and leave out the name of Edison. As I have shown in the chapter on the Development of the Art, Mr. Hubbell has seen all the latter-day developments of blanket-weaving. He saw the art deteriorate, and then set himself to work to stem the tide of ignorance and carelessness which bid fair speedily to wreck what his far-seeing vision knew might be a means of great wealth to an industrious and struggling people. He spoke the Navaho language fluently, lived in the very heart of the reservation and was in daily contact with some of the most progressive men and women of the tribe. He took them into his office and talked with them, one by one. As rapidly as was possible he eliminated the use of cotton warp, showing the weavers that, while its substitution for the wool warps saved them much time, it made the blanket so much inferior that he could not pay anything like the same price for it. Then he eliminated certain dyes from his trade. He refused to keep the colors that the Indians used so recklessly when they had once broken loose from the old traditions of pure colors. Then, slowly but surely, he discouraged the use of Germantown yarn, and urged the thorough cleaning and scouring, carding, spinning, and dyeing of their own wool. During all this time he was urging the weavers to higher endeavor, and giving special privileges and favors to those who showed not only skill and originality of design, but general acquiescence in his endeavors to improve the art. The final result has been that now he has gathered around him by far the finest set of weavers on the whole reservation; he has found out the class of work best done by certain women, and who are the "color artists" for the making of that style of fancy blankets in which color plays the most important part. Then, too, he has learned from practical experience, what designs of pure Navaho origin please the most exacting patrons, and these he has had copied in oil or water-colors, and they line the walls of his office by the score.

Hence, when a certain type of blanket is needed, he can point to the design, or, if necessary, loan the painting of it to the weaver to whom he commits the order. If this particular weaver fails as a dyer of good colors, he supplies her with wool he has had dyed by some other woman who is a dyeing expert. Thus he gains the best kind of work, and can supply anything makeable by a Navaho weaver, with sureness, accuracy, skill, and speed.   That his name is synonymous with honorable and upright dealing goes without saying, for no man can stand as he does with the Navahos without being—as the Indians would say—"a walker on the beautiful way."

Another Gallup, N. M., firm that is perfectly reliable and trustworthy is the C. C. Manning Company.   In 1894 Mr. Manning went to the Navaho Indian Agency, at Fort Defiance, as Assistant Engineer for Government Irrigation Work that was being done for the benefit of the Navahos.   In the spring of 1896 he left the government service and bought out the reservation trading store of W. E. Weidemeyer, where he remained in daily contact with the Navahos for the space of ten years.   In 1906 he sold out and went for a visit to California and southern Arizona, but in three years, longing for the largeness of his Indian trading life, he returned and repurchased his old store.   Ever since then he has been engaged in the Navaho trade, though now his company transacts a tremendous wholesale business with the various traders on the reservation, having their large warehouses, etc., at Gallup.   During the year 1911-12 they found sale for Navaho blankets for which they had traded to the amount of forty thousand dollars, independent of the blankets sold by the manager of their Navaho Reservation store, who finds his own market and never sends his supply in to be disposed of by the firm.

While the Manning Company does an almost exclusively wholesale business, they assure me that if any would-be purchaser wishes to write to them they will either send such blankets as may be desired, or will refer the purchaser to one of the Indian traders with whom they do business, whose word and goods may be relied upon.   To those, however, who wish to purchase in quantity, the Manning Company offer special facilities. Trading over a large part of the reservation and buying from a score or more of those who deal actually with the Indians they secure a wide variety of styles, weaves, and designs that make their stock an especially desirable one to select from.   In addition to this, there are a number of first-class weavers who have learned that this company is willing to pay them a high price for every superior blanket that is brought direct to them; hence they secure quite a number of extra choice specimens in this manner.

A Navaho trader who makes a specialty of a mail-order business in the finer grades of Indian blankets, and whose statements as to the quality of his goods may be implicitly relied upon, is J. A. Molohon, Crystal, N. M.   Mr. Molohon is the successor by purchase of J. B. Moore's trading-store, from which a large number of excellent blankets have been sent out to satisfied customers.   Some seventeen years ago Mr. Moore entered the Indian trading business and in his district began to do for the Navahos what Messrs. Hubbell and Cotton had done in theirs.   Little by little he succeeded in improving the products of their looms by introducing new ideas in preparing and dyeing the yarn. He established reasonably fixed grades of qualities in which he did an extensive business. This was no easy task. The Navaho woman is as conservative in many respects as is her husband. She changes slowly. As I have shown elsewhere, when Mr. Moore entered the field, the Navaho blanket had deteriorated and was a discredited product, undesirable, and largely unsalable. Two gigantic barriers, therefore, had to be broken down, the one on the side of the Indians, the other on the part of the American purchaser. It required courage, persistence, and knowledge of the Navaho to change the weavers' methods, and several years passed ere he secured blankets of the quality he desired. His methods were an innovation. To send the wool away and have it scientifically and thoroughly cleansed and prepared for dyeing was a great trouble and expense, but it paid in the end.

Soon a few of the more thorough weavers saw how much better the dye would "bite in" to this well-scoured wool. They were thus induced to a more thorough cleansing of their wool, and when they received a higher price for the blankets made of such wool, they began to fall in line with Mr. Moore's further suggestions for the improvement of their work. The result is the blankets from the Crystal weavers are highly desired, and as Mr. Molohon is equally particular with his predecessor, the business has continued to be carried on in the old and well-established lines. The Molohon Company offers no cheap grade blankets. They have only two grades or classes. The first is their "ER-20" grade, which is made entirely from specially scoured wool, dyed in the yarn with special dyes and carefully prepared mordants, so that the fastness and truth of the colors is assured. The wool is then issued to the weaver who has proven her capacity, with general instructions as to the kind of blanket desired. The design is left largely to her own will, thus ensuring the individual character so much desired. These blankets vary in size from 45 x 76 inches to about 6 x 9 feet, but blankets of any size may be ordered with the assurance of receiving exactly the quality desired.

The Molohon second, or "T-XX" grades, are selected blankets from those brought in by the Indians, where there has been no special scouring or dyeing of the wool under the trader's personal supervision. Most of these blankets come from weavers who are earnestly striving to get into the Molohon class of first-class weavers, hence they have an incentive to do their utmost. This results in a higher class blanket than that secured by the indifferent trader.

The address of J. A. Molohon & Co. is Crystal, N. M.

Another of the oldest and most reliable of Indian traders is the C. H. Algert Company, of Fruitland, N. M. They are wholesale dealers only and have a large trade all over the United States. I first made the acquaintance of Mr. Algert over twenty years ago when he was the Indian trader at Tuba City, Ariz. Our acquaintance ripened into friendship, and ever since I have had more or less continuous dealings with him. A few years ago he took into partnership his former clerk and assistant, June Fautz, and they removed to Fruitland, N. M., where their business has considerably enlarged as the years have gone by. The C. H. Algert Company does an almost exclusive business with the traders of the northern part of the Reservation, extending clear across from New Mexico to California and to the borders of southern Colorado, Utah, and Nevada.

Their specialty is a good, reliable grade of standard, native wool, undyed, and outline blankets, with a steady supply of the extra qualities of all these types. It was from Mr. Algert that I bought my first native wool undyed blankets, especially those in the grays, blacks, and whites, and while he was at Tuba City, he was most conscientious, constant, and thorough in urging upon the weavers of his district the improvement of this class of weave. Indeed, he has done more to promote the general improvement of the art in this line than any other trader. On several occasions I have been present at his trading-post when he has gathered together as many as two or three thousand Navahos, not only to give them a good time in their feats of horsemanship, etc., but also to foster among the weavers a desire to improve the quality of their blankets.

Since his removal to Fruitland, he has discontinued immediate dealings with the Indians and deals only with the traders, supplying them with everything that they need in exchange for the blankets, etc., sent in. His firm handles thousands of dollars worth of blankets each year, and is known for its square and honorable dealing.

Elsewhere I have referred to the endeavors made by the Hyde Exploring Expedition to improve the condition of the Navahos and further their interests by pushing the sale of their blankets on a large scale. Their successor was the Benham Indian Trading Company, which finally concentrated all its efforts in its chief store on South Broadway, Los Angeles, California. For many years it conducted a successful business here, the direction of affairs being in the hands of Mr. A. M. Benham, whose responsible assistant was Mr. L. L. Burns, who held an interest in the firm. At Mr. Benham's death some two or three years ago, Mr. Burns bought out all other interests and organized the Burns Indian Trading Company, which has carried on the work of its predecessors on the same high plane. Like Fred Harvey, Mr. Burns has scoured the country for old and rare blankets of all good weavers, and many collections owe some of their most valued specimens to him. Especially in rare bayetas and old Chimayós has he been successful.

Mr. Burns has also accomplished for the Chimayó blanket what Mr. Hubbell and Mr. Molohon are doing for the Navaho. He brought several Chimayó weavers and their looms to Los Angeles and there personally supervised their work. The Burns Company deals in every kind of genuine Indian goods, and sells at both wholesale and retail. It also makes a specialty of mail orders.

Recently Mr. Burns has found a new and congenial field for his laboriously-acquired Indian knowledge. As is well known, Los Angeles is the home of moving picture film makers. Thousands of feet of Indian plays are made monthly. Mr. Burns has organized the Western Costume Company, and he and his associates give expert technical advice and practical assistance in the correct costuming and staging of Indian and western plays. They have a large stock of blankets, squaw dresses, etc., such as are described in these pages, and it is an interesting fact to note the development of this new industry in connection with *Indian Blankets and Their Makers.*

In conclusion: While mine is a busy life and I have no such commodity as "spare time," I shall always be glad to place my services at the disposal of any one interested in securing a collection of Navaho blankets of a superior order.

INDEX

INDEX

A CATALOGUE OF SELECTED DOVER BOOKS
IN ALL FIELDS OF INTEREST

DESIGN BY ACCIDENT; A BOOK OF "ACCIDENTAL EFFECTS" FOR ARTISTS AND DESIGNERS, James F. O'Brien. Create your own unique, striking, imaginative effects by "controlled accident" interaction of materials: paints and lacquers, oil and water based paints, splatter, crackling materials, shatter, similar items. Everything you do will be different; first book on this limitless art, so useful to both fine artist and commercial artist. Full instructions. 192 plates showing "accidents," 8 in color. viii + 215pp. 8⅜ x 11¼. 21942-9 Paperbound $3.50

THE BOOK OF SIGNS, Rudolf Koch. Famed German type designer draws 493 beautiful symbols: religious, mystical, alchemical, imperial, property marks, runes, etc. Remarkable fusion of traditional and modern. Good for suggestions of timelessness, smartness, modernity. Text. vi + 104pp. 6⅛ x 9¼.
20162-7 Paperbound $1.25

HISTORY OF INDIAN AND INDONESIAN ART, Ananda K. Coomaraswamy. An unabridged republication of one of the finest books by a great scholar in Eastern art. Rich in descriptive material, history, social backgrounds; Sunga reliefs, Rajput paintings, Gupta temples, Burmese frescoes, textiles, jewelry, sculpture, etc. 400 photos. viii + 423pp. 6⅜ x 9¾. 21436-2 Paperbound $4.00

PRIMITIVE ART, Franz Boas. America's foremost anthropologist surveys textiles, ceramics, woodcarving, basketry, metalwork, etc.; patterns, technology, creation of symbols, style origins. All areas of world, but very full on Northwest Coast Indians. More than 350 illustrations of baskets, boxes, totem poles, weapons, etc. 378 pp.
20025-6 Paperbound $3.00

THE GENTLEMAN AND CABINET MAKER'S DIRECTOR, Thomas Chippendale. Full reprint (third edition, 1762) of most influential furniture book of all time, by master cabinetmaker. 200 plates, illustrating chairs, sofas, mirrors, tables, cabinets, plus 24 photographs of surviving pieces. Biographical introduction by N. Bienenstock. vi + 249pp. 9⅞ x 12¾. 21601-2 Paperbound $4.00

AMERICAN ANTIQUE FURNITURE, Edgar G. Miller, Jr. The basic coverage of all American furniture before 1840. Individual chapters cover type of furniture—clocks, tables, sideboards, etc.—chronologically, with inexhaustible wealth of data. More than 2100 photographs, all identified, commented on. Essential to all early American collectors. Introduction by H. E. Keyes. vi + 1106pp. 7⅞ x 10¾.
21599-7, 21600-4 Two volumes, Paperbound $11.00

PENNSYLVANIA DUTCH AMERICAN FOLK ART, Henry J. Kauffman. 279 photos, 28 drawings of tulipware, Fraktur script, painted tinware, toys, flowered furniture, quilts, samplers, hex signs, house interiors, etc. Full descriptive text. Excellent for tourist, rewarding for designer, collector. Map. 146pp. 7⅞ x 10¾.
21205-X Paperbound $2.50

EARLY NEW ENGLAND GRAVESTONE RUBBINGS, Edmund V. Gillon, Jr. 43 photographs, 226 carefully reproduced rubbings show heavily symbolic, sometimes macabre early gravestones, up to early 19th century. Remarkable early American primitive art, occasionally strikingly beautiful; always powerful. Text. xxvi + 207pp. 8⅜ x 11¼. 21380-3 Paperbound $3.50

MATHEMATICAL PUZZLES FOR BEGINNERS AND ENTHUSIASTS, Geoffrey Mott-Smith. 189 puzzles from easy to difficult—involving arithmetic, logic, algebra, properties of digits, probability, etc.—for enjoyment and mental stimulus. Explanation of mathematical principles behind the puzzles. 135 illustrations. viii + 248pp.
20198-8 Paperbound $1.75

PAPER FOLDING FOR BEGINNERS, William D. Murray and Francis J. Rigney. Easiest book on the market, clearest instructions on making interesting, beautiful origami. Sail boats, cups, roosters, frogs that move legs, bonbon boxes, standing birds, etc. 40 projects; more than 275 diagrams and photographs. 94pp.
20713-7 Paperbound $1.00

TRICKS AND GAMES ON THE POOL TABLE, Fred Herrmann. 79 tricks and games—some solitaires, some for two or more players, some competitive games—to entertain you between formal games. Mystifying shots and throws, unusual caroms, tricks involving such props as cork, coins, a hat, etc. Formerly *Fun on the Pool Table*. 77 figures. 95pp.
21814-7 Paperbound $1.00

HAND SHADOWS TO BE THROWN UPON THE WALL: A SERIES OF NOVEL AND AMUSING FIGURES FORMED BY THE HAND, Henry Bursill. Delightful picturebook from great-grandfather's day shows how to make 18 different hand shadows: a bird that flies, duck that quacks, dog that wags his tail, camel, goose, deer, boy, turtle, etc. Only book of its sort. vi + 33pp. 6½ x 9¼.   21779-5 Paperbound $1.00

WHITTLING AND WOODCARVING, E. J. Tangerman. 18th printing of best book on market. "If you can cut a potato you can carve" toys and puzzles, chains, chessmen, caricatures, masks, frames, woodcut blocks, surface patterns, much more. Information on tools, woods, techniques. Also goes into serious wood sculpture from Middle Ages to present, East and West. 464 photos, figures. x + 293pp.
20965-2 Paperbound $2.00

HISTORY OF PHILOSOPHY, Julián Marias. Possibly the clearest, most easily followed, best planned, most useful one-volume history of philosophy on the market; neither skimpy nor overfull. Full details on system of every major philosopher and dozens of less important thinkers from pre-Socratics up to Existentialism and later. Strong on many European figures usually omitted. Has gone through dozens of editions in Europe. 1966 edition, translated by Stanley Appelbaum and Clarence Strowbridge. xviii + 505pp.
21739-6 Paperbound $3.00

YOGA: A SCIENTIFIC EVALUATION, Kovoor T. Behanan. Scientific but non-technical study of physiological results of yoga exercises; done under auspices of Yale U. Relations to Indian thought, to psychoanalysis, etc. 16 photos. xxiii + 270pp.
20505-3 Paperbound $2.50

Prices subject to change without notice.
Available at your book dealer or write for free catalogue to Dept. GI, Dover Publications, Inc., 180 Varick St., N. Y., N. Y. 10014. Dover publishes more than 150 books each year on science, elementary and advanced mathematics, biology, music, art, literary history, social sciences and other areas.